Underglobalization

Underglobalization

Beijing's
Media Urbanism
and the Chimera
of Legitimacy

Joshua Neves

DUKE UNIVERSITY PRESS | DURHAM AND LONDON | 2020

© 2020 Duke University Press
All rights reserved
Designed by Drew Sisk
Typeset in Portrait Text, SimSun, and Univers by
Westchester Publishing Services

Library of Congress Cataloging-in-Publication Data
Names: Neves, Joshua, [date] author.
Title: Underglobalization : Beijing's media urbanism and the
   chimera of legitimacy / Joshua Neves.
Description: Durham : Duke University Press, 2020. | Includes
   bibliographical references and index.
Identifiers: LCCN 2019032496 (print) | LCCN 2019032497 (ebook)
ISBN 9781478007630 (hardcover)
ISBN 9781478008057 (paperback)
ISBN 9781478009023 (ebook)
Subjects: LCSH: Product counterfeiting—Law and legislation—
China. | Piracy (Copyright)—China. | Legitimacy of
   governments—China. | Globalization—China.Classification:
   LCC KNQ1160.3.N48 2020 (print) |
   LCC KNQ1160.3 (ebook) | DDC 302.230951—dc23
LC recordavailableathttps:/ /lccn.loc.gov/2019032496
LC ebookrec ordavailableathttps:/ /lccn.loc.gov/2019032497

Cover art: Xing Danwen, detail from *Urban Fictions*, 2004.
Courtesy of the artist and Danwen Studio.

Chapter 5 was originally published in "Videation: Technological
Intimacy and the Politics of Global Connection," in *Asian Video
Cultures: In the Penumbra of the Global*, edited by Joshua Neves and
Bhaskar Sarkar (Durham, NC: Duke University Press, 2017).

CONTENTS

VII   ACKNOWLEDGMENTS

I   INTRODUCTION After Legitimacy

33   **1** Rendering the City
       Between Ruins and Blueprints

61   **2** Digital Urbanism
       *Piratical Citizenship
       and the Infrastructure of Dissensus*

94   **3** Bricks and Media
       Cinema's Technologized Spatiality

120 **4** Beijing en Abyme
       Television and the Unhomely Social

150 **5** Videation
       *Technological Intimacy and the
       Politics of Global Connection*

169 **6** People as Media Infrastructure
       *Illicit Culture and the
       Pornographies of Globalization*

199 NOTES
227 BIBLIOGRAPHY
245 INDEX

ACKNOWLEDGMENTS

This has been a slow book about fast changes. And like most first books it is indebted to many people for their guidance, care, and, perhaps not least of all, patience. This book grew out of my graduate work in film and media studies at the University of California, Santa Barbara. I must first thank my dissertation committee. Bhaskar Sarkar gave me a home from the first day and mentored my research with generosity, rigor, and fun! This book could not have been written without his stimulation and friendship. Lisa Parks brought me into the world of media studies; she inspired an interest in experimentation and a penchant for engaging problems that matter rather than preformed disciplinary questions. Her interventions hover over this manuscript. Michael Berry provided a steady hand, pushing me to dig deeper into Chinese cinema and cultural studies, indulging the strange turns in my project, and providing valuable feedback. Swati Chattopadhyay shaped my thinking about spatial practice and the city. She pushed me to develop postcolonial critiques and, perhaps most of all, precision with conceptual language. The failings here are all mine! Finally, Charles Wolfe was a model of academic bigheartedness; his door was always open and he patiently engaged my ideas and anxieties, responding with wisdom. I must also thank Bishnupriya Ghosh, my spectral committee member, whose zest and dynamic thinking have had a tremendous impact on this research and beyond. Finally, I want to thank the entire film and media faculty at UCSB for their support, big and small, especially Peter Bloom, Edward Branigan, Michael Curtin, Anna Everett, Constance Penley, Greg Seigel, Cristina Venegas, and Janet Walker.

I was fortunate to be a part of the first cohort of PhD students in film and media at UCSB, and I must also thank my peers. I remember fondly the hours passed with Hye Jean Chung, Chris Dzialo, Regina Longo, Dan Reynolds, Jeff Scheible, and Nicole Starosielski, among many others. Our work on the *Media Fields* conference series and journal remains a bright spot. This book also could not have been written without the support of many students, scholars, and filmmakers from my years in Beijing. Thanks especially to Wang Wo and Zhu Rikun for the amazing and difficult work with the Li Xianting Film Fund, to Yang Shu and Wang Wenhuan for their research support, and to JP Sniadecki for our travels and bringing me into the SEL community. I am grateful to Yomi Braester, Chris Berry, and others for the stimulating Summer Program in Chinese Film History at the Beijing Film Academy, among many other interactions. Finally, thanks to the many panelists and interlocutors, too many to name here, who have engaged this work over the last ten years, especially Ruoyun Bai, James Cahill, Jenny Chio, Jinying Li, Eng-Beng Lim, Ralph Litzinger, Ramon Lobato, Anna McCarthy, Pang Laikwan, Luke Robinson, and Nishant Shah.

This research was also supported by an Andrew W. Mellon Postdoctoral Fellowship at the Jackman Humanities Institute, University of Toronto. I thank the community of fellows and my colleagues in Cinema Studies and Visual Studies for our rich conversations. At Brown University, I received generous funding from the Pembroke Center and the Seed and Salomon Awards. I am also grateful for the mentorship of my MCM colleagues, especially Wendy Hui Kyong Chun, Lynne Joyrich, and Phil Rosen. I completed this manuscript at Concordia University and want to thank to my colleagues in film studies and across the Montreal community—many of whom have commented on parts of this manuscript, including Luca Caminati, Michelle Cho, Yuri Furuhata, Thomas Lamarre, Masha Salazkina, and Marc Steinberg, among others. I also want to thank the Canada Research Chairs Program, the Social Science and Humanities Research Council (SSHRC), and the Canada Foundation for Innovation–funded Global Emergent Media Lab for supporting the final stages of writing and editing. Cheers to our graduate students, especially Weixian Pan, for their help with the final manuscript. Finally, I would like to thank the two anonymous reviewers for their generous engagement, and, at Duke University Press, Drew Sisk for the book design, and Courtney Berger at Duke University Press for her wisdom and support over the past few years.

Chapters 3 and 4 originated as the articles "Cinematic Encounters in Beijing," *Film Quarterly* 67, no. 1 (2014): 27–40, and "Beijing en Abyme: Outside Television in the Olympic Era," *Social Text 107* 29, no. 2 (summer 2011): 21–46. Chapter 5, "Videation: Technological Intimacy and the Politics of Global Connection," also appears in *Asian Video Cultures: In the Penumbra of the Global*, edited by Joshua Neves and Bhaskar Sarkar (Durham, NC: Duke University Press, 2017). Thanks to the readers and supporters of these early pieces, as well as the many friends and colleagues who have provided critical insights over the last few years.

Many friendships and loved ones have also shepherded this project over the past decade. I remember my dear friend and collaborator Graham Bury. Graham passed away during the writing, and this book is in his memory. I also thank my family for all their support, especially as this research has often sent me far from home. Finally, to my dearest Meg Fernandes, who has been a fellow traveler on this project and many other adventures besides. She has not only improved this book with her ideas and passion, but brought joy and beauty into our world these last years. I would not have wanted to do any of it without her wonder and love. I dedicate this book to the memory of Graham Bury; to my mother, Eden; my grandmother, Mary; and to Meg.

INTRODUCTION

After Legitimacy

You have failed, you have done wrong,
says the modern orientalist.
—EDWARD SAID

In July 2007, Beijing TV aired a story about local food stalls that served steamed buns (*baozi* 包子) filled with fat-soaked cardboard instead of pork. The money-saving tactic caused an uproar in the city's media and was broadcast nationwide on China Central Television (CCTV), leading people to speculate about food safety and the everyday flavors of getting ahead in the capital. Shortly after the report aired it was retracted by the station as itself a fake. The journalist, Zi Beijia, allegedly staged the story based on hearsay using migrant workers. He had hoped to the boost the ratings of *Degrees of Transparency* (*Toumingdu* 透明度), a program he produced for Beijing TV's Life Channel. Soon after, Mr. Zi issued a formal apology and was arrested. The fake story about the fake baozi, however, did not go away. The media and passing conversations revealed a rampant belief that the fake buns were in fact real—that is, actually filled with fatty pulp—and that the retraction, apology, and arrest were put on by government intervention.¹ Unsavory practices that contributed to the negative "made in China" image, it was thought, would not to be tolerated in the Olympic era—a period intrinsically linked to China's twenty-first-century media urbanism.

Regardless of the story's truth,² the string of fakes, or more precisely uncertainties, underline a host of issues related to media, development, and legitimacy in contemporary China—and globally. In the very same week in July 2007, the former head of China's State Food and Drug Administration, Zheng Xiaoyu, was executed for accepting bribes to approve substandard and tainted medicine. The proximate months were equally marred by repeated controversies, at home and abroad, over poisonous infant formula, contaminated toothpaste, intellectual property (IP) violations, performance-enhancing drugs, human rights abuses, artificial rain, images of stubborn "nail houses" (*dingzihu* 钉子户), campaigns against corruption and pornography, and confusion over the high steroid levels of Beijing's poultry. This latter fact hit the news as part of a campaign boasting that Olympic athletes would eat from a separate food supply chain. Residents wondered why their food was not fit for visitors.

What troubles is not that people modify food with cheap ingredients for economic advantage, or that information is manipulated and put to various ends—such stories are overwhelmingly ordinary—but rather the fear that one's ability to discern paper food and bad news has somehow been diminished. The story about the alleged cardboard buns is filled with this confusion—they are literally con-fused—pointing to changing notions of how the state and citizens should act, the commercialization of media industries, and new discourses of (il)legitimacy that are irresolutely *after* socialism. These mushrooming experiences of disorientation, extralegality, and social endangerment are at the center of underglobalization, though it is often said to be something else entirely. While these examples are specific to the People's Republic of China (PRC), this felt sense of uncertainty also extends across the continents, shored up by anxieties about fake news, failing ecologies, massive inequity, resurgent fascisms, neoliberal reasoning, and more. Put differently, illegitimacy—as a marker of illegality, abnormality, and crisis—is both a protocol and an outcome of globalizing processes.

While the mundane example of the cardboard bun privileges a key period in my own research—the years framing the 2008 Beijing Olympic Games—the uncertainties it projects have only intensified in subsequent years: from stories about picture-perfect fake Apple stores, false reports of former Premier Jiang Zemin's death, and the confiscation of "miracle pills" allegedly made from dead babies, to evidence of pervasive academic fraud; widely reported ghost cities; the global fascination with the detention of figures like Liu Xiaobo, Chen Guangcheng, and Ai Weiwei; and salacious tales of corruption. The latter is exemplified by the 2012 Bo Xilai and Gu Kailai scandal, including Bo's dismissal as Chongqing party chief and removal from the Politburo, and Gu's conviction for the murder of British businessman Neil Heywood. The opaqueness of Beijing's polluted skyline is more than a metaphor.

In this way, the cardboard baozi is emblematic of a new social mode where fake is broadly defined to conflate a range of meanings and practices. Fakes are not genuine (not pork), second-rate (not as good as pork), harmful (poisonous, lacking in nutrition), and punishable (by arrest, execution, pedagogical intervention), and, at the same time, can be a productive strategy to lower costs, increase ratings, and assert control over an epistemological or social field (e.g., state intervention, street-level doubt, fake news). This emerging cultural, economic, and political logic, or *illogic*—which extends far beyond the commonplace discussion of counterfeit goods and media piracy—is the focus of this book. It centers on struggles over legality and legitimacy, and their deep embeddedness in the technologized city, during a period that I term the *Olympic era*: from Beijing's victorious Olympic bid in July 2001, to the nineteth anniversary of the Chinese Communist Party in 2011, and into the speculative future of the 2022 Beijing Winter Games.

The Fake

The fake—variously figured as *jiahuo* 假货 (faked goods) or *fangmaopin* 方冒品 (counterfeit), *daoban* 盗版 (pirated), *kelong* 克隆 (cloned), *gao* 稿 (copied),[3] or *shanzhai* 山寨 (a common term for copies of branded products, especially electronics),[4] among many other such terms—emerges and is put into discourse under a particular set of historical conditions. The cultural theorist Akbar Abbas describes this "historical marker" as the process of "faking globalization." He argues that fakes appear when cities are "just about to enter the world economy and become exposed to media representations of global commodities." The fake, for Abbas, is part of a historical stepladder that disappears, or reappears in bona fide forms, when a city or country integrates more fully into global structures; it is a *symptom* of development.[5]

Abbas's well-known essay is an emblematic frame for this book. I build on a number of his insights about the transformation of Chinese cities, informal and piratical practices, and their relation to globalization. But ultimately, I disagree with his conclusions about fakes, design, and development. I take these up more fully below. In short, whereas Abbas turns to design culture as a geopolitical fix, perhaps as a kind of pharmakon, I locate the problem elsewhere. This book begins to theorize a larger process of *faking globalization*— what I reconceptualize as *underglobalization*—examining the frictions and folds between an emergent China and prevailing hegemonic structures. Put differently, it moves beyond the common focus on counterfeit objects, pirate consumption, and benevolent norms. Instead, it examines multiplying conditions of illegality and illegitimacy, and the basic relation of such conditions to dominant models for development and futurity (from district governments to the World Trade Organization): illegal citizens and cities, erratic legitimacies newly tethered to media infrastructures and performativities, and a global condition that, despite its own triumphalist rhetoric, is profoundly antidemocratic, unequal, and unjust.

As a starting point, I share Abbas's concern with the inadequacy of our current frameworks for meaningfully engaging Asian urbanism, illicit assemblages, and forms of political action. Instead, "we must come up with new terms and new frameworks" to engage this complex media urbanism at all.[6] This is particularly true of Chinese media/area studies' deep narrowness—which too often emphasizes national culture and discrete fields such as literature, cinema, and the new. Such frames are largely uninterested in inter-Asian or intermedial dynamics, or in the crucial social and political interpenetrations that make illicit life meaningful. Instead, they rely on what Bhaskar Sarkar calls an "additive" model of the global—where, if you add up all of the areas, you have a world.[7] Against such a static world picture, pirate culture and politics make sense only as part of a mutating system of prescribed and proscribed imitations, and the structural harmonizing of legal regimes, economic norms, and aspirational lifeworlds.[8] This is what has led political scientists like Edward S. Steinfeld—not to mention publications from *The Economist* to *Foreign Affairs*—to argue that "China's rise doesn't threaten the West"; instead, the architecture of globalization has developing nations "playing our game."[9]

Let me briefly rehearse a few of Abbas's arguments in the "Faking Globalization" essay. He begins by offering three concepts for engaging Asian cities and their ineluctable relation to globalization: Gilles Deleuze's "any-space-whatever," Mario Gandelsonas's "X-urbanism," and Abbas's own riff on the latter term, *X-colonialism*.[10] Together these concepts, while distinct, theorize a shift in the experience of the city and of everyday life that are deeply uncertain—not unlike the confusion of chewing on a cardboard baozi. The first term describes processes of fragmentation and disorientation, both in cinema and in spatial practice (such as Deleuze's theorization of the "movement image" and focus on postwar ruins and shantytowns), where, as Abbas puts it, space describes "places we do not yet understand, or no longer understand," and affect refers to "emotions we do not yet have, or no longer have a name for."[11]

Such unmooring is amplified by new modes of replication that have transformed the image and experience of the city in ways that are affectively felt but are often unregistered by visual knowledge—a mode of visuality or repetition that makes it difficult to see.[12] Drawing on Gandelsonas's X-urbanism, and resonant with theorizations of digital culture, Abbas describes this replication as *fractal*. Its logic disrupts previous urban forms, like the unicentric model of downtown and suburb, not by contesting the whole or adding a new discrete dimension, but through "the replication, on a smaller scale, of the whole."[13] X-urbanism is a model of reproduction or diffusion that basically challenges existing ideas about social and political space—where, for instance, the richest and poorest are not separated by continents but live as neighbors, worlds apart—transforming the import of repetition itself (as imitation, model, transfer, atmosphere, digitization, etc.). Finally, Abbas argues that fractal replication matters beyond urban form or developmental gestures and is crucial to how colonialism transforms itself as a structure of dominance—the X-colonial. As above, this presence is hard to describe, not where one expects it to be, affectively powerful but unnamed, and yet vital to the performativity of legitimacy and control. It is, in other words, spectral. I develop this idea in chapter 1 in relation to the experience of ruins and of planning's new visual culture.

It is when Abbas turns to the fake that the essay becomes most illuminating and most infuriating—a paradoxical mode of theorizing that he relishes. He moves through a wide range of examples—from Orson Welles's *F Is for Fake* (1973), Swiss watch *ebanchés* (movements), and the "original-fake," to the politics of fake consumption—demonstrating how fakes can destabilize our very categories of authenticity and drive puzzlement.[14] What is useful in Abbas's analysis of the fake is that he refuses simple moralizing or the familiar invocation of legal regimes to manage the piratical. The RAND Corporation's report *Film Piracy, Organized Crime, and Terrorism* is emblematic of such narratives, linking the financial losses of US movie studios to the criminal acts of cartels and terrorists.[15] Such reasoning justifies both direct and covert interventionism the world over, turning pirates into terrorists and affluent white male hackers into darling CEOs of Silicon Valley–style tech-utopias. Instead, he takes the contradictions of the fake seriously. Abbas argues that the fake never exists in isolation—rather, it depends on experts, legal regimes, technology, developmental logic, and so on—and that its value is as a "symptom of a set of social, economic, and cultural conditions" that we must consider how to change.[16]

At the same time—and this is what I find most significant—Abbas sees a clear limit on the social and political value of the fake and informal or piratical practices, and on their capacity to disturb the condition of globalization itself. He writes: "When something is faked, global order is not disturbed; in fact, the fake confirms, rather than subverts the global division of labor, made worse now by the fact that it is developing countries that condemn *themselves* to the (fake) production of First World designs. The fake is not, as it is sometimes represented to be, capable of being politically subversive of the global order."[17] He arrives at this conclusion after a curious comparison of Richard Rosecrance's developmental parable of "head" (designing) and "body" (manufacturing) nations, and Ziauddin Sardar's postcolonial challenge to global commodity consumption in the form of Malaysian street piracy. Abbas finds each claim, in a different way, to be too optimistic. The former assumes that foreign investment, technology transfer, and manufacturing capacity will lead assembling nations to grow their own heads, becoming designers. It does not account for basic inequities, the experience of lag and enforced imitation, or whether in fact this "meanwhile" will ever arrive. On the other hand, Sardar's understanding of the "gentle inversion" of "in-cluded" Malays, with their fake fashions and cloned mobile phones, emphasizes the timeliness of the fake as an immediate form of technology transfer. But its short-term gains, for Abbas, confirm rather than subvert the global order.[18]

Against these two optimisms—one hegemonic, the other a form of making do—he abruptly concludes the essay with another inversion: the problem with the fake is not its lawlessness and radicality, but that it is "too rule-bound and conservative." While provocative, the claim leads to a narrow understanding of the fake and faking it, and, in my view, a deeply problematic conclusion: "the best way to go beyond the fake is not through legislation" (all good so far!), "but to encourage the development of design culture." To be fair, his provocations about design are intriguing if far too vague—that it "falsify" rather than "fake," that it stop making crap that is so easy to copy, and that it include those responsible for the informal economy.[19]

What I want to emphasize here is this: Abbas erects a threshold for what constitutes transformative practice, and clearly locates the value of the fake in the narrow context of high-value commodity design (e.g., in designing, not making). What is surprising is how unsurprising the conclusion is: it is a familiar call to avant-garde production that is pedagogical in its idealizations, fits easily within the global creative economy and China's own innovation ambitions, and is oddly dismissive of real conditions of precarity, abandonment, and the becoming illegal of everyday forms of life. At best this call for design merely reverses the head–body problem, sending manufacturing further down the food chain. Hence his playful suggestion that the West fears China's power to design more than its power to copy: "once China can also design, it will be unstoppable."[20] The question of what design creates and for whom requires more attention.

From Fake Things to Illegal Life

Abbas's thresholding and symptomatic reading of the fake are important because they are familiar. In one way or another his arguments are reiterated by much of the best work on informal media, piracy, and other forms of

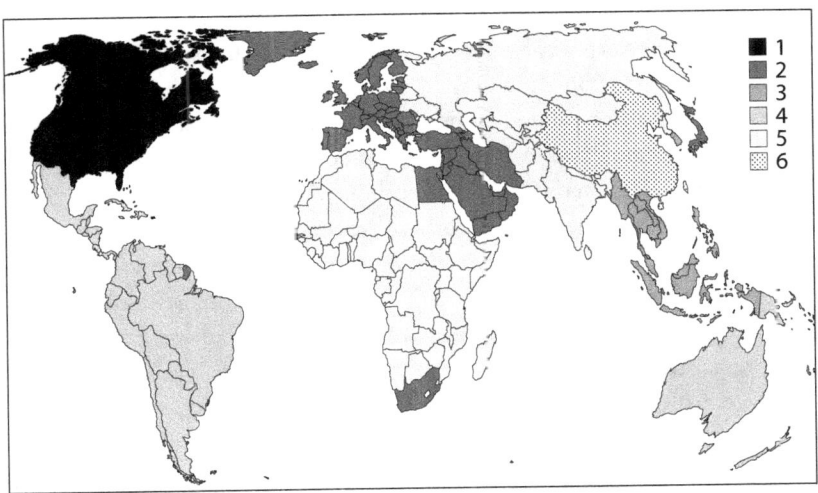

Map I.1 DVD region coding quarantines China into a single zone. Adapted from "Map of DVD Regions with a Key" by Monaneko, available under GNU Free Documentation License.

make-do politics and sociality. Many such works—including what I take to be seminal books in media studies, such as Pang Laikwan's *Creativity and Its Discontents*, Ramon Lobato and Julian Thomas's *The Informal Media Economy*, Joe Karaganis's *Media Piracy in Emerging Economies*, and Ravi Sundaram's *Pirate Modernity: Delhi's Media Urbanism*—explore the piratical but also establish a clear limit to the value of the illicit and the informal as political thought and action. Thus, while fake practices may draw attention to real problems, and are titillating in their transgression and shoddy inventiveness—as with discussions of local make-do practices like shanzhai, *jugaad*, and *gambiara*—such practices are hardly the stuff of serious cultural engagement or political theory. This gap between the meaningful and the trivial, center and edge, draws our attention to an epistemological block: the discursive construction of piracy impedes understandings of actually existing forms and practices.[21] While the piratical announces a broad array of social forms and relations—from the DIY and the survivalist to indeterminate zones and the blatantly illegal and antisocial—it also helps us to conceptualize a particular relationship to legality and legitimacy shored up by media globalization. I will return to this idea shortly.

There are, of course, good reasons for dismissals. Concerns about fakes and faking it are also familiar: piratical practices may be illicit but they are not self-consciously political; at best they are "prepolitical," and thus fail to

INTRODUCTION 7

constitute anything like a counterpublic;[22] informal practices are apertures to formality and thus are easily incorporated by the existing state and corporate structures; focusing on the informal and make-do practices is just more of the romance industry shored up by cultural studies and related fields, where resistance is located and evocatively described, but nothing changes; pirate production steals from the legitimate economy, but damages artists and small-scale producers the most; piracy is best described as a "global pricing problem" and should be understood in relation to access and economic concerns;[23] pirates challenge the rule of law upon which democratic life is built; piracy enables short-term inhabitations for subaltern and popular populations but also brings "them to the edge of permanent technological visibility" and surveillance;[24] unregulated practices lead to real dangers like the production of fake infant formulas or medicines that harm or kill people, and thus "forgeries can't be romanticized";[25] piracy is merely a symptom, the real action is elsewhere; among many others.

These are important issues and are taken up at different points in this book. But routine dismissals, and the general policing of the boundary between real and fake, also do a certain kind of political work. They have become automatic and inhibiting rather than critical and enabling.[26] It is by now required to point out the limits of piracy before discussing its minor potentialities, mere footnotes to core problems. Against such dismissals, piracy and fakes—as modes of cultural, economic, and political life under conditions of illegality and illegitimacy—have more to tell and teach us. At the same time, the idea that fakes are merely symptomatic of development and disappear in so-called developed zones demonstrates the force of hegemonic claims of globalization—which is to say they are fictions. Such claims get to the heart of late capitalist logics, including deep collaborations between ostensible democracies and autocracies, and the marketization of control via commonsense categories like *creativity, authenticity, security, futurity*, and even *civil society* and *citizenship*.[27] The linkage between the cognitive economy, legal regimes, and state violence (in its banal and catastrophic forms) demands more attention.

Legal activist Lawrence Liang, in the widely circulated online documentary *Steal This Film* (2006), describes the imbrication of intellectual property and militarized violence as the repression of human potential. Liang asserts: "One cannot speak of the gap between the possible and the proscribed without actually looking at what exists between the two. And what exists between the two are legal fictions backed by extreme capabilities of violence. So, it's a terrorism of the mind that actually sustains concepts like intellectual property.

It's a terrorism that's grounded on an idea of a brutal repression of that which is actually possible."[28] Liang's critique of intellectual property and the creative economy—as a "terrorism of the mind"—inverts discourses of the pirate and terrorist, and it is a sharp reminder of what the creative economy produces. What it produces is the power to adjudicate, and to violently enforce distinctions between, real and fake things, affects, and ways of life—what we can call the *creation of legitimacy*. The flip side is a surge in gatekeeping, disciplinary actions, and illegitimacy (where illegitimacy means not sanctioned by the law and its recognizable signs or trademarks). These less visibly violent forms of brute repression are at the heart of underglobalization. Further, they shift our attention to the forms of difference and disposable worlds—what Neferti X. M. Tadiar terms "remaindered life-times"—that many neoliberal critiques, because they focus on top-down economic domination, have proven less suited to theorize.[29]

This is to recalibrate our focus from *what piracy is* to *what piracy does*. As Liang argues, a "shift in focus from the discursive and moral representation of the illegal deed to the wider social world in which the deed is located allows us to bring into light the very nature of the law that names a particular act as an illegal one."[30] A key task in this context is to repopulate the techno-economic discourses that diminish and dispose of human beings and social worlds. For example, the first part of this study addresses how the inhuman address of urban plans, devoid of people but richly rendered in vital and verdant hues, catalyzes modes of *piratical citizenship*—contested forms of urban belonging enacted by illegal but socially legitimate claims on media, infrastructure, and citizenship itself.[31] Further along this thread, the book concludes by considering how human infrastructures and the "social network of hands" recast sprawling policing projects, like China's National Anti-Pornography and Anti-Piracy Office (Quanguo saohuang dafei gongzuo xiaozhu bangongshi 全国扫黄打非工作小组办公室), which combines copyright enforcement with nebulous antistate or pornographic targets. What is not potentially illegal in this context? Each of these, and the chapters in between, is centered on a shift from examining fake things to theorizing the antagonisms of illegal life.

These debates are not new. They recall, among other things, the mottled practices associated with popular shanzhai (literally "mountain fortress" 山寨) and *jianghu* (literally "rivers and lakes" 江湖) culture, among other lawless zones in China's past and present imagination. Often traced back to the fourteenth-century text *Outlaws of the Marsh* (*Shuihuzhuan* 水浒传), shanzhai and jianghu draw our attention to time and space outside the familiar, such as the alternative worlds of *wuxia* (martial arts 武侠) literature and cinema.

Taiwanese scholar Josephine Ho describes shanzhai as various outlaw communities and modes of "self-preservation and self-protection" that emerge during particularly troubled times in Chinese history. She adds: "with only limited resources afforded by the defensive geographic location, and pressed by the desire for survival, these fortresses had also been known to sometimes resort to highwayman or Robin Hood–style robberies."[32] Now applied to copycat electronics that disassemble and remake global brands like Apple and Samsung, shanzhai productions mark a tentative position outside the economic order that has been both celebrated for its vitality and, at the same time, condemned as criminal or primitive.[33] Critically, the concepts stake out communities at the edge of the social—what we might think of as quotidian if structural heterotopias—sites that are at once integral to the cognitive economy and drive an informal politics of assembly. This line between creative and menial labor, the socially valuable and socially tolerated, for example, is the focus of chapter 5.

Similarly, these contemporary forms recall Marcus Tullius Cicero's 2,000-year-old proclamation that pirates, because they operate outside of territorial sovereignty and ordinary jurisdiction, are the "enemy of all" (*hostis humani generis*). Under Roman law, and subsequently international law, piracy came to define a new legal category distinct from individuals and states.[34] It carves out an alternative "legal geography," both inside and beyond the state, that denies subjects legal status in the world.[35] As Daniel Heller-Roazen argues, they can neither be considered "common criminals" under the civil code, nor "be represented of lawful enemies, for by virtue of their enmity with respect to the general collectivity they fail to constitute an association with which there might be peace as well as war."[36]

As such, the pirate is legitimized as the universal enemy of humankind and thus can be killed by anyone. This startling and resilient formulation—durable because this logic continues to enable slow and catastrophic violence toward various nonstate actors; terrorists; immigrants and refugees; sexual, gender, religious, and racial minorities; as well as those operating in indeterminate legal zones, such as the sea—captures how piracy troubles legal and social legitimacy, and seeps into ordinary life.[37] This includes the possibility of "the collapse of the distinction between the criminal and the political." Put differently, the zone of illegality ordained by the "enemy of all" leads to a transformation of the idea of war.[38] It relocates warfare to seemingly mundane levels of the social—immunizing some from risk, exposing others—consolidating new legal regimes centered on the exclusion and eradication of illegal forms of life. What matters here is how illegal or piratical subjects, practices, and sites—placed outside of and endangered by the whole—are recast and proliferate under neoliberal cum postsocialist legitimacies and governance. This illicit assemblage, and not counterfeit IP or uncreative Asians, is the real problem specified by underglobalization. In this way, *Underglobalization* contributes to decades-long debates about colonialism and development, ranging from Walter Rodney's foundational critique, *How Europe Underdeveloped Africa*, to Tomás Gutiérrez Alea's 1968 film *Memories of Underdevelopment (Memorias del Subdesarrollo)*.[39] That questions of underdevelopment are central to recent Chinese cultural production, and that China is now the power tied to the underdevelopment of Africa, among other areas, signals the importance and complexity of this problem.

It is worth noting here that the "enemy of all" does not neatly map onto Carl Schmitt's well-known articulation of the "state of exception."[40] The exception operates on the dichotomy of "law" versus "no law," where, in theory, the law is operative or it is suspended, and the sovereign is the one who can decide. In contrast, piracy inaugurates a paradoxical formation. It is a legal category that makes the exception permanent, extralegal—which is to say it is only ever partially a legal formation to begin with. The idea of piracy in international law is thus not based only or even primarily on the authority to decide on the state of exception—on, that is, the power to suspend democracy during crisis—but rather the entangled power to decide on the state of normality and inclusion, and thus abnormality and exclusion, *distinct from legal norms*. This is the power to determine real and fake, human and inhuman. In other words, the logic of *hostis humani generis* offers its own challenge to understandings of sovereignty. And this challenge, following Achille Mbembe's intervention in a parallel context, is *necropolitical* rather than biopolitical. As Mbembe puts it: "sovereignty means the capacity to define who matters and who does not, who is *disposable* and who is not."[41] Here, most basically, we find the troubling and peculiar linkage between fake things and fake life.

To be clear, I agree with Schmitt's foundational claim that sovereignty rests on the power to decide rather than on legal norms. Indeed, my aim is to push his Hobbesian notion that authority and not truth makes laws into the mundane world of media urbanism and global contact.[42] To do so requires challenging the scale or intensity of what constitutes meaningful events or crises. The exception is not invoked for the banal, the chronic, the pathology of the normal. As Elizabeth Povinelli forcefully argues in *Economies of Abandonment*, in much of the disposability, exposure, and killing that proliferates across the global system, "nothing happens that rises to the level of an event let alone crisis." Rather, it suggests a "dispersed suffering" for which the state of exception need not ever be invoked.⁴³ Schmitt's exception thus needs to be pushed to its extreme—which is to say, to its most banal. When left only to ponder the possible limit or suspension of the system itself, the exception becomes a kind of ruse, misrecognizing the real emergency. This transposition, in my view, is entangled with another important shift: the waxing of legitimacy and waning of legality as sovereign forces across the global system.

In this regard, a basic aim of this book is to reorient research about piracy and the fake away from a narrow focus on copyright and related violations, which spectacularize headlines about northern loss and southern larceny—and toward concrete failures in legality, democracy, and globalization. These are not simply China's failures, as Euro-American pundits and scholars have it, but are intrinsic to the global system that it cocreates. Bourgeoning and global forms of illegality include illicit relationships to water, food, housing, electricity, medicine, education, political representation, labor, religion, mobility, gender, imagination, technology, cities, and citizenship itself. Beyond the focus on discrete commodities or legal regimes, this book begins by learning from postcolonial studies and engagements with the Global South, by tracing everyday urban forms and media practices, and by emphasizing "political society" over more familiar civil and public spheres—including critiques of the limits of such spheres in the People's Republic of China.⁴⁴

A related problem is the tendency to subordinate the political aspects of piratical and illegal practices to their economic effects. In addition to assuming the logic of WTO-style claims about creativity and development—which requires the adoption of legal protocols that benefit patent-holding nations (like the Trade-Related Aspects of Intellectual Property Rights or TRIPS), enabling new forms of "information feudalism"⁴⁵—this subordination transforms political claims into developmental crises to be solved by technocrats. Similarly, research on informal (media) economies and the survival sector, which examines how unofficial economic activities operate outside of or in partial articulation with state and corporate structures, tends to take a narrow economic view.⁴⁶ While such work has been crucial in reorienting the basic terrain of cultural production, distribution, and consumption—acknowledging that what had been called fake, shadow, or the edge is indeed the center for most people—its focus on the unmeasured, unregulated, and untaxed has downplayed or ignored how informality and pirate practices animate social and political systems. Piratical practices matter well beyond strict economic concerns, hysterical narratives of law-breaking and lost revenues, production contexts, or even the consumption side of the global economy and its emphasis on producing consumers. Indeed, one of the chief arguments of this book is that informal and illicit culture and creativity—as modes of underperformativity—not only open up new economic zones, fostering circulation, contact, and local value, but also drive a new *distribution of the social*.

Global Political Society

The fiction of law has been exposed by globalization. Put differently, sovereignty is to legality what competing sovereignties are to legitimacy. By this I mean simply that the overlapping spatial and temporal controls intensified by globalization basically transform legal effects and affects. If the imag*inational* allowed for a relatively coherent sense of territoriality, jurisdiction, and the law, then global flows and permeabilities constantly disregard, resituate, and remake these claims. In the context of intellectual property and piracy, Shujen Wang describes the problematic enforcement of global copyright at distinct scales as a shuttling between liminal spaces: "between copyright legislation and law enforcement, between global copyright governance and national/local compliance, between global actors and national networks, and among different levels of juridical spaces and overlapping sovereignties."[47] Following Saskia Sassen and Aihwa Ong, among others, Wang argues that national-global models are insufficient to make sense of what is a "polycentric legal order" consisting of "multiplying and overlapping sovereignties."[48]

Overlapping sovereignty describes multiscalar negotiations and a crucial shift in the textures of legality and legitimacy. This emergent confusion is a many-headed hydra. On the one hand, it emphasizes a range of debates in international affairs. As Richard Falk asks, "can international actions be regarded as legitimate even if they are not legal? And are legal actions in the global arena sometimes deemed illegitimate?"[49] Falk and his coeditors have in mind a range of current issues in international law, including military interventions—which are often understood by international bodies to be legitimate even if they are illegal (and vice versa). Sovereign states are not supposed to invade one another, but in certain cases (and importantly not in others) public opinion and institutions like the United Nations or states like United States or the People's Republic of China may sanction such interventions as moral and political goods. Here, legitimacy trumps legality.[50] In other cases still, as Falk notes, they proceed regardless of legitimacy and legal will. The US invasion of Iraq in 2003 or China's excursions into the South China Sea are widely seen as both illegal and illegitimate.

This tension, focused on top-down formations in the above examples, signals a larger contemporary shift whereby legality and the law—in ad hoc, opportunistic, and at times rabidly antiprogressive fashion—give way to contested forms of legitimacy. As I develop throughout this book, overlapping sovereignty might be better considered and theorized as forms of *overlapping legitimacy*. This, in my view, is an essential ramification of proliferating conditions of under-, extra-, and illegality—and the constant negotiation between what is (il)legal and what is socially (il)legitimate. It returns us anew to Schmitt's political theology: that the sovereign is both inside and outside the law, because of the capacity to suspend it, is also to note the turtles-all-the-way-down logic of the argument. If not legality, then upon what does this authority rest? My modest answer to this question is that the workings of political society—wedged between state and civil and corporate spheres, local to transnational—bring us sharply into contact with the portable legitimacies and contests over authority that undergird contemporary forms of political subjectivity.

If competing sovereignties suggest routine exceptions and the uneven enforcement of the law—as sovereign claims multiply, expanding and contracting across scales and contact zones—then the law itself is diminished. Thus, while legal regimes speak in a loud voice and continue to buttress hegemonic global projects, they must also seek out new forms of legitimation. This observation is consonant with critiques of how neoliberalism(s) divides populations—fostering new modes of social legitimacy and illegitimacy. Consider two distinct if entangled examples. First, critiques of contemporary economic reason emphasize the increasing division between those living with legal rights and protections—now recast as privilege—and those squeezed outside the licit realm. This is to ask, as Tadiar does, "which individuals inhabit and qualify for the investor model of subjectivity and its structure of temporal experience?"[51] And which fall away as bad investments or illegal citizens? Another emblematic example is what legal activists like Vandana Shiva term "biopiracy." Biopiracy describes how Western patent systems treat local biodiversity and knowledge as "empty of prior creativity and prior rights," and hence open to outside claims of "ownership" and "invention."[52] This clear and exploitative gap between what is legal and what is legitimate also helps us to observe, as Shiva notes, that the "promotion of piracy is not an aberration in the US patent law. It is intrinsic to it."[53]

Competing legitimacies—from subnational to transnational—fill the space left by uncertain juridical powers and the paradoxical condition of weak law (e.g., overlapping, unevenly enforced, at sea), on the one hand, and growing conditions of under- or illegality on the other. From illegal squatters who make moral claims on housing or education to transnational alliances that mobilize public will for illegal interventions—including those against violence

Figure I.1 A graphic forest surrounds a construction site in Beijing—exemplifying the banal ways media become enmeshed with the city. Photo courtesy of Wang Wo.

and genocide—legitimacy increasingly bleeds into and reanimates any universal sense of the law as a political infrastructure. The recourse to legitimacy marks the instability and the failure to harmonize, or at the very least the massive gaps within, legal protocols. This recalls another of Heller-Roazen's recuperated terms, the *littorum*. The littorum designates the indeterminate zone where land meets sea, and where the fluctuations of the moving shoreline put all rights under dispute, thus challenging sovereignty and its claims on land, property, and the rule of law itself.[54]

A basic assumption of this book is that popular politics are increasingly situated in gray zones outside or between civil and state recognition—which is to say, public culture for many increasingly takes on the patina of the piratical. The proliferation of extralegal lifeworlds, where social actors must negotiate from a position beyond and between states and civil-corporate spheres, requires new critical engagements with popular politics and public cultures.[55] A crucial starting point is to move beyond the idealized self-descriptions that shore up elite democracies and the package of exported modernity, the sphere that continues to overdetermine democratic discourse, as well Eurocentric dismissals of robust political life in China and across Asia. Instead, this book seeks to engage and extend Partha Chatterjee's theorization of "political society," a concept developed in *The Politics of the Governed* and extended in numerous essays and lectures, as well as the work of other scholars, including Taiwanese cultural theorist Chen Kuan-hsing.[56] Political society expresses the workings of popular politics in zones where legitimacy matters more than legality. The concept has much to offer to understandings of political negotiation in China—and globally. It designates a political sphere that meets few of the definitional requirements of democratic theory and is yet where unfettered democracy, including its excesses, seems to actually be in action.

Underglobalization examines how pervasive discourses about *global civil society* are challenged and recalibrated by attending to its underbelly—*global political society*. This is especially important given the role of NGOs and other pedagogical institutions in China. I situate this transition in more depth in the first part of the book, but let me begin to locate political society within debates about public culture in contemporary China—though my larger interest might be described as the space between China and the world. Following the student movement and massacre in Tiananmen Square, the collapse of the Berlin Wall, both in 1989, and the dissolution of the Soviet Union in 1991, the concepts of civil society and the public sphere emerged as key tools for thinking about political negotiation and the desire for democracy in postsocialist and postcolonial states across the world. Such conceptions attempted to build on Jürgen Habermas's notion of the bourgeois public sphere, first translated into English in 1989, in order to identify those emergent realms where new democratic capacities might lurk.[57] From religious organizations to new café cultures, scholars were quick to project a familiar modernity onto a range of states—from Poland to the People's Republic of China.

This impulse was critical to many treatments of the failed student movement and state violence in Beijing and cities throughout China, culminating in numerous books and a special issue of *Modern China* in 1993.[58] The symposium "'Public Sphere'/'Civil Society' in China?" debated a spectrum of issues related to China's presocialist civil formations and the appropriateness of Habermas's ideal public sphere for thinking about non-Western contexts. The editor of the volume, Philip C. C. Huang, usefully suggested that Habermas's public sphere should be understood as part of a typology of public spheres—which included the bourgeois public sphere, among other variants—and that the concept could be reworked to engage contemporary Chinese politics. To do so, he productively theorized a "third realm" between state and society, in which both sets of actors participated.[59] This third zone is an early recognition of the importance of something like political society for examining China's transformation.

International debates, however, continued to flounder around the weight of overdetermined concepts like the public sphere, with their idealization of particular state-society relations, and ethnocentric views of the world—not to mention the neglect of Chinese intellectuals and the substantial democratic gains of China's socialist past. In the US context, scholars like Nancy Fraser turned to a critique of "actually existing democracies" in order to demonstrate the degree to which the celebrated public sphere relied on the exclusion of women and those marked by racial, economic, or sexual difference.[60] Such interventions were vital to debates about the workings of the public sphere and led to an explosion of work on "counterpublics."[61] While important works by scholars like Pheng Cheah, Bruce Robbins, Michael Warner, and Lauren Berlant, among others associated with the journal *Public Culture*, transformed the very notion of publics, they also led to stagnation in many areas, where, after a sidebar noting the awkwardness but necessity of the concepts, one could go ahead and use them.[62]

My interest here is to move away from cookie-cutter or reformulated applications of civil society and the public sphere. Instead, Chatterjee's theorization of political society is crucial throughout this study. The force of Chatterjee's conceptual innovation is that it returns us to the space of political negotiation itself. As Nivedita Menon asserts in the introduction to a 2010 collection of Chatterjee's essays, *Empire and Nation*, political society theorizes "the domain where democracy seems to be actually in action, but which meets none of the standards set by political theory for what is permitted to count as democracy—rationality, deliberation, reasonable justification, control over excess, non-violence."[63] Rather than exporting notions of state-society relations, Chatterjee shifts attention to the basic back-and-forth practices through which people create pressure and claim the services and things they need to live. This includes both those denied political subjectivity and rights and those engaged in the more formalized fields of rights-based negotiations (e.g., civil society). "To effectively direct those benefits toward them," he writes, the governed "must succeed in applying the right pressure at the right places in the governmental machinery."[64] Perhaps most significantly, as Chatterjee and urban theorists like AbdouMaliq Simone have shown, it is these self-generating, collective practices—generally dismissed as aberrations—that provide the basis for theorizing the social formations of the future.

Chatterjee's insights must also be located in the context of China's actually existing social struggles, and be modified to account for the critical role of media. The former is exemplified by what the political scientist Xi Chen terms "contentious authoritarianism"—a phrase that describes pervasive and normalized social protest in China, as well as the fact that "beneath the surface of noise and anxiety," China's political system remains stable.[65] As Xi puts it, China represents a seemingly peculiar case "of a strong authoritarian regime having accommodated or facilitated widespread and routinized popular and collective action for a relatively long period of time."[66] The latter—the critical role of media forms and infrastructures—is the focus of Ravi Sundaram's *Pirate Modernity: Delhi's Media Urbanism*. Sundaram argues that political society, as developed by Chatterjee, is "surprisingly devoid of technocultural networks."[67] The current experience of media urbanism, for Sundaram, emphasizes both the ways that technology has "now seeped into the everyday lives of urban residents," as well as how "media has changed the flesh of infrastructure," thereby transforming the material and imaginary city.[68] Extending Sundaram's insight to social relations and media urban practices in Olympic-era China is one of the key aims of this book. It contributes to debates over the media city, examining how political society is taken up and transformed by a wide range of media practices, forms, and spaces. Chapters 1 and 2 trace the politics of urban planning's visual culture and of inhabiting the model city; chapters 3 and 4 examine contests over emergent media and spatial legitimacies, focusing on ambient television and the explosion of new movie theaters; and chapters 5 and 6 trace the politics of global connection and technological intimacy, examining microelectronics labor and the hand-to-hand assemblies of street piracy—what I call "people as media infrastructure."

The work of Chen Kuan-hsing, one of the leading voices of inter-Asian cultural studies, is also key to this discussion. In particular, Chen takes seriously Chatterjee's theorization of political struggles in non-Western social formations and resituates political society in the context of Taiwan and East Asia more generally. He offers the concept of *minjian shehui* 民间社会—which roughly corresponds to "people's" or "folk" society, emphasizing a certain "in-betweenness"—to describe the "space where traditions are maintained as resources to help common people survive the violent rupture brought about by the modernizing of state and civil society."[69] This emphasis on local cosmologies in working out locally situated but global processes is central to political society's transnational relevance. As such, Chen's intervention also foregrounds the generative role of interreferencing across Asia(s), and other marginalized locales, as central to contemporary cultural and political theory. Chen describes the potential of *Asia as Method*: "The potential of Asia as method is this: using the idea of Asia as an imaginary anchoring point, societies in Asia can become each other's points of reference, so that the understanding of the self may be transformed, and subjectivity rebuilt. On this basis, the diverse historical experiences and rich social practices of Asia may be mobilized to provide alternative horizons and perspectives. This method of engagement, I believe, has the potential to advance a different understanding of world history."[70]

Building on this insight, *Underglobalization* draws on inter-Asian cultural studies and parallel engagements with urban politics in Africa and South and East Asia—archipelagos of diverse and dynamic world-building projects. Abbas's Hong Kong, Chen's Taiwan, Neferti X. M. Tadiar's Manila, Brian Larkin's Kano, Ravi Sundaram's Delhi, AbdouMaliq Simone's Dakar, Swati Chattopadhyay's Calcutta, Ziauddin Sardar's Kuala Lumpur, Néstor Canclini's Mexico City, Chua Beng Huat's Singapore, among many others, are critical to generating a fresh set of intersections and concerns for approaching media, urbanism, and political society in China. These sites, while distinct, share the burden of development, including the double movement of incessant Western criticism for failing to do modernity right, and the failure of development plans themselves to meet the needs of states and local populations.

Underglobalization

Such is the ambivalence of development projects. They are at once massively destructive, displacing many, but may also bring about new infrastructures and improve living conditions for sectors of the population. About this context, I have often been asked whether I think that the images of destruction and displacement that figure in my research "are bad." While I do not think this is a particularly useful question, it does point to at least two key issues. The first is the problem of the North American scholar imposing an external set of assumptions and values to evaluate Chinese aspirations. Part nativist critique and part anxiety about how orientalism lives on, it queries: Is this not just more of the same criticism—like those that fill the popular press, international relations books, legal indictments—pointing to China's excessive, authoritarian, backward, and counterfeiting ways? On the other hand, are not massive new infrastructure projects like metro systems, roads, business districts, public monuments and parks, and new housing to replace the often-dilapidated courtyard houses of the inner city an important public good? Is this not an area where China's state-led development clearly outperforms that of its G7 peers? Just observe the disappointment of Chinese tourists when they disembark at New York's shabby John F. Kennedy airport. And more to the point: how do such ambitions and images of the city differ from the package of global modernity endorsed by dominant economies like the US, the UK, Germany, or Japan?

Why is China's development constantly critiqued while the larger system it cocreates remains, for many, the global ideal?

To be clear, my analysis of postsocialist-cum-neoliberal media and developmental projects, as well as various responses to living transformation, is not interested in reiterating the same old complaints about the Chinese state—especially not those that isolate China as the bad object in order to reinforce ideas about the "free world" and the munificent West. Or that advance yet another argument in the genre: China will rise or China will fall. Those fallacies are as reckless as the picture of the cunning and excessive Chinese. Instead, this book begins to theorize a larger process of *underglobalization*—part of a more general theory "of which Western theory is just a particular case."[71] In this sense, the critiques lodged against China in this book are not exceptional (i.e., not about China alone); rather, they are emblematic (i.e., they describe a global condition). This is to eschew the still dominant and often racist West-East binary and to examine political conditions of inequity and aspiration in their local and global dimensions. It is a project that takes seriously Chinese specificities while challenging the civilizational world picture, where essentialist differences of monolithic civilizations cover over differences that matter.[72] Contra civilizational geopolitics, this book adopts an inter-Asian and southern perspective, pointing its critique at global economic and political projects, and not simply the purported excesses of the PRC.

This is not to disregard the very real issues China poses for those interested in social equity, ecological preservation, and democratic futures. But neither can these problems be taken apart from the global, to which they are intimately tied. We need to return with renewed critical force to the deep failures, structural violence, and antidemocratic pulses that sustain and are sustained by the idea of the West, including its imbrication with globalization. For starters, this is to acknowledge the role that hegemonic imitation and transfer play in global processes—from the harmonizing of intellectual property required by the World Trade Organization and the protocols of the World Bank, to the exported models for productive, consumer, and debt-driven lifestyles. That these are widely understood to be practices of equality and progressive change gives the lie to claims that copying and informality are simply the backward practices of lazy and cunning southerners.

Routine developmental fables, which have traveled across Asia in recent decades (from Japan, Taiwan, and South Korea to China, India, and the ASEAN countries), cover over the significance of imitation as a *global* and not merely a developmental phenomenon. This is to challenge the fallacy that fringe or developing nations "cheat" the well-meaning economies of the core and, at the same time, incessantly hinder themselves. Even left-leaning scholars of intellectual property like Lawrence Lessig distinguish between "good" remix cultures, which are innovative and "add value," and "bad" Asian piracy, which is "theft plain and simple."[73] While the problem of the fake is generally narrated through the lens of Asian sameness and excess—from rote memorization to authoritarian compliance—what is at stake here is a shifted understanding of transformation and, ultimately, an understanding of Asia and the non-West as not only counterfeit zones but also centers where new and non-Western forms of life are (re)produced.

As in diverse locations ranging from Scotland to South Korea, innovation and the cultural creative industries (*wenhua chuangyi chanye* 文化创意产业) are critical to contemporary Chinese policymaking and rhetoric, and to China's transition from manufacturing and export processing into a global designer (and rights holder) of film, TV, publishing, fashion, high-tech, pharma, urbanism, and the like. This creative turn complements China's "Going Out Policy" (*Zouchuqu zhanlüe* 走出去战略), initiated in 1999, encouraging the spread of overseas investment and influence. Fascination with the innovation industries has led to new government committees and plans, university departments, urban districts, smart initiatives, Confucius Institutes, and numerous recent books and essays in and about Asia, and throughout the world. In the Chinese context, for instance, Wang Jing's *Brand New China: Advertising, Media, and Commercial Culture* (2008); Michael Keane's *Created in China: The New Great Leap Forward* (2007) and *Creative Industries in China: Art, Design, and Media* (2013); Hu Huilin's *The Development of Cultural Industries and National Cultural Security* (*Wenhua chanye fazhan yu guojia wenhua anquan*, 2005); Pang Laikwan's *Creativity and Its Discontents: China's Creative Industries and Intellectual Property Rights Offenses* (2012); Winnie Wong's *Van Gogh on Demand: China and the Readymade* (2014); and Fan Yang's *Faked in China: Nation Branding, Counterfeit Culture, and Globalization* (2015), to name just a few, offer a wide range of approaches to the politics of creativity across national and global registers.

I will return to the cultural creative industries throughout the book. What I want to establish here is this: first, the creative industries extend far beyond culture and are enmeshed with media urbanism and broader geopolitical concerns; and second, formal creative and design industries, while framed as solutions to global inequity, are instead its underlying logic.[74] My aim is to bring into relief the crucial role of creative capitalism, including its Chinese characteristics, in attempting to harmonize legitimacy across subnational and supranational scales. As Pang argues, the discourse of creativity has shaped contemporary imaginaries that see China as a pirate nation and, at the same time, have led Chinese upper classes to widely embrace the idea that creativity is the key to modernization.[75] Creativity thus frames the allure and legal power wielded by the knowledge economy.

What is generally called creativity or innovation is enmeshed in thicker processes of simulation and replication that are central to hegemonic globalization. If we shift our focus from value-added content, authorship, and ownership, what comes into view is the degree to which global platforms require faking, imitation, and transfer as the price of admission. Postsocialist and neoliberal governmentality—or what we might simply call globalization in its dominant form—works both by goading much of the world to copy its structures and, at the same time, by perpetually belittling developing nations for not copying right or the right things, for copying too much, or for copying too well. From trade agreements to international standards, mimicry is far from an aberrant logic; it is the norm—functioning as a kind of software update for the developing world. This "transfer" is what is undercut by global processes.

Against this thrust, faking can also be understood as a basic and powerful reluctance or refusal to copy and to implement the specific procedures or templates associated with hegemonic global modernity—whether enforced by international institutions, state policy, or local government. This is to give a name to contemporary forms of underdevelopment—what we can call *underglobalization*. The term *underglobalization*, rather than signaling developmental lag or failure, points to the ways various actors undermine or underperform national and global protocols. The concept helps us to theorize the illicit or underworldly practices—often illegal but valid in their own contexts—at the center of this book. Key examples include emerging forms of piratical citizenship; struggles over eminent domain practices and the resulting demolition of housing and relocation of tens of thousands of Beijing residents (*chaiqian* 拆迁); claims on the technologized city, including struggles over ambient television, cinematic spectatorship, and street piracy; and mundane forms of creativity—from menial factory labor to the hand-to-hand sociality of street piracy—that are widely dismissed as mere imitation and yet drive social infrastructures and urban belonging. These reorientations turn our attention to the situated and sophisticated engagements with illicit forms by a wide range of popular and subaltern actors.

To take seriously faking as a social practice is not to romanticize what can be dangerous and antiprogressive. But neither is it to dismiss tensions over growing illegalities and illegitimacies, as is the habit of political avant-gardism and the deep-seated elitist fear of the popular that informs much of cultural and political theory. Instead, we need to examine how quotidian, ad hoc, and informal practices and semiotics drive disregarded forms of political action and social timeliness, keying in on wide-ranging struggles over the city, citizenship, and the present tense. This, in my view, suggests a useful temporal intervention into current social thought and the emphasis on *longue durée* and utopian transformations. Focusing on the informal, the survivalist, and the piratical challenges the theological dimension of radical critique—the pie-in-the-sky ethos that continually defers social equity into the revolutionary future. While radical critiques remain vital, critical social theory still has much to learn from mundane tactics and popular negotiations. The point is to understand how people find ways to inhabit the present. Finally, this is not merely to romance resistance—as the by now banal critiques of cultural studies and related fields have it—but to learn from and to transform debates about cultures of democracy. Even when they appear in unlikely times and places.

The Olympic Era

Postsocialism describes the complexity of China's reform and opening (*gaige kaifang* 改革开放), and especially life in the post-1989 or "post new period" (*hou xin shiqi* 后新时期). These competing logics include the continued rule of the Communist Party and the everyday if residual relevance of Chinese socialism, as well as China's transition to a marketized mode of cultural production and integration into the global economy—where it is now a prime mover.[76] Much scholarship, for example, has focused on the contradictions and ambiguities animating life *after* socialism. A related thread emphasizes the significance of China's transformation and capitalist compromise for what we now call globalization. Zhang Xudong argues that the condition of postsocialism "does not disappear into but becomes intertwined" with global postmodernity.[77] Similarly, what Jason McGrath calls "postsocialist modernity" describes the mutual entanglement of China and the global, where each is transformed.[78]

But Arif Dirlik, who coined the term in the late 1980s, perhaps offered the most useful if now anachronistic explanation of Chinese postsocialism.[79] For Dirlik, postsocialism not only described the new reality at the end of the grand Maoist project and command economy, but the possibility to rethink Chinese socialism anew. While tied to a particular historical moment and interest in theorizing postsocialist challenges to global capital, it remains explanatory, and its idealism remains appealing. Writing in 1989, Dirlik argues:

> Postsocialism is of necessity also postcapitalist, not in the classical sense of socialism as a phase in historical development that is anterior to capitalism, but in the sense of a socialism that represents a response to the

experience of capitalism and an attempt to overcome the deficiencies of capitalist development. Its own deficiencies and efforts to correct thereby resorting to capitalist methods of development are conditioned by this awareness of the deficiencies of capitalism in history. Hence postsocialism seeks to avoid a return to capitalism, no matter how much it may draw upon the latter to improve the performance of "actually existing socialism." For this reason, and also to legitimize the structure of "actually existing socialism," it strives to keep alive a vague vision of future socialism as the common goal of humankind while denying to it any immanent role in the determination of present social policy.[80]

Dirlik's analysis continues to resonate strongly with the present. It highlights, for example, two notable tendencies of the Xi Jinping era: permanent economic development and a reinvigoration of socialist language and imagery. The latter, in particular, is highlighted at the October 2017 Communist Party Congress, which saw "Xi Jinping Thought on Socialism with Chinese characteristics for a new era" enshrined in the constitution and, more recently, term limits abolished.[81]

Rather than suggest a simple return to Dirlik's proposal, I am interested in a parallel track proposed two decades ago by Ralph Litzinger. Litzinger calls for a decolonization of scholarship on postsocialism "by way of the ethnic margins" (while not simply identifying "the ethnic minority other [as] the quintessential sign of resistance and rebellion").[82] The question of how to write marginal communities—here: the illegible, illegitimate, illegal—into the analysis of contemporary China and of the global system has once again emerged as a pressing issue. While Litzinger's call remains vital on its own terms—and critical studies of race and ethnicity are much needed in the face of still overwhelming Han- and northern China–centered analysis—my aim is also to invert familiar approaches by making what is epistemologically at the edge, the center. This study seeks to transform approaches to the postsocialist-global by emphasizing burgeoning illegal and illegitimate forms, including how these widespread practices enact their own social infrastructures, modes of legitimacy, and political agencies.

Across this study, I employ the conceptual periodization or chronotope of the Olympic era in place of the fraught and familiar concept of postsocialism. I argue that the Olympic era consolidates postsocialism as a way of life—which is to say that what has routinely been called "postsocialist China" has become something else altogether. While the term *postsocialism* retains a certain analytical value, particularly as it links up with other postcommu-

Figure I.2 The official website of the International Olympic Committee (IOC) greets visitors with a snow-dusted image of the Great Wall and Beijing 2022.

nist and postcolonial societies and research, it often obscures more than it reveals. On the one hand, it severs critical ties with prereform China(s). On the other hand, it frequently serves as a placeholder for what is assumed to be ungraspable, a descriptor for a condition that is taken to be too fast, opaque, and complex—an unknowable afterlife. As a historical marker, postsocialism is unconvincing. It remains overly invested in the duality through which a monolithic "socialist" period is opposed to a dynamic and confused "post" (or posts). In this context, gaige kaifang and the years bracketing the suppressed student movement in Tiananmen Square and Deng Xiaoping's 1992 southern tour (*nanxun* 南巡) are very often taken as *the* turning points in the rise of China. While significant, such tales of transformation make static what is in fact dynamic and ongoing change.

The "post" in postsocialism suggests both transformation (*zhuanxing* 转型) and stability (*wending* 稳定). Stability is a fascinating concept. It suggests solidity, steadiness, sanity, strength, and security, as in the permanence of the Chinese state, the importance of social harmony for economic growth, and the need for rational planning and enforcement (e.g., five-year plans, sacrifice). But stability requires constant interventions and rigid policing, and poses important problems for transformation after socialism. Development and stability, interestingly, presuppose contradictory tempos and imaginaries for Chinese modernity. Development suggests the unfolding, evolution, or modernization of China, while stability insists on its fixity, security, and immutability. This fact is explained by the dual emphasis on discourses of limitless modernization and celebrations of a changeless

INTRODUCTION 25

cultural heritage. The Olympics, as a developmental medium, spectacularizes and links these spatiotemporal fascinations, stitching together a harmonious image of the ancient and the technologized future city (see figure I.3). Similarly, events like China's sixtieth anniversary celebration on October 1, 2009, national filmic spectaculars like *The Founding of a Republic* (Han Sanping and Huang Jianxing, 2009) and *The Founding of a Party* (Han and Huang, 2011), and CCTV's annual new year's gala also scramble to connect China to this bipolar imaginary. What they share is a focus on the past and the future that disappears the present.

This paradoxical vector is central to what I term the Olympic era. The Olympic era clears fresh space for the consideration not only of China's relationship to the past—it is, in part, a repetition[83]—but also of the continued significance of technological development and models of the future. Integral to such shifts are contemporary processes of *media urbanism*—for which the Olympics are an emblematic global form. Such mega-events not only require the material remaking of the city, they also prepare the city as an image for global circulation, transforming it into a media capital.[84] The media capital produces new feelings of legitimacy via monumental and mundane infrastructures and habits, and the proliferation of mediated forms. While the book is not explicitly about the Beijing Olympics, I take the 2008 and 2022 Games as a periodizing blueprint for analyzing the cultural politics of transformation in twenty-first-century China.

Underglobalization examines the cultural logic of the fake across different media technologies that shape politics, development, and aspiration in Olympic-era China. This analysis centers on cinema and television practices, urban space, and design, tracing how Beijing functions as a pivot for public communication about the future of the social body. Specifically, I interrogate a range of contested claims on the social: planning's visual culture, ambient TV, film and video exhibition, electronics labor and technological intimacy, and the entanglement of piracy and pornography. In this context, I argue that digital cultural economies and the turn to the creative industries underscore how "faking" and "legitimacy" operate as confused forms of postscocialist, neoliberal, and neocolonial emergence and control. In this way, piratical culture and politics constitute a set of prescribed and proscribed imitations that both sustain the world system and dismiss of Chinese modernization itself as counterfeit, false, or excessive. Arguing for a shift from global civil society to global political society, this study asks how mundane and mediated practices of faking (and its myriad cognates) undergird and transform globalization as we know it.

Beijing as Method

This book draws on research I conducted during several extended trips to Beijing between 2007 and 2016, including regular summer visits and a continuous stay of fifteen months in 2007–8. The research unfolded in three stages, beginning in the mid-2000s as a representational and ethnographic study of Beijing's film and TV cultures and their relationship to Olympic-era development. In the course of conducting my fieldwork, as it became clear just how vital new screen technologies were to remaking the city, I began to expand my analysis beyond urban cinema, television programs, and planning discourse. Instead, I was struck by the proliferation of digital forms and practices across the city—construction-site billboards and planning imagery, ubiquitous screens (from buses to building façades), new movie theater construction, electronics markets and optical disc piracy, mobile phones and digital video cameras, and so much more. Crucially, these media urban forms were both out of sync with dominant ideas about new media—which tended to see China as backward and to ignore local digital cultures—and also beyond the purview of cinema studies, visual studies, Asian studies, anthropology, and related fields.

Building on these insights, the second stage of my research begins from actually existing media phenomena in the city, relying on observation and attention to spatial practices, materials gleaned from personal and professional relationships, formal and informal interviews, participation in archiving and film festival communities,[85] and photography and video projects.[86] One starting point, for example, was to walk or cycle the major arteries and narrow alleyways in the inner city (within the Second Ring Road), among other sites associated with Olympic urbanization (e.g., the Olympic Green, central business district, 798 Art Zone, Haidian District, among others), in order to better apprehend the relationship between media technologies and demolition and construction projects. On many trips, I was accompanied by a photographer and graduate students from Peking University and Beijing Normal University. My approach was to map new developments in the city, and based on street-by-street observation I began to focus on—and to photograph, describe, and archive—a cluster of objects and sites that were clearly significant but that remained underexplored. Everywhere I went during this stage, I encountered a clash between older and informal media practices and new, more centralized forms of address. Countertop TVs were replaced by new state-corporate displays; independent film festivals were pressured by flashy cinemas and state-run galas; colorful images of the ancient or future city covered over demolished neighborhoods; antipiracy and antipornography campaigns were performed in public squares and filled newspapers, banners, and television news.

This perambulatory mode of meeting the city through the camera was not only a way to map social and media space; it was also a way to meet people. Residents, visitors, even the police were quick to share their own stories, suggest other locations, offer interpretations, tell you to move on. While I conducted informal interviews with neighbors and shopkeepers, construction managers and print shop workers, activists and filmmakers, my research departs from traditional ethnography and its focus on informants and community dynamics. Instead, I became more and more interested in the role of media technologies, alongside people and institutions, as agents of change. In this way, I prefer the terms *sociography* or *technography* to describe the method of this project. The former I borrow from Elizabeth Povinelli, via James Clifford, to describe a shift from traditional ethnographic thick description toward "a way of writing the social from the point of view of social projects."[87] Extending Povinelli's interest in alternative social projects, my research engages and writes the social from the point of view of *technologized social projects*. This is what is meant by the concept of media urbanism across this book.

This focus on technologized sociality was also informed by collaborations at the Li Xianting Film Fund and documentary archive in Songzhuang—an artist hub in Beijing's eastern suburbs. This includes regular participation in the China Documentary Film Festival (Zhongguo jilupian jiaoliu zhou) and Beijing Independent Film Festival (Beijing duli yingzhan), interviews with filmmakers, production of a documentary film focused on China's railways (*The Iron Ministry*, 2014, directed by JP Sniadecki), and long evenings spent watching films and discussing politics. Here is where I first became fascinated with how activists and filmmakers established informal archives to keep and share their work and utilized piracy networks to distribute their films, where I observed police interventions push festival screenings into private living rooms or other cities far from the capital, and where I observed many Chinese friends leave for North America, Europe, and Australia. In this way, I began to understand the tension between locally legitimate practices and pervasive illegality. Put differently, examining media piracy led me to much broader and more significant problems.

As my research went on, it became increasingly clear that to make sense of Beijing's media urbanism I would need to better understand the larger medial and political dynamics that shaped widespread discourses about piracy, imitation, and informality—what I would eventually call *underglobalization*. To that end, I expanded the scope of the research once again. My aim was to contribute to important debates in media and cultural studies but also to refuse the disciplinary limits articulated by those fields. As I became more focused on piratical social practices, and on the normalized condition of illegality, I also recognized that understanding these practices only in terms of media or intellectual property—the contours of dominant discourse—was to miss the point. Thus, the final stage of this research brought me more squarely into contact with social and political theory, including postcolonial studies, Asian cultural studies, political science, and sociology. By working between the spaces and objects from my technographic research, and larger theoretical engagements with social, economic, and political change in China and the Global South, I came to appreciate the contradictory role of imitation or faking as a global logic—legality and legitimacy were at loggerheads. This emphasis on the becoming illegal of everyday life also helped me to understand the way that official media objects and practices—by providing narratives of danger or economic loss, enabling policing, shaping social aspirations, training the sensorium, and so on—inform more insidious systems of political and economic exclusion and violence.

Structure of the Book

This book examines illegality and illegitimacy as global techniques and techniques of being global. It engages practices and sites of faking or underglobalization at multiple scales and across contact zones—shifting attention from fake objects to illegal citizens. It takes the routine dismissal of and anxiety over forgery, failure, and falsity as the chief line of inquiry—as the real symptom—asking: How or in what ways is faking altering or undermining globalization as we know it? What role does this process play in China's own contested desires for development? How does faking capacitate models of social, political, and economic practice or collaboration—that is, new social projects and understandings of authenticity—across a range of actors, street-level to the state, local to global? And what does it mean to bring informal, illicit, and fringe practices—overlooked social and political infrastructures—to the center of critical analysis and social thought? If underglobalization is not merely yet another southern flop, marking anachronistic habits and cities, then perhaps its variegated forms can provide models for building new societies. What I termed "after legitimacy" at the start of this introduction is thus to name not legitimacy's end, but rather the founding of critical projects on the back of socially legitimate, if illegal, forms of life.

Chapter 1, "Rendering the City," offers both a history of a particularly salient moment in Beijing's transformation and a reinterpretation of what this remaking means in the context of media and political theory. The chapter examines how ruins and blueprints constitute the sensorium of the technologized city. It centers on how Beijing is produced as a set of competing vectors—between past and future—and how these dominant modes of experience make claims on its present. Of particular importance is Sundaram's idea of *media urbanism*—a synthetic concept that brings together important material and imaginary practices. This includes the long-standing tension between culture and development itself. Rendering the city thus takes seriously planning's visual culture and adapts a mode of reading the city that is attentive to design's address as well as the imbricated politics of dispossession. It concludes by developing an approach to the politics of the governed suited the emergent sphere of political relations in China. Chapter 2, "Digital Urbanism," extends the discussion of the future-function of culture begun in chapter 1. It traces how media publics engage and seep into official designs and blueprints—creating their own (un)civil contracts. The chapter also lays out the conceptual foundation for the book's focus on popular politics and public culture. This infrastructure of dissensus is traced across media urban practices, including digital video and documentary, urban billboards, contemporary art, and a range of dynamic claims on city surfaces and everyday life. Drawing on what the RAQs Media Collective calls "seepage," it theorizes how *piratical* or *illegal citizens* are both managed by official structures and penetrate and transform them.

The next two chapters build on the approach to digital urbanism established in the opening chapters by examining two important sites that proliferate in the media city. Chapter 3, "Bricks and Media," begins with China's booming movie theater business. It both describes this transition and theorizes shifting modes of technologized spatiality that pit the gloss of state-led blockbuster projects against informal and alternative video cultures. This includes massive political crackdowns on China's independent film festivals and other unofficial forms. By exploring a range of specific exhibition sites, it traces both how Chinese state–market clusters increasingly reach a global audience and, at the same time, how they seek to control local screens and shape commonsense space and imaginaries. Similarly, chapter 4, "Beijing en Abyme," examines both technological changes in ambient TV culture—from handheld devices to subway television—and how official structures attempt to choreograph state-society relations at the interface. The chapter takes an intermedial approach, pushing the study of television outside the home as well as into the gallery and the cinema. The title "Beijing en Abyme" points to the proliferation of screens and images showing Beijing's transformation in the city itself, as well as how the congruence between TV and the state transforms the television into a volatile form for public communication. This includes the unhomely social, the spectral laborers who make new technologies but are pushed out of frame by media development.

The final two chapters move from site-specific issues in Beijing to a larger politics related to technology, social change, and global intimacies. Chapter 5, "Videation: Technological Intimacy and the Politics of Global Connection," centers on the unhomely laborers alluded to in the previous chapter. Moving beyond the spectacular image of worker suicides, the chapter traces everyday forms of intimacy and technomobility. It pays particular attention to the threshold between creative designs and menial labor, centering on what I call *videation*: video culture's overlooked habits, actions, and results. The chapter examines China's own neoliberal forms of abandonment and opens up what constitutes meaningful cultural production. It also considers the media savvy of workers who use low-fi video infrastructures to project their own desires and to refuse the fractured citizenship assigned to them by the state. Chapter 6, "People as Media Infrastructure," both builds on this discussion and acts as the book's conclusion. It brings the book full circle by returning to the question of pirate culture and sociality. But it does so not through an interest in intellectual property but rather by exploring the social life of informal media in Beijing, or what I call people as media infrastructure. This chapter engages media infrastructure studies and seeks to extend them to people's actions in the city. An important framing element for this chapter is the National Anti-Pornography and Anti-Piracy Office (Quanguo saohuang dafei gongzuo xiaozhu bangongshi). The office and its campaigns demonstrate the confused intersections of legality and legitimacy that propel this study, and draw our attention to both competing legitimacies and what I theorize as the "pornographies of globalization." The latter phrase describes the forms of social timeliness generated by piracy's hand-to-hand sociality, and returns us to the larger illicit assemblages that frame the book.

Rendering the City
Between Ruins and Blueprints

The theory that will explain Indian democracy today or the theory that will explain China's capitalism today will actually be a far more general theory of which Western theory will just be a particular case.
—PARTHA CHATTERJEE

Power is a measure of work. Which is what maps do: they work.
—DENIS WOOD

This chapter charts Beijing's media urbanism through two imbricated figures: *ruins* and *blueprints*. Ruins express the action or materiality of decay, disaster, and destruction. Blueprints, on the other hand, signify both the process for reproducing technical designs (in white and cyan) and, in common language, plans, designs, and models in general. The imbricated shift from the image and experience of ruins, a dominant preoccupation in the audiovisual culture of the 1990s and into the 2000s, to the political space of the blueprint is at the heart of China's transformation (*zhuanxing*) in the Olympic era. It is part of a thicker process of state-market-led creative destruction that displaces prior social forms and institutions with a new imagination of citizens, cities, and the future.[1] In this chapter, I am interested in how the capital is produced as a set of competing vectors—partitioned between the fading past and the future perfect, and how it circulates across subnational and transnational scales as/in media. I refer to this fabulation as *rendering the city*. Rendering draws our

Figure 1.1 Cyanotype image of a construction site in Beijing's Dongcheng District. Created by Graham Bury and the author. Courtesy of Pam and John Bury.

attention to both low-fi and high-tech processes for generating images from models (and vice versa)—and thus the production of digital lifeworlds—as well as etymologically entangled forms of reproduction: the collection of rents, legal judgments, or the rendering of fat. Rendering is, in other words, a form of alchemy.

What I am calling ruins and blueprints are key textures in the sensorium of the technologized city. They are key because of the significance each takes on across state, market, and citizen projects—not to mention the voluminous work on China's urban transformation. But these vectors are too often divided by studies of cultural production. It is this division that the synthetic concept *media urbanism*, adapted from Ravi Sundaram's work on contemporary Delhi, re-fuses.[2] Distinct disciplinary concerns tend to isolate specific media forms,

Figure 1.2 Beijing National Stadium, aka the Bird's Nest. is one of the many architectural projects associated with Olympic-era development. Architect: Herzog and de Meuron.

artifacts, and modes of production from the messiness of spatial practice and popular politics. On the one hand, ruins and demolition have been the terrain of art historians and scholars of film, literature, anthropology, and the like (e.g., from scar literature to the New Documentary Movement). Blueprints and planning's visual culture, on the other hand, belong to designers, urbanists, and policy debates—constituting a mere background in studies of media and urban change.[3] Such well-worn disconnections fail to account for planning's visual culture as *media* and as processes of *mediation*.[4] This division also reproduces a similar tendency in social theory to understand development and culture in opposition. Arjun Appadurai, for instance, critiques the habitual thinking that links development with the future, and culture with tradition and the past.[5] The culture–development dichotomy inserts a gap in our spatial and temporal conceptions of social worlds—a gap this chapter seeks to bridge.

If development is routinely associated with progress and futurity (overly temporal, "what will be"), culture is widely understood as its obstacle, the lived baggage slowing planned economic and political transformation (overly spatial, "what was" or remains). Hence China's transformation is linked to pedagogical "civilization" (*wenming* 文明) campaigns to improve the quality, *the culture*, of its citizens (*renmin de suzhi* 人民的素质)—attempts to accelerate and recalibrate lived attributes to fit new designs.[6] Examples include everything from campaigns teaching urbanites how to queue for the subway, to stop spitting in public, or to move a step closer to the urinal to antipiracy demonstrations, new urban districts modeling consumer lifestyles, and plans or models of the urban body itself. What Appadurai terms the "capacity to aspire" thus indicates both the state's recognition that culture is key to refashioning its subjects (e.g., by improving their quality, reshaping their habits and aspirations, etc.) and, at the same time, is a crucial resource for subaltern and popular claims on the present. My aim in what follows is to explore this tension—the jostling of ruins and blueprints—paying close attention to the *future-function* of culture.

Creative Destruction and Spectral Life

The cyanotype images that open this chapter (see figures 1.1 and 1.3) perform the politics of rendering the developmental city in twenty-first-century China. Two examples out of hundreds of pictures from a collaborative photography project documenting street-level media in Beijing, the cyan-blue landscapes transform the view of the city *in transition* into a blueprint: a two-dimensional schema marked by a limited tonal range, shallow depth, soft focus, and ease of reproducibility.[7] In this regard, the handmade cyanotypes are a way of making use of my research archive to *demonstrate* the "New Beijing" (*xin Beijing* 新北京). Demonstration in this context is supplemental: a mode of capture and critique that touches upon the rhetoric at hand. It is an approach to research and to theory that aims for more than analysis by gesturing to a certain atmosphere, affect, or imagination that is vanished by analytical distance. Printing high-resolution color images in the bluish tint of ferric ammonium citrate and potassium ferricyanide both reproduces the flattened aesthetic and mode of address that defines future projections of the city, and is an aperture into design's sensorium—even as that sensorium, its aqueous blues, mossy greens, and sci-fi silvers, has become formulaic, computational, hyperreal.

Figure 1.1 frames the spatiotemporalities of the razed city *and* the model city. It displays a vinyl-printed landscape fencing in a construction site. In the left of the frame, lush visions of Beijing's green and technologized future (muted by the cyan palette): verdant parks, blue skies, car-filled boulevards, and new high-rises. In contrast, the right side of the image opens onto a dirt lot razed for new buildings and a new subway line in Beijing's Dongcheng District. A lone leafless tree in the background contradicts the dense urban forest that fills the construction site's outer wall, giving the lie to the politics that continually says that demolition, speculation, and the new necessarily lead to a healthy, thriving, and unpolluted future. The photograph stages the untimeliness of living in a model or ghost city: a zone saturated by past and future, but seemingly devoid of the present (and presence): *now* is a living in images.[8]

The picture also captures the poles of "accumulation by dispossession," David Harvey's term for how primitive accumulation lives on in the context of financial globalization—drawing out the friction between modernization and changes in quality of life. It is a crucial aspect of what Joseph Schumpeter, writing decades before, called "creative destruction" in describing the endless mutation intrinsic to capital: it "revolutionizes the economic structure from within, incessantly destroying the old one, incessantly creating a new one."[9] Harvey's neoliberal update focuses on the centrality of dispossession to these processes, such as amassing wealth through the privatization of public resources, by dismantling prior egalitarian narratives and institutions, and by providing an outlet for surplus capital through investments in megastructures and large-scale development projects. Crucially, it produces new feelings of legitimacy via monumental infrastructure and mediated forms.[10] As Harvey puts it, distinct neoliberal systems undergirding the global economy destroy not only political institutions and powers, but also "divisions of labor, social relations, welfare provisions, technological mixes, ways of life, attachments to the land, habits of the heart, ways of thought, and the like."[11]

This latter point is crucial to critiques of the China critique. For example, the political scientist Lin Chun notes the importance of socialist-era advances in education, health care, workers' rights, collective land ownership, and state protections, among other areas, to the economic successes of the reform era.[12] She writes, "Chinese socialism as one of the grandest modern projects of social emancipation—in spite of the destruction amid its colossal construction—cannot be dismissed."[13] As such, Lin challenges narratives that suggest China's crisis of development is the result of its backwardness and "incomplete market transition," arguing instead that such crises are better understood in relation to the "reform's shattered promises" for justice, equality, and democracy. In short, creative destruction takes on specific dimensions as it unfolds in China—even as it is linked to the country's phenomenal growth, including celebrations of its capacity to lift millions out of extreme poverty and its new role as a model for development across Asia and the South—unleashing new proliferations of capital that are prime movers of what has come to be intimately known as globalization.

My aim here is to extend Harvey's well-known analysis to the spectral or mediated dimensions of urban dispossession. These spectral forms both push beyond what we think we know about speculative urbanization, and offer a

Figure 1.3 Cyanotype picturing Qianmen's haunted redevelopment. New construction, background, mirrors the renderings projected on a construction site billboard in the foreground. Created by Graham Bury and the author. Courtesy of Pam and John Bury.

useful interpretive strategy. Here I draw on Bishnupriya Ghosh's examination of the spectral dimensions of security technologies in recent Bollywood horror films. Ghosh begins with two pictures of real estate speculation: a property advertisement for Singaporean-style luxury apartments in Mumbai and a documentary image of migrants living at the edge of the vertical city. The relation between these two images or lifeworlds is one of vertical security. In films like *Bhoot* (Ram Gopal Varma, 2003) or *1920* (Vikram Bhatt, 2008), among others, elevators, guards, audiovisual surveillance, and air-conditioning are not only characters but take on peculiar affective significance. Ghosh calls this dynamic the *"techno-aesthetic of security."* It at once habituates spectators to new ways of living—as they anxiously monitor dangers below—and nurtures personal investments in financial globalization. But the very technologies that "remove, sequester, or immunize" against perceived social and ecological dangers also take on an affective quality that *possesses* its viewers.[14] As Ghosh puts it, the spectral is a form of recognition that "*opens* the human sensorium to mediatized traces" of the *unhomeliness* and unrest produced by speculation, among other forms of legal and nonlegal dispossession. Put more sharply, it orients human awareness "toward the concrete remainder of the global."[15] Ghosh's examination of how a haunted coexistence infuses and directs the sensorium of the present, even while many are dispossessed, positioned as backward or merely aspirational (i.e., not present), offers a crucial insight about the experience of the technologized city—of reading ruins and renderings.

This is because, as Jacques Derrida observes in his writing on the displacement of time and the political, we are no longer theorizing a zone of pure presence or ontology. Instead, he discerns an emergent technological presence. Derrida writes: "And if this important frontier is being displaced, it is because the medium in which it is instituted, namely, the medium of the media themselves (news, the press, telecommunications, techno-tele-discursivity, techno-tele-iconicity, that which in general assures and determines the spacing of public space, the very possibility of the res publica and the phenomenality of the political), this element itself is neither living nor dead, present nor absent: *it spectralizes*."[16] Derrida calls this spectral zone beyond ontology a *hauntology*. It is a means to open up ontology's obsession with, and capacity to see only, its own retrospective chain of presence and origin—and thus its posited futures. Hauntology insists upon a "constitutive displacement" within ontology itself, implying radically distinct forms of cohabitation, sociality, and politics.[17] To say that *time is* "constitutively" *out of joint*, Ernesto Laclau suggests in his reading of Derrida's hauntology, is to say that "the ghost is the condition of possibility of any present."[18] As this brief genealogy suggests, the spectral aspects of contemporary media urbanism are both unseen and constitutive of social relations.[19]

What interests me in these theories of dispossession and mediation is their capacity for temporal critique and for charting the connectivities, habituations, and claims made by those excluded by, while attempting to live within, legitimate society. To say that media *spectralize*, that they sensitize the sensorium to that which is occluded, immunized, or distant, presents a striking methodology for apprehending everyday and popular forms, making meaningful contact across difference and dominance. What Ghosh brings into view is how the intense connections articulated by financial globalization and pervasive technologies—such as the fascination with security and luxury condos in popular cinema—have a tendency to generate unsettling remnants. What's more, these traces are experienced sensorially through embodied spatial encounters and are not easily analyzed through familiar tropes like allegory or the unmasking of ideology. My aim in what follows is to extend Ghosh's *postphenomenological* gaze to ruins and blueprints.[20] These techniques of rendering the city both shore up the gloss of state-market development and open onto the (ghostly) politics of dispossession.

Ruins

The now-infamous Third Plenum of the Eleventh Party Congress in 1978 ushered in an era of economic reforms, inaugurating a shift from rural-led modernization to what Robin Visser has termed "urban aesthetics."[21] During the 1980s such transformations were focused on the restructuring of the agricultural economy and on investment in Special Economic Zones (SEZ), which created industrial cities overnight in places like the Pearl River Delta. At the same time, Beijing began its massive remaking from socialist capital to the political and cultural center of the new China. Beijing's 1991–2010 masterplan intensified this reconstruction by seeking out foreign investment, encouraging private enterprise, and designating both new sites of preservation and a central business district.[22] As art historian Wu Hung notes, new planning strategies began to change the face of the city in the 1980s, but its material transformation "reached the level of a visual spectacle only during the 1990s, when Beijing was turned into an oversized demolition and construction site."[23] Following the launch of the "Old and Dilapidated (or Hazardous) Housing Renewal" (*Wei jiu fang gaizao*) plan in 1991, part of a larger process of *weigai* dating back to the 1970s, it is estimated that more than 400,000 households were displaced by large-scale demolition and relocation projects in Beijing in that period alone.[24] This process greatly intensified in subsequent years and reached its peak in 2001.[25] This included the destruction of the traditional *hutong* (Beijing's alleyways and courtyard housing; 胡同), the relocation of hundreds of thousands of residents, and the sprawling of city concentrically outward—forming a new megalopolis.

An important response to the intensified condition of razing and rebuilding in the 1990s is the fascination with ruins as a mode of engaging the social.[26] Prior to the postsocialist period, images of ruins were rare in Chinese cultural production. As Wu notes, contrary to the European traditions that routinely pictured ruins in artworks, there was a "taboo in pre-modern China against preserving and portraying architectural ruins."[27] While ruined cities or palaces were remembered in poetry, visualizing such images of decay and destruction was uncommon, even ominous. Cultural exchange between Europe and China produced some interest in the aesthetic of ruins; however, it was not until the 1970s and 1980s that ruins played an important part in cultural debates. "Scar" art and literature (*shanghen yishu yu wenxue* 伤痕艺术与文学) provided notable examples from that period through their engagement with the traumatic excesses of the Cultural Revolution and, as Michael Berry notes, "provided a cathartic release of the pain, sorrow, anger, and disillusionment that so many people felt."[28]

In contrast, the 1990s witnessed a particular modality of ruination that is the product of demolition and dispossession.[29] Unlike the lingering ruins of war, continuous revolution, or the ancients, demolition transforms proximate time and space in particular ways. While Beijing's Old Summer Palace (Yuanmingyuan 圆明园), segments of the Great Wall, or even Mao's portrait—three notorious instances of *preserved* ruins—make the past present, preserving it in an anachronistic state, demolition's transmutation works in the opposite direction: it shifts the present to the past. Flattening the built environment thus produces a peculiar logic of disappearance that seeks to either erase or museumify. In either case, the infamous "拆" character (*chai*, meaning demolish), which covered Beijing buildings in the 1990s and 2000s, announces not only a spatial maneuver (e.g., presence to absence), but also a temporal shift from living to dead. It is not surprising that it is during this period that Beijing's vernacular architecture takes on new historical significance, prompting fresh debates over the politics of preservation and qualities of life in the city. Such (dis)appearances are aligned with the destruction of urban memory, loss of community, and new forms of homelessness, as well as corruption, legal disputes, and new urban formations. Yet ruin sites—whether quickly covered over, rebuilt, or abandoned—belong to the present physical and mnemonic fabric of the city in significant ways.

In dialogue with the gloss and order of official projections, audiovisual cultures during the 1990s examine urban subjects living between ruins and blueprints—a space of prolonged uncertainty. Numerous scholars, including Wu, Visser, Wang Jun, Zhang Zhen, Sheldon Lu, Jason McGrath, Zhang Yingjin, Yomi Braester, and Lu Xinyu, among others, have contributed to the discourse on demolition and reconstruction in contemporary cultural production.[30] Sheldon Lu goes so far as to suggest the term *Chai-na* to describe the logic of demolition (chai) at the turn of the century.[31] Building on such work, my aim here is to develop a particular understanding of ruin aesthetics and its relation to media practice. A useful starting point is noting how photographers, artists, and filmmakers—including many amateurs and emergent activists—responded to widespread demolition, producing a rich body of work that both documents and reanimates the city in/as ruins. These works deconstruct blueprints and master planning by capturing the contradictory textures that make up urban life after 1989. For my purposes here, I want to underscore three multimodal aspects of ruins aesthetics: street realism, archiving and preservation, and the occupation of new surfaces for public communication.

Street realism includes a broad set of tactics that directly challenge the official representational strategies associated with "socialist realism," leitmotif (*zhuxuanlü* 主旋律) films, the illustrated lecture format of so-called special topics programs (*zhuantipian* 专题片), and, I would add, the official address of the masterplan and similar modes.[32] Central to urban cinema, the New Documentary Movement, and contemporary art is an interest in the site-specificity of the everyday. The overlapping modes of "on-the-spot realism" (*jishi zhuyi* 纪实主义) and "on the scene" (*xianchang* 现场) videomaking, to take two well-known concepts from independent cinema, emphasize the importance of capturing real time and space.[33] These approaches entail much more than the economic necessity of using public and proximate locations. Instead, documentary and fictional films like Wu Wenguang's *Bumming in Beijing: The Last Dreamers* (1990) or Zhang Yuan's *Beijing Bastards* (1993) sought a spontaneous dialogue between filmmaker, urban subjects, and the city itself, participating in a broad reconfiguration of subaltern and popular cultural production. These documentary aesthetics capture a street-level view of the city through on-location stylistic devices, including nonprofessional actors, low-fi handheld cameras, natural lighting, synched sound, and ordinary encounters.

As the titles of Wu's and Zhang's films indicate, Beijing serves as a critical location and subject—one might even say a cinematic character—in numerous productions in the period. Popular films like Chen Kaige's *Farewell My Concubine* (1995); Zhang Yang's *Shower* (1999); Feng Xiaogang's *Sorry Baby* (1999), *Big Shot's Funeral* (2001), and *Cell Phone* (2003); Zhang Yuan's *Green Tea* (2003); Xiao Jiang's *Electric Shadows* (2004); Wu Shixian's *Waiting Alone* (2005); Gun Jun's *Dream Weavers: Beijing 2008* (2008); Huang Jianxin's *The Founding of a Republic* (2009); and Xu Jinglei's *Go Lala Go!* (2010) exist alongside indie films and documentary works. Examples include Zhou Xiaowen's *No Regret about Youth* (1992); Ning Ying's Beijing trilogy *For Fun* (1992), *On the Beat* (1995), and *I Love Beijing* (2000), as well as *Perpetual Motion* (2005); Zhang Yuan's *The Square* (1994), *East Palace, West Palace* (1996), and *I Love You* (2001); Wang Xiaoshuai's *Beijing Bicycle* (2001); Lu Xuechang's *Cala, My Dog!* (2002); Zhang Yibai's *Spring Subway* (2002); Pan Jianlin's *Good Morning, Beijing* (2003); Jia Zhangke's *The*

World (2004); Lou Ye's *Summer Palace* (2006); Li Yu's *Fish and Elephant* (2001) and *Lost in Beijing* (2007); Wang Wo's *Outside* (2007); Zhao Liang's *Petition* (2008); Wang Miao's *Beijing Taxi* (2010); and Wang Jiuliang's *Beijing Besieged by Waste* (2011), among many others.

These films document the real and imagined city during a period of intensive transformation. In fact, Urban Generation filmmaking has in part been understood as a mode of witnessing and of preservation. Zhang Zhen's influential collection *The Urban Generation*, published ahead of the Olympics in 2007, centers on the cinema's role in "bearing witness" to postsocialist urbanization. If Fifth-Generation filmmakers are noted for their stylistic engagements with fringe peasant and minority communities, "the swath of yellow earth," then the Urban Generation is defined by the "ubiquity of the bulldozer, the building crane, and the debris of urban ruins."[34] Yomi Braester, among others, has dubbed the tendency across fictional and documentary works to make records of the city the *documentary impulse*. He convincingly argues that contemporary cinema's archiving impulse operates "against the developer's shortening of duration though ready-made models," projecting instead a "preservational chronotope [that] slows down the events to lived time and turns the spectator into an eyewitness who moves through the city and records the change."[35] As such, the velocity of demolition and reconstruction has led to cinematic strategies to *preserve* the city in sounds and images, even as the city's materiality gives way to new shapes and practices.

Relying on similar on-the-spot impulses, artists Song Dong, Rong Rong, Xu Bing, Wang Jinsong, Yin Xiuzhen, Wang Zhan, and Zhang Dali, among many others, have examined the destruction of the urban body, freezing the disappearing city into photographs, performances, and video.[36] In a series of Beijing images from 1996 to 1997, for example, the photographer Rong Rong famously documented the ruined remains of traditional hutong housing (see figure 1.4). Devoid of human subjects, the images capture the residues of once-vibrant spaces, including dragons on the wall of a former restaurant, Chinese New Year paintings, and pin-ups of Marilyn Monroe and Chinese fashion models forgotten and left hanging on fragments of a wall. Regarding Rong Rong's ruin images, Wu Hung writes: "these images do not register a specific past, nor are they associated with the present or future. What they help construct in the photographs is a complete breakdown between private and public spaces. Ruins in Beijing and in these pictures are places that belong to everyone and to no one. *They belong to no one because the breakdown between private and public space does not generate a new kind of space.*"[37] Wu's reading reiterates the idea that ruins evacuate the present, breaking down existing space

Figure 1.4 Rong Rong's *Ruins* series captures Beijing between ruins and blueprints. Series: *Ruins*; Title: "1997 No.1 (1) Beijing." Courtesy of the artist and Three Shadows +3 Gallery. Copyright the artist, Rong Rong.

and social forms. But we can perhaps revise his assertion that because ruins belong to *no one* they fail to generate a new kind of space. Instead, lingering sites and images open onto new and volatile forms of communication—both on the street and across media.

In addition to street realism and the construction of an urban archive, artists like Zhan Wang, Yin Xiuzhen, and Zhang Dali use ruins to construct new avenues of public communication. Zhang Dali's diffuse graffiti and ruins sculptures, also examined by Wu, link up with a long tradition of using city surfaces to make claims on the social (e.g., "big character posters," so-called *dazibao*, and the Democracy Wall).[38] Between the years 1995 and 1998 it is estimated that Zhang spray-painted some 2,000 images of his trademark bald head throughout Beijing. By the late 1990s, the graffiti style had mutated to include the novel practice of emptying out his image, creating gaping holes in the remains of mostly demolished structures (see figure 1.5). These "holes" functioned as windows that telescoped the new and old, preserved and demolished.

The ubiquity of Zhang's ruins graffiti and sculptures resulted in a public controversy in 1998 when the images were widely discussed in Beijing's newspapers and magazines.[39] It was only at this point that the artist revealed his identity to the public. In one interview, Zhang notes: "The head is a condensation

Figure 1.5 Zhang Dali's photographic dialogues turn the ruined city into a medium for public communication. *Demolition*, 1998. Copyright Zhang Dali, courtesy of the artist.

of my own likeness as an individual. It represents me communicating with the city. I want to know everything about this city—its state of being, its transformation, its structure. I call this project *Dialogue*."[40] Zhang's ephemeral icons, with their imminent disappearance, seize on the city as a surface that can be used for public communication If demolition had shifted homes and neighborhoods into the past—transforming them into ruins—myriad artists and filmmakers sought to reclaim these sites for/in the present. Such operations signify more than record-making or witnessing. Instead, they claim and inhabit social space *in practice*, exploding the spatial and temporal gap instituted by the overlapping logics of demolition and design.

Figure 1.6 Demolished hutong in Chen Kaige's omnibus short *100 Flowers Hidden Deep* (2001).

Of particular interest in this context are the space and time of ruins. Rather than demarcate a limited field of architectural remains, muddy rubble, and the like, ruins capture the asynchronous modality of both demolition and reconstruction. Emerging concrete slabs and flattened tracts of land are equally out of joint. These coexisting sites/sights shifted the present into a separate and fragmented register that marks them as belonging to the past or future—but never the here and now. This is why unfinished skyscrapers and building cranes are often more jarring or uncanny than the bulldozed earth, corrugated fencing, or colorful graphic projections that mark the recently razed. Both ruins and blueprints haunt the present with their peculiar forms of spectrality. Moving through the city requires that urban residents concurrently imagine a jostling assemblage: the memory of demolished places (e.g., a favorite restaurant or neighbor), the present tract of living residues and emerging structures, and the various material and imaginary representations projecting the future of the site.

In this official language, ruins render the present past while blueprints defer the present into the future. Together, these modalities trigger a shift in the experience of the present that marks it as always not quite here or there,

Figure 1.7   Unfinished towers, building cranes, and razed neighborhoods haunt Beijing's landscape in Ning Ying's *I Love Beijing* (2001).

perpetually fragmented or unfinished. It produces the present as a sacrificial time—where transformation is an end that is without end. This fractional present requires the supervision and guidance of the state to actualize and stabilize the social body—the city and its image become linked in new political ways. The documentary impulse is an important response to this clash. Recording and archiving the everyday, however, is only part of the story. It emphasizes culture's relationship to its past, where artists, filmmakers, and intellectuals remember and provide traces to capture and mourn a city whose changes outpace them. On the other hand, what of culture's future capacities? This question is the focus of the remainder of this chapter and of chapter 2. How do social actors not only bring the city back into lived experience, but also make claims on its possibilities into the hereafter? In what follows, I first address planning's visual culture from the perspective of formal state-market projections.

Blueprints

The counterpart to demolition and urban ruins is Beijing's reconstruction—a project that transforms the city itself into a model or blueprint. In contrast to the idea of the map, which relies on cartographic conventions to produce a detailed survey of geography *after the fact*, the blueprint brings together an entire field of cultural production invested in the *yet to come*: plans, models, renderings and digital design, air quality predictions, civilization campaigns, five-year plans, GDP forecasts, and related projections. I employ the commonplace understanding of the blueprint to indicate a detailed plan, proposal, or

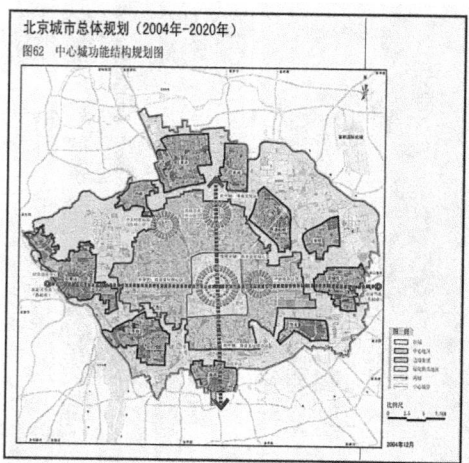 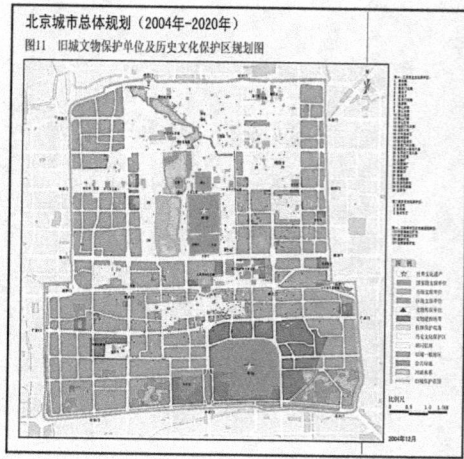

Figure 1.8 Beijing's 2020 master plan exemplifies official modes of urban address. City functions and axes, left; projected areas of preservation, right.

gesture, as well as the capacity for easy duplication, circulation, and address. Blueprints describe the atmospherics of design in the Olympic era and the widespread use of futurity logics—visions of the capital itself—as a medium of public communication. In particular, I want to draw attention to the blueprint's role as both a highly designed model and a copy—a template designed for reproduction and implementation. This basic logic of repetition is at the heart of contested legitimacies and processes of underglobalization.

Planning's audiovisuality plays a critical role in constructing the *imaginary* of development before demolition and reconstruction commence. It materializes new social imaginaries that orient (and over-orient) the present as future. As Dilip Gaonkar writes in a special issue of *Public Culture* dedicated to "new imaginaries," social imaginaries are "ways of understanding the social that become social entities themselves, mediating collective life."[41] A range of theorists, from Cornelius Castoriadis to Charles Taylor, have employed the concept to understand the "enabling but not fully explicable symbolic matrix" through which people make sense of the world and imagine their collective social life.[42] My argument to this point is that ruins and blueprints constitute the contested social imaginaries of transition.

We might also connect this symbolic matrix to Frederic Jameson's concept of "cognitive mapping"—a symbolic process crucial to how individuals locate themselves in a global system and prepare as political actors. Relatedly, what we might lightly term "cognitive rendering" builds on Jameson's insights but also offers a shift in emphasis from the propositional logic of the map. As Dennis Wood puts it, "all maps do assert that *this is there*."[43] Wood continues: "far from being pictures of the world maps are instruments for its creation; that is, they are not representations but systems of propositions, arguments about what the world might be."[44] Renderings or blueprints intensify the map's "this is there" point of view. They are not only propositions, but maps of future states: *this will be there*. The question I want to underline here is this: How does one locate oneself and develop political strategies in a world that is both spectrally present and yet to come?

Beginning with Beijing's 1991–2010 masterplan (*zongti guihua* 总体规划), adopted in 1993 and replaced by the 2020 masterplan in 2004, planning discourses and imaging strategies emerged as a critical texture in Olympic-era visual culture. In Beijing alone, numerous planning institutions and popular culture outlets incessantly produce and circulate depictions of the city in its distant and detailed views.[45] This includes billboards and public service announcements; cinema and TV; a wide range of print media; images of new business, residential, and commercial districts; media events like National Day celebrations or the 2008 and 2022 Olympics; a new culture of ceaseless expos; and Beijing's Planning Exhibition Hall, among others. The Exhibition Hall, complete with scale models of the future city (which are never quite up to date), is perhaps an emblematic example.[46] Opened in 2004, it contains not only scale models of the city, heritage sites, the Olympic Park, and the central business district, but also exhibitions and 2D, 3D, and 4D cinema projections showcasing the masterplan, megastructures, transportation development, preservation projects, sustainable water and electricity practices, and the like. Short features like *New Beijing* or *Beijing's Transportation of the Future* create fast-paced CGI journeys into the future of the metropolis. *Future Beijing* (*Weilai Beijing*), for example, opens in swirling soft focus as a computer-generated flyover shot soars over the city's central axis—its traditional buildings are instantly transformed using a time-lapse aesthetic. As the scene dissolves, a voiceover narrator exuberantly proclaims: "Beijing, an Oriental capital with a more than 3,000-year history, is now ready to take off on a new historical runway."

Urban plans themselves are a crucial part of this public address. No longer internal documents limited to officials and experts, they seep into everyday life in numerous forms—constituting a technique of common sense. Images from Beijing's 2020 masterplan produce an urban geometry that highlights symbolic structures and development procedures. Areas to be preserved, demolished, or constructed anew are seamlessly indicated with arrows, colors,

Figure 1.9 2D, 3D, and 4D cinematic recreations of Beijing's future feature prominently at Beijing Urban Planning Exhibition Hall. Courtesy of the author.

text, or bold lines. Movement seemingly occurs unimpeded across an urban field defined only by flat roadways, emblematic sites, and large multiblock clusters—one imagines steering a floating avatar in a digital world. Simultaneously, long shots of urban development emphasize political boundaries, and occasionally topography, capturing the central role of Beijing as a political and media capital. It is a hub that satellite cities orbit and a regional vector that provincial and rural zones, if they desire development too, must move toward and imitate. There is no room for variegated human rhythms in such displays.

Daniel Abramson, writing from an urban planning perspective, describes images from Beijing's masterplan as projecting a "picturesque aesthetic." As with discussions of city plans elsewhere, he is critical of the static bird's-eye view and, in particular, the capacity of "city-scale preservation" to flatten out urban differences and the street-level experience of city life. Beyond restrictions on building height, traditional urban grids and symmetry, city colors (gray bricks, green trees, yellow roof tiles), sight lines along the main axes, land use, and so on, the plan's abstract rationalizations do not provide site-specific prescriptions for preservation and change. He writes, "official preservation

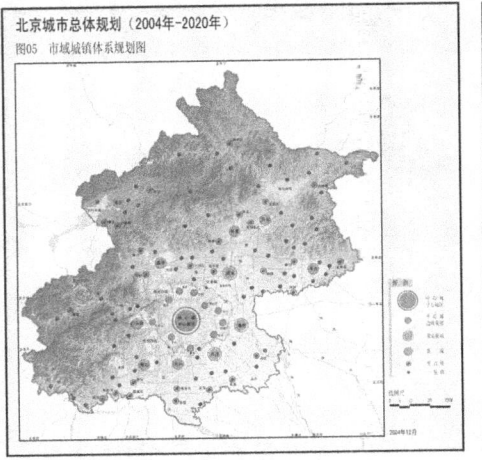 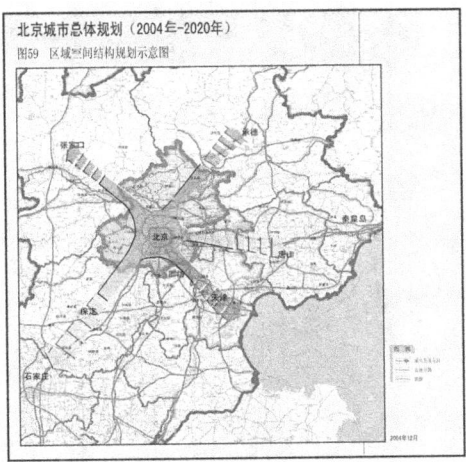

Figure 1.10 The 2020 masterplan projects Beijing's relationship to satellite towns and the region.

policy was so focused on an idea of what constituted Beijing's 'classic' overall historical geography, that it failed to appreciate important local variations."⁴⁷ The vagueness of the "picturesque" is easily modified through constant exceptions, and by deals between developers, officials, and district governments.

Abramson's discussion is notable as one of a few sustained engagements with the cultural work of urban planning as a mode of visual culture and address in contemporary China—though numerous studies emphasize the entangled responses of artists, filmmakers, and the like. Rather than relegate such visions to the domain of urbanists and designers, however, the audiovisuality of development can be productively brought into a wider exploration of media urbanism and the contests to produce the capital as a future tense—"Beijing will be a beautiful city"—during a period of perpetual de-/reconstruction. Indeed, we can highlight three distinct if overlapping modes of projecting the future city. These modes signal the importance of audiovisual cultures, in their material and immaterial forms, to the imaginary of transition and the production of new legitimacies.

The first mode, emphasized by Abramson's planning perspective, is the use of two-dimensional, diagrammatic plans of urban space (see figures 1.8 and 1.9). These views from on high reproduce the city as a series of geometric relationships that transform redevelopment into a technical problems: widening roads, adding a central business district, allocating sites for preservation

Figure 1.11 Planning images attached to construction site walls use multiple visual modes to depict the historically rooted futures of Beijing's Dongcheng District. Courtesy of the author.

and tourism, and connecting Beijing to raw materials and commerce. Such images depoliticize the destruction of neighborhoods, relocation of residents, influx of migrant workers, and privatization of collective space. Projections from the 2020 masterplan reproduce a rationalized picture of development through their repetition on billboards, in print, on the web, and on TV, as well as in Olympic media and Beijing's own planning museum, which sits on the edge of the city's largely demolished southern slums. In chapters 3 and 4, for instance, I focus on how this transitional logic is consolidated through cinematic and televisual spatialities in the city.

Planning's visual culture is also an important part of street life, often serving as *in-between* architecture announcing future buildings or neighborhoods. An important example of this materialization in the city, taken up further in chapter 2, is the use of billboard-like images to cover over construction sites and other urban transformations. These ubiquitous renderings demonstrate how planning imagery proliferates, including its mixed aesthetics and mode of address. The use of beautifying landscapes in Dongcheng District is a good illustration. Stretching across several blocks, the images and text offer a "tour of Dongcheng District," including its imperial heritage, important cultural sites, and traditional courtyard (*siheyuan* 四合院) housing. For example, text on the construction-site walls describes the transformation of Dongcheng's traditional architecture:

> As a historical and cultural conservation district, Dongcheng has preserved courtyard residences built since the Yuan Dynasty. Throughout the hutongs and alleys in Dongcheng, these courtyard houses are converted into restaurants, clubs, hotels, galleries, teahouses, theaters, and bars, constituting a major part of Dongcheng District's tourist attractions. Gege Fu used to be the private residence of Emperor Kangxi's twenty-fourth son, Prince Zicheng Wang. Empress Dowager Cixi later bestowed this residence on Princess Rongsou after her wedding. Now in Gege Fu, you can taste the famous Manchu Han Imperial Feast, experiencing the prestigious and luxurious life of imperial officers. The impressive imperial feast and waiters in Manchu costumes create the illusion of being back in the Qing Dynasty over one hundred years ago. . . . Now, there are hundreds of modern service facilities, such as restaurants, hotels, teahouses, and bars, that combine traditional courtyard houses and ancient garden architectures. Therefore, Dongcheng is a perfect place to experience Beijing's traditional culture and modern life.[48]

These mediations oscillate between the promise to experience the capital's rich history and the potential of its future states. The "now" invoked suggests a confused temporality—between old or renovated heritage sites and a range of "modern service facilities" that, at the time, only existed in the large printed plan on the wall of a construction site.

A second and related mode of address belongs to digital design and architecture and, in particular, the process of using computer programs to generate images and models. This practice is commonly referred to as *rendering*. Rendering's digital aesthetics relies not on the symbolic logic of the plan, but on a mixture of the iconic and quasi-indexical properties associated with computational photographic realism. Unlike most plans and blueprints, which largely function as policy templates or technical instructions, rendering produces lifelike visualizations of entire urban ecologies. Depictions of buildings, neighborhoods, and new infrastructure signal the technological and environmental rhetoric of Beijing's Olympic slogans: "Green Olympics, High-Tech Olympics, People's Olympics." Warm digital blues and greens are combined with futuristic silver hues to create a technologized future city that is defined by its media monuments, transportation infrastructure, business and residential towers, urban consumers, green belts, rivers, and pollution-free skies.

Figure 1.12 Beijing's "Water Cube" (*shuilifang*), National Aquatics Center, is one of many Olympic-era structures designed to circulate as an image. Publicity image from the Beijing Olympic Committee.

Figure 1.13 Tourists pose for pictures on the Olympic Green in the lead-up to the 2008 Games.

Simultaneously, skylines of the traditional city—city walls and gates, pagodas, temples, and the rooftops of the Forbidden City—are routinely used to recall the mythology of China's continuous history, and to support a preservational logic that is geared toward tourism and the construction of an inelastic past.[49]

The "Water Cube" aquatics center embodies the technological address of the new city. Its molecular design draws on scientific discourses—sustainability, efficiency, computer-aided design, nature—to create a structure modeled on water bubbles. Importantly, the innovative design itself emerges as a medium through which the urban fabric is recast. At every level, proclaim design videos, magazine articles, TV programs, exhibits, billboards, and so on, the structure's minutest details have been designed so that the floor tiles filter and recycle water, the cubic membrane heats pools and air, and natural light reduces electricity consumption. These facts are driven home through anatomical sketches of its cellular makeup and renderings that envisage the formation of a new collective space without insides or outsides. The media city is permeable—a stylistic element repeated by Paul Andreu's National Theater, and Herzog and de Meuron's Bird's Nest National Stadium, among other recent projects—filled with digital beings that crowd its open squares, are lit by its ecological hues, and are able to revel in its seamless pleasures. Of course, most people will encounter these high-design locales only through media such as TV, the internet, and print.

Computational design thus produces a digital aesthetics in both its material and representational forms. Architectural renderings of the Water Cube, among many other new structures in the capital, are constructed through a combination of soft-focus geometries, rich manipulated hues (colors that are too colorful), unlimited visibility, and, contradictorily, the fading of adjacent life. It mimics the visual effects of blockbuster films with imagery that is uncanny in its ability to be at once lifelike and not quite like life. The building's temporality is thus inscribed in its conceptualization through and as "new" media. Digital strategies are even employed at the level of mise-en-scène so that the Water Cube resembles its projected image. This tendency to exist before being built is an important part of the social life of renderings. Internal and external lighting, structural gloss and coloring, easy visibility from the central axis or from automobiles on the Fourth Ring Road, and so on, construct the site/sight—and infrastructure in general—as a mode of address. It is a rationale that replays development's particular hold on the city. The city need not work so long as its images do. Thus, as water and air pollution and desertification plague northern China, and Beijing in particular, the Water Cube demonstrates the scientific promise of cool blue purity.

Next, cinematic visual effects are key to material and imaginary reworkings of the urban. This aspect has been of the most interest to scholars in media and cultural studies and can be expanded to include a range of motion pictures beyond contemporary independent cinema and entertainment forms. From Olympic promotional fare and tourism films to animated features, media events, web videos, real estate showrooms, and TV series, the cinematic constructs vital imaginaries for urban development. Borrowing stylistic elements from both the plan and renderings, cinematic productions also rely heavily on documentary modes as well as flyover shots, computer-generated spaces, montage, time-lapse, monumentality, maps/plans, and teleological narratives that deliver a clear endgame: Beijing 2008, Beijing 2022, and so on.

Of particular importance is the way cinematic futures rely on nonrepresentational elements: simulated camera movements, alternating aerial shots and extreme close-ups, frenetic pacing, and progressive transitions to create a mode of address that borrows from science fiction—and, following Ghosh's argument above, shores up spectral contact zones. Such claims are reiterated by metaphors for urban design that understand the modern city itself as *like* the cinema. For example, Steven Holl's Linked Hybrid "MOMA" project at the northeast edge of Beijing's Second Ring Road—a high-end residential compound now replicated in urban districts throughout China—describes its porous and looped layout as a "cinematic adventure." What's more, a state-of-the-art cinema, with transparent walls allowing moving pictures to seep into the lavish garden and shopping area, is located in the center of the circular plan.

These cinematic modes also come together in the many promotional clips and movies that animate the Olympic era. Olympic shorts like *Charming Beijing, Chinese Seal, Dancing Beijing, Beijing: Candidate City, The National Stadium*, and *We Got It* exist alongside the award-winning *Fuwa* cartoons (Olympic mascots 福娃); feature-length works like *The Road to the Green Olympics, The One Man Olympics, Bird's Nest: Herzog & de Meuron in China*, and *Dream Weavers: Beijing 2008*; and media events like the unveiling of the Olympic emblem broadcast from the Temple of Heaven, and the opening and closing ceremonies of the Games themselves. Such multimodal cinematic productions construct a thick description of the city that is simultaneously rooted in its documentary image and future projections.

What interests me here are the claims associated with planning rhetoric—claims to be documentary images of sites that do not yet exist. Not only will they have been there—it is as if they always already were. Beijing's media monuments broadcast the promises of market socialism, even while they buttress a "hurry up and wait" ethos that is used to perpetually delay social equity, ecological care, and rights of assembly, while rationalizing the need for centralized and harmonious governance. The technological sublime of the Water Cube, CCTV towers, the Bird's Nest, and so on, give volume to the present and are proof that the future is worth the wait. In this sense, the characterizations of postsocialist *excess*—the *too much* logic that animates so much discourse about China (e.g., the *New York Times*' Olympic series "Choking on Growth") turn out, in fact, to be less and not more. The over-orientation of the masterplan delimits and fixes the future in a particular image and vector. It does not produce excess, but instead forces social bodies and spaces into certain grooves—patterns or ruts, depending on the perspective. This is to say that blueprints are primarily political rather than technical representations. They project a set of conditions through which a certain modality of development, and of history, can take place.

As AbdouMaliq Simone puts it in his study of urban Africa, *For the City Yet to Come*, "cities remain, at least 'officially,' inscribed in a narrative of development. But development as a specific *modality of temporality* is not simply about meeting the needs of citizens. It is also about capturing the residents to a life aesthetic defined by the state so that they can be citizens. It is about making ethical beings; about holding people in relations that make them governable."[50] Simone reminds us that development itself is composed of multiple and conflicting modalities, including the desire to modernize production on the one hand, and the uneven schemes to improve citizens and quality of life on the other. His challenge to the pedagogical logic of Western-oriented development discourse is to locate the informal, invisible, and spectral ways that both citizens and noncitizens develop their own social capacities and are able to "extend themselves across a larger world and enact . . . possibilities of urban becoming."[51] Building on Simone's understanding of everyday design formations, the terms *ruins* and *blueprints* developed in this chapter do not signal a simple top-down linearity, where one replaces the other, or where only the state and market have their say. Instead, they represent a spectrum of temporal claims and desires on the material space of the city, on history, and upon (non)citizenship practices.

Watching the City

In this final section, I draw on the work of (post)colonial political theorists Ariella Azoulay and Partha Chatterjee to focus and extend the preceding discussion of ruins and blueprints, and of Beijing's digital urbanism. I begin with what Azoulay terms the "civil contract of photography." My aim is to bring her provocative analysis of visuality, responsibility, and refusal to bear on the visual logics of urban design. Azoulay's theorization stems from pictures of injury and displacement—such as photographs of Palestinians in the Occupied Territories—and the sense that such images show more than "what was being done to" those displaced.[52] Instead, they articulate a space of political relations that exceed the mediations of state and nation. Importantly, this "civil political space" works against the image bank of the dominant culture (what Azoulay terms "planted" pictures): "Because photographs, unlike planted pictures, have no single, individual author, in principle, they allow civic negotiations about the subject they designate and about their sense."[53] Her articulation makes two valuable points about reading and unraveling hegemonic visuality. First, such images belong to *no one*, and as such the spectator is not simply addressed by the photographs, but is an "addressee" who can produce and disseminate her own meanings from the images. This is more than romancing resistance, as critics of cultural studies have it—instead, it is basic to notions of the public that underlie democracy. Second, the pictures capture an entangled set of social relations that include the photographer, the photographed subject, and the spectator. Thus, the ensemble restores the *captured subject* to a position of relevance and capacity—and does not simply focus on photographers and viewers, as is the habit in many visual fields.

To trace this civil political space, Azoulay argues, we need to stop *looking at* photographs and start *watching* them. She writes: "The verb 'to watch' is usually used for regarding phenomena or moving pictures. It entails dimensions of time and movement that need to be reinscribed in the interpretation of the still photographic image. When and where the subject of the photograph is a person who has suffered some form of injury, a viewing of the photograph that reconstructs the photographic situation and allows a reading of the injury inflicted on others becomes a civic skill, not an exercise in aesthetic appreciation."[54] The civic skill of "watching" insists on more than the common idea that photography essentially captures something that *was there*. Rather, it also testifies to the "fact that the photographed *people* were there." And assuming that the photographed people are *still there* at the time of watching, Azoulay continues, allows us to reanimate the political relations of the governed.[55]

She proceeds by reinstating a basic fact in political theory: citizens *too* are governed. This actuality is too often forgotten because the legal and ideological bonds between state and citizen seem to operate above and against noncitizens and others acting outside of rights-based discourses. Azoulay's aim is to disrupt the formal affinity between state and citizen, and instead to energize the space of relations *among the governed*—including both citizens and noncitizens. In this context, "political duty" is primarily a responsibility to one another, rather than "toward the ruling power."[56] This sense of social responsibility flies directly in the face of biopower and bourgeois pedagogical projects that often pit citizens against noncitizens on issues ranging from migration, jobs, health, and housing to noise, sexuality, piracy, and the myriad ways of life pushed to the edge of the licit city.

To make sense of this mediatic relation, one thread of Azoulay's project is to examine the politics of the gaze in photographs of vulnerable subjects. She asks: "Does their use of photography express a civic skill that they possess?" and "Why are they looking at me?" Such questions recalibrate the politics of witnessing associated with images of displacement and disaster. It suggests a temporal shift that refuses the assumption that what is captured in such pictures is "over and done with"—an assumption that would foreclose the political assemblage at issue here.[57] Thus, Azoulay argues, when a Hebron merchant whose business has been destroyed by occupying forces stares into the camera, it is not primarily to demand remuneration for lost property. Rather, it is to refuse the position of noncitizenship imposed on him by the state, and to demand "participation in a sphere of political relations within which his claims can be heard and acknowledged."[58] Azoulay's theorization critically grounds the civil duties of spectatorship and image-making, as well as the political volatility associated with the distribution of images—the way that captured subjects utilize official media to transmit their own social projects and to alter the ways they are governed.

Partha Chatterjee's theorization of political society pressures Azoulay's civil contract in generative ways.[59] Drawing on Antonio Gramsci's distinction between civil society and political society, Chatterjee inserts a gap between a civil politics or contract and its uncivil counterpart. While Azoulay's point about the governed (including citizens and noncitizens) is well taken, the civil politics it imagines are at times out of sync with the emergent sphere of political relations in China, in Asia, and in much of the world. Put otherwise, civil participation, recognition, and solidarity are only one of the vectors in this dynamic. I will develop this distinction further in chapter 2. My aim here is to bring Azoulay's and Chatterjee's understandings of the politics of the governed into conversation. This is not a matter of replacing one line of thought with another, but rather of articulating how these civil and uncivil processes are knotted and diverge—and of how uncivil political relations proliferate under contemporary conditions of illegality and the increasing sway of state-corporate capital. In short, each brings into view a distinct aspect of this political sphere: Azoulay's model is tilted toward the responsibility of citizens toward those who are governed unequally beside them, and toward rejecting state projects to concretize this partition. On the other hand, Chatterjee's political society is pragmatic and spectral, even perhaps dangerously so. It emphasizes the contingent politics of social actors whose interactions with the state happen (at least partially) outside of official, legal, or civil organs—yet whose pressure is essential to everyday forms of belonging and survival. Chatterjee's example of negotiations between squatter communities and local governments,[60] for example, make central quotidian forms of resiliency and abandonment, especially the mundane, dull, and cruddy politics that fail to achieve the status of a disastrous event and to cohere into a grand political narrative.[61] Such is popular politics in "much of the world."

How can we extend the (un)civil contract of photography to think about ruins and blueprints—especially mediations of the latter? We can begin with the suggestion that one stop looking at plans, and related designs, and start *watching* them—a tactic that can be imported from the vibrant work on Chinese documentary and alternative cinemas, and that is crucial to unraveling dominant forms of digital urbanism. For Azoulay, much of photography's civic power and address to the spectator is sutured to the photographed person who stares out from the frame. The question "Why are they looking at me?" allows her to recalibrate the field of social relations and, most importantly, "our interrelations within it."[62] But *no one* has been captured in the plan, model, or blueprint. There is no one looking at me, at you. Watching these images thus requires a different order of impressing time and movement, and of reading—especially if we are to move beyond the politics of textuality or spectatorship alone and chart the operations of actually existing democratic pulses. The first task is to *repopulate* planning's picturesque and hauntingly inhuman address. If the very presence of people in Azoulay's photographs suggests a social skill on the part of the photographed, shoring up a new political space and modes of contact, then plans ask us to watch for and to render the disappeared gazes, to find apertures back to the ground of representation, and to imagine inhabiting demolished and transitional worlds. This includes the spectral remnants produced by embodied spatial encounters, and their capacity to reorient perception, with diverse media forms and the city itself. Tracing how social actors apprehend, engage, and seep into such blueprints to create new (un)civil contracts is the focus of chapter 2.

Digital Urbanism

Piratical Citizenship and the Infrastructure of Dissensus

The political reality, which is plain for anyone to see, is that China has many laws but no rule of law; it has a constitution but no constitutional government. The ruling elite continues to cling to its authoritarian power and fights off any move toward political change.

—"FOREWORD," CHARTER 08

The core of the problem, as I see it, is that democracy is neither a form of government nor a form of social life. Democracy is the institution of politics as such, of politics as a paradox.

—JACQUES RANCIÈRE

The popular online video game *The Big Battle: Nail House vs. Demolition Team* (*Dingzihu dazhan chaiqiandui* 钉子户大战拆迁队) animates China's transformation through acts of contentious dispossession. The game draws on a rich iconography of so-called nail houses (*dingzi hu*), lone holdouts in redevelopment zones, particularly the iconic nail house of Chongqing, capturing both the disputed nature of demolition and relocation, and the mundane ways that digital imaginaries seep into everyday life.[1] The objective of the game is to save the beset home from destruction crews and hired thugs. In dozens of my own attempts I failed to get past the fourth of seven levels—a detail corroborated by many online commenters, including one player who notes: "I have

Figure 2.1 In *The Big Battle* residents attempt to defend their homes from a developer's wrecking crews.

already got 70,000 [points] in the game but my house was still demolished." She continues: "It tells us that the demolition team is not defeatable . . . the only thing we can do is to wait and die." *The Big Battle* was played nearly two million times in the first two weeks after going online in August 2010.[2] Its fascination, despite limited graphics and gameplay, indicates the degree to which struggles over urban space and political legitimacy have penetrated cultural consciousness.

This chapter extends the notion of rendering the city, developed in chapter 1, by examining how people find ways to inhabit the model/media city. I call this contested occupation *illegal* or *piratical citizenship*—a dominant form of political subjectivity in the era of underglobalization. Piratical citizenship is defined by both its democratic potentialities and uncertain or illegal relations to law and state, as well as its *media logic*: informal media technologies and publicities are critical to making urban demands and altering the way subjects are governed. This jittery political and medial infrastructure is the form of management and recognition exercised by digital urbanism. It is how the city is controlled and pressured, populated and remade. Adapting Ravi Sundaram's "media urbanism," I emphasize *digital* urbanism to call attention to the normative thresholds that segregate digital culture in China, and elsewhere, from idealized forms of technomodernity in the Global North.³ The very textures of these media worlds assign them to distinct developmental and aspirational time zones. Consequently, they are tied to the production of new legitimacies and ways of life. "Technology," as Sundaram observes, has shifted from the realm of the expert and official institution and "now seep[s] into the everyday lives of urban residents, their debates, their conflicts, their dreams and desires."⁴ In what follows, I trace the media infrastructures and inhabitations that mark a crucial moment of Beijing's transition (circa the 2000s), paying close attention to the intersections of documentary video, planning and construction-site billboards, digital art and handmade signs, among other (in)formal technologies of distribution and dissensus.

Public Culture and Popular Politics

Central to this analysis are a range of debates about media and public culture, especially as they pertain to the postcolonial and postsocialist non-West. My starting point is to extend the work of scholars of Asian media and politics, like Sundaram, Chen Kuan-hsing, Xi Chen, Lu Xinyu, Chris Berry, and others. These theorists provide useful ways out of the often dead-end discussions about public capacities in China and across Asia. For example, in his work on Chinese documentary and public space, Berry argues that we should toss aside the one-dimensional perspective that understands a nation-state to either have civil society and a public sphere, or not. Instead, he asserts, we need to think through what kinds of public *spheres* exist in practice: "Who are the actors in that public space? What protocols govern what they do in that space, including the discourse they can produce? What is the scope of the space produced?"⁵

Similarly, Chen suggests that we reimagine the normative concept of *civil society* as an analytical category, "enabling us to better understand the locations and directions of the social forces at work."⁶ This is, on the one hand, to demystify a concept that does a good deal of work in shoring up Euro-American modernity as a template for national and global becoming. It internationalizes critiques about the constitutive inequality of actually existing democracies—with their deep-seated divisions based on class, race, gender, sexuality, post/coloniality, and so on—even while North Atlantic countries attempt to export their own package of modernity qua liberal democracy to the world.⁷ On the other hand, provincializing dominant models of democratic publicity is also to dispute the pedagogical and legalistic roles played by civil society institutions and their coalitions. As Chen argues, intellectuals need to rethink their own positions within civil society—an institutional context that, in the name of civility, works against subaltern populations and popular democracy.[8]

While the existence of robust civil society institutions and a public sphere are often used to distinguish between democratic and authoritarian zones—for example, between India and China, but even more between West and East—these idealized political spheres are also increasingly overwhelmed and corrupted by corporate capital and the market state, among other incursions. This fact challenges current models of political action as well as the swagger with which Euro-American modernity is held up as an ideal for the world. To be sure, we need to continue to take seriously civil society as a realm of political mediation. But we should do so with renewed caution, especially toward its pedagogical and salvific rhetoric, and with an eye toward the inequalities it instantiates: like the state, civil society can be sharply antidemocratic. Recalibrating idealizations of civil society and the public sphere, then, has the power to reorient our attention from ossified distinctions between Easts and Wests, and toward the vibrating geopolitics that undergird actually existing globalizations. As a consequence, mainstream discourses about global civil society need to make way for new engagements with *global political society*.

Political activity for many takes place in the shadow of the civil society and outside the legal recognition of the state. This shift demands fresh theorizations of popular politics and public culture in both familiar "elite" democracies and the perceived outliers of the world system: state capitalism, military juntas, theocracies, single-party (post)socialism, and so on. These latter sites, in particular, are too often understood to lack meaningful political spheres and energy—assumptions that reinforce adherence to status-quo governmentalities. My aim here is to build on Partha Chatterjee's idea of "political society"—a framework for examining the workings of democracy in zones marked by informality, illegality, weak entitlements, fractured citizenship, and other uncertain relations below and beyond the law. This sphere meets few of the definitional requirements of democratic theory, and yet it is where popular and locally rooted democratic potentialities are operational.[9] Put differently, civil society is the *real* to political society's *fake*. To fake, in this context, is not only to forge, copy, or improvise (e.g., to opportunistically reroute official infrastructures), but also to refuse to engage—to undermine or underperform official protocols, and instead draw on homegrown capacities and legitimacies. These situated, piratical, and often illegal politics—forms of *underglobalization*—are the foundation on which democratic potentialities are built.

But this notion of informal democracy—where public culture becomes a pirate relation—must also be adapted to our technologized habitus. Here

Sundaram's *Pirate Modernity* is illuminating. He usefully adapts the concept by noting that Chatterjee's analysis fails to recognize the significance of "techno-cultural networks" within political society itself. Instead, it suggests "a politics before media."[10] While perhaps problematic in its invocation of a before and after—new media are not so new—Sundaram shows how media have technologized political culture and urban life in ways that are yet to be appreciated. In this context, the tactics employed by the governed are met by both new mediatic pleasures and techniques of urban control—from techno-consumer lifestyles, surveillance, and illicit norms to biopolitical strategies for managing air quality, traffic accidents, epidemics, and the like. Focusing on contemporary Delhi, Sundaram notes that political society *after media* must account for the emerging "technologies of civic liberalism" that are used to rationalize and institute a seemingly permanent crisis of the urban. Of particular significance is how risk and uncertainty are deployed to create an urban atmosphere that requires constant interventions. Such hoopla, he suggests, assists elites in reclaiming the city from the politics of representation.[11]

Sundaram's provocative reading of civic liberalism's transformative effects, however, is out of sync with the Chinese context, where liberal discourses butt up against the single-party state, among other (post)socialist residues. This is to make two points. First, while each instance requires paternalistic interventions to stabilize the contagious city, they assume radically different subjects and spheres of action. Studies of Chinese politics, for example, emphasize how the state gobbles up or is coextensive with civil society and publicity. Organizations associated with resident welfare, housing, health, courts, media, and the like, rather than constituting distinct spheres of influence and debate, are part of the official apparatus or remain deeply marginal. The enfolding of state and civil forms is thus largely defined by the former's infusion into public and private zones, making any distinctions between them hazy or ad hoc. Such tensions are amplified by arbitrary arrests, the censorship of information, severe limits on speech, assembly, and the press, combined with a massive migrant population, development-led environmental degradation, the proliferation of Special Economic Zones (*Jingji tequ* 经济特区), and pervasive but illegal protest. But political activity and protest, while widespread, are forced to adopt techniques that can rarely aspire to be public in the spectacularly mundane sense of the so-called social movement society[12]—and hence require different modes of engagement.[13]

These and other distinctions notwithstanding, Indian and Chinese urban strategies since the late 1990s have utilized similar governmental techniques. In each case political elites have sought to divide the population—into citizens and non- or lesser citizens—and to legitimize emergency interventions whereby urban problems are resolved outside the social and political sphere.[14] For Sundaram, this matters because it circumvents the electorate and consolidates a new role for appointed technocrats and the courts—animating a public culture marked by perpetual crisis.[15] In the Chinese context, where electoral politics are not the chief issue, too limited and local, similar governmental techniques also undergird its reliance on crisis resolution. Such scenes are crucial for shoring up the legitimacy of the party state by substantiating its commitment to stability and the harmonious society (*hexie shehui* 和谐社会) and to building coalitions between the party elite and the growing urban middle classes. For example, anxieties about migrants, petty criminals, sex workers, food safety, piracy (from medicine to media), educational opportunities, pollution, traffic, noise, ethnic minorities, even the desire for development itself, are all good indexes of how proper citizens are set against the unruly rest.

These sundry examples throw into relief the potent and transnational tendency for modernity and democracy to be pitted against one another. As such, we must account for the failures of democratic institutions, spaces, and processes (e.g., civil society and the public sphere), including their crucial role in animating hegemonic forms of globalization. By extension, we must also challenge the banal notion that the corruption of public/political domains belongs to the developing world and the non-West. Instead, the proliferation of political society and piratical citizenship—in China but also globally—draws attention to an increasingly postdemocratic condition.[16] This is also to highlight the peculiar formalization of illegal and illegitimate forms of political subjectivity. As Chatterjee argues, state legitimacy at once relies upon dispossession and ongoing primitive accumulation for economic growth and, at the same time, must act to (unevenly) ameliorate the effects of precarity "since this carries the risk of turning [the dispossessed] into the 'dangerous classes.'"[17] While gaps between privilege and precarity are only intensifying, even normalizing, this tension also points to the deeply ambivalent nature of political society. It is a space of tactical action where marginal groups can pressure governmental machinery, but it is also opportunistically employed or facilitated by administrative structures in lieu of substantial and legally binding social contracts.

What Xi Chen calls "contentious authoritarianism" provides a useful articulation of something like political society in contemporary China. My interest here is to establish the utility of political society beyond electoral democracy—even as its specific incarnations drive new divisions and explode prior notions of a shared third-world history.[18] Chen's notion of contentious authoritarianism describes, on the one hand, the dramatic rise and routinization of social protest in China (distinct from traditional petitions or *xinfang* 信访), but also, on the other hand, enduring social stability and the persistence of the rigid state.[19] Eighty-seven thousand such "collective incidents" (*quntixing shijian* 群体性事件) were registered by the Public Security Bureau in 2005, and that number has grown steadily in recent years.[20] The same is true of the rapid increase of organized labor strikes.[21] Chen thus describes a zone of political volatility that is illegal and yet widespread and accommodated. Counterintuitively, he argues that the Chinese state facilitates contentious politics as a way to control crises and maintain legitimacy.[22] Managing irruptions has become its raison d'être. This uncertain condition is a good parallel to Sundaram's "civic liberalism," suggesting something like state or "party liberalism" as a technology of governance in contemporary China.[23]

The consolidation of extralegal political space and relationships is what I introduced, above, as *illegal* or *piratical citizenship*. It describes the conditions of political recognition where political society, and not rights-based mechanisms, is the norm. The concept can be understood in parallel to what Nikhil Anand has termed *hydraulic citizenship*.[24] Built around the ethnographic study of water systems in Mumbai, Anand understands hydraulic citizenship as a mode of claiming the city through the generation and application of pressure: "You need pressure to make water flow."[25] Incorporating a range of technical, political, social, and material agents, he shows how different ways of creating pressure, both legal and illegal, enable a wide range of groups to direct water toward themselves and occupy the city. "Hydraulic citizenship" is a form of *belonging* that is brought about by "social and material claims made to the city's water infrastructure."[26]

Anand's analysis, while specific to its context, is also instructive for thinking about the tensely mundane condition of fake citizenship and mediated pressure at the center of this book. Citizenship is always marked by contingency, performativity, and negotiation, but its *becoming illegal* (piratical, fake, informal, etc.) consolidates trends in neoliberal cum postsocialist technologies of government that are decidedly unequal and unjust—including models of self-entrepreneurialism and abandonment, familiar jingoisms and sacrificial aspirations, the privatization of public imaginaries and the commons, and the pitting of state–citizen projects against those dispossessed by the new city. In the context of Beijing's material and imaginary remaking, piratical citizenship helps us to understand the social projects and forms of urban belonging enacted by claims on the city's media infrastructure—including how informal and illicit practices pressure or seep into official structures.

The Aesthetics of Development

Dream Weavers: Beijing 2008 (*Zhu Meng 2008*, directed by Gu Jun) is the official documentary of Beijing's Olympic transformation. Shot over the course of seven years, the film weaves together a series of stark juxtapositions. The documentary opens with TV footage of elated crowds and dazzling fireworks in celebration of the July 2001 announcement naming Beijing as host of the twenty-ninth Olympiad. It cuts to a slow pan over the rooftops of courtyard housing and the soon-to-be-demolished Gao family home in Wali Village. The matriarch, Gao Guilan, dutifully describes how her home will be razed to make way for the Olympic Green—one of nearly four thousand displaced families to be relocated. Another quick cut takes us to November 2002, and to design competitions at the Beijing Municipal Commission of Urban Planning (see figures 2.2–2.4), where global firms pitch their plans for Olympic venues. On the soundtrack, the clatter of shouting voices and fireworks gives way to the quiet haze and pigeon whistles of courtyard life and, finally, to the official address of a planning conference: a government official describes the significance of locating the Olympic Park at the northern end of the city's traditional central axis. Three minutes into the film the voiceover montage exuberantly weaves these spatial and historical dynamics together, exclaiming: "The National Stadium and Wali Village, two seemingly unrelated names, have become synonymous in 2002 because of the Olympics. As an iconic construction project bearing the dreams of the Olympics, countless eyes are on the design competition for the national stadium. Simultaneously, over three thousand households in Wali Village are beginning to plan the details of their relocation."

These juxtapositions succinctly capture the aesthetics of development undergirding new urban imaginaries: projecting the at once instant and deferred temporalities of modernization, old and new ways of living, ideologies of transition and sacrifice, and the importance of techno-scientific planning as a mode of address. The documentary continues in this fashion, crosscutting the Gao family's move to a modern high-rise apartment with scenes highlighting the construction of Olympic stadia, training sequences featuring young gymnasts and track star Liu Xiang, and preparations by special forces units charged with Olympic security. In each case, the hardships of training and transition are dramatized but ultimately justified by the ends. The film, in fact, can be described as the official demolition (*chaiqian*) and reconstruction story of Beijing—directly responding to over two decades of

Figure 2.2 *Dream Weavers* juxtapositions provide an official narrative for Beijing's transformation: Olympic bid celebrations, 2001.

Figure 2.3
Grandma Gao's soor-to-be-demolished home in Wali Village.

Figure 2.4
Design competitions for new Olympic Park development.

disputes over redevelopment, unfair compensation, and massive changes in the quality of life.²⁷

What interests me about this polished and moving documentary is not its propagandistic tone—such patriotic developmentalism is typical around the world—but rather how it seeks to rigorously establish legitimate modes for living out transformation. This includes the promise of the model city: new roadways, subway lines, high-speed railways, a massive airport terminal, new megastructures like the National Stadium (the Bird's Nest) and the National Centre for the Performing Arts (the Egg), as well as new housing, shopping districts, and telecommunications infrastructure. But it also projects an ideal citizen—modeling how subjects should act, relate to the state, and articulate their aspirations. This includes paternalistic relationships with district governments, expectations about consumption and quality of life, and civil or resilient responses from those asked to forgo, improve, or migrate. The Gao family relocation is presented as an ideal template for the difficult but necessary changes tied to the urbanization process. Tellingly, these difficulties are largely constructed as a generational gap between Grandma Gao and her children. The gap takes on the familiar peasant versus urbanite trope—where urban subjects are associated with *quality* (or *suzhi* 素质) and rural people are subject to improvement.

While resigned to yet another massive change, Grandma Gao also speaks quite frankly, even breaks down in tears, about leaving her family home and moving to the city. But the family is not really moving to the city so much as the village is being swallowed by its expansion. The Gaos will move a short distance to a new development and watch as Wali Village is remade into a high-tech Olympic Green and a stage for global media spectacle. In contrast to Grandma Gao's seen-this-before acquiescence, her son and daughter-in-law are exuberant about leaving the country for the city and starting a new life. This idealism is framed by the birth of their daughter, Tongtong, on December 31, 2002. Little Tongtong is literally a child of the Olympic era. Through the film, she serves to mark time and progress, functioning as a kind of a mascot for life in the new city. But while excited about leaving the countryside, the young family are anxious about the complexities of relocation. In one scene, they imagine the cost of buying a new apartment—130 square meters, at 4,000 RMB per square meter, equals more than 500,000 RMB—and worry whether government compensation will be sufficient. This anxiety is presented in a moving sequence, just minutes later, showing the family seated around a table during the 2003 Spring Festival. As China Central Television's (CCTV) broadcast of the New Year's Gala (*Yangshi chunwan*

央视春晚) plays in the background, the extended family both celebrate the passing of another year and express trepidation about where the next one will find them.

The film also takes care to explore detailed differences between the Gao family home in Wali Village and the family's new home in the city. For example, in the opening sequences, the camera dwells on the dilapidated state of the old courtyard-style home, its primitive kitchen with a coal stove, separated living spaces, and Grandma Gao's shuttling of a bucket of water. When, four years later, we catch up with the family at little Tongtong's kindergarten near the Bird's Nest Stadium, and next in their new apartment, the viewer is struck by their change of lifestyle. The village courtyard has been replaced by a small bright apartment in a high-rise complex, complete with air-conditioner, gas stove, and other conveniences. One of the film's producers greets Grandma Gao by telling her that she looks much "younger than last time." And indeed she does. She wears new clothes, has a fashionable haircut, and even her teeth—the subject of earlier close-ups and marker of her peasant status—have been replaced, now white and sparkly. She enthusiastically states that "life is much better than in the village," and now she "has fewer worries." Grandma Gao adds, with pride, that each of her three sons now owns a car. What is more, this new urban living is stimulating and rewarding. We see Grandma Gao patrol the streets as part of the neighborhood committee and, later, become a volunteer for the Olympic Games. In one scene, she and little Tongtong attend a rally to learn English so they can welcome visitors. Changes in the material city promise to reshape the bodies and habits of its residents too.

Importantly, the process of compensating the Gao family for their home in Wali Village, and of finding and purchasing a new apartment, is all but elided in the film. A single scene of a government official posting the terms of relocation, followed by friendly officials carefully measuring the dimensions of the Gao's residence are all we learn about the process. But this elision is significant because the process of demolition and relocation has been and remains intensely controversial across China. This is both because of the traumatic scale of redevelopment, but also because its specious protocols have spurred petitions and protests, mass sit-ins, traffic blockages, suicide attempts, and violence.[28] Contentious modernization projects draw our attention to widespread land grabs, privatization and speculation, fraud, and illegal government actions that are important to Beijing's transformation in the 2000s, but that also continue in the capital and nationally. The 2011 and 2016 anticorruption protests in Wukan, Guangdong, or the November 2017 crackdown on migrants in Beijing's suburbs are just two well-documented illustrations of this ongoing process.[29]

Dream Weavers, alongside an array of official designs and discourse, refuses the ambivalent and violently unjust aspects of redevelopment. While there is no doubt that new infrastructure and urban renewal projects have improved living standards for many people, the reverse is also true. Modernization projects can only be understood in relation to widespread dispossession and disenfranchisement (as indicated by China's massive "floating" population and regularized protests), as well as the articulation of new urban lifestyles and citizenship practices. That this telos of development is seen as the solution to poverty, abandonment, and vulnerability, and not its underlying cause, is crucial to underglobalization. Put differently, *Dream Weavers* projects an official modality of development that relegates (non)citizens "to a life aesthetic defined by the state so that they can be citizens."[30] Other forms of social and political life fall away as illegal, counterfeit, or backward.

Distribution and Piratical Citizenship

In contrast to the smooth promise of official transformation, street-level and activist media provide a different vantage onto the politics of model living. The 2006 documentary *Meishi Street* is perhaps the best-known example of this contentious urbanization. The collaborative video project documents residents' protest of the planned demolition of the Dashalan'r neighborhood, at the southwestern corner of Tiananmen Square, ahead of the 2008 Olympics. Produced by visual artists Ou Ning and Cao Fei, who shot additional footage and were its editors, the bulk of the film was recorded with a camcorder by Meishi Street resident Zhang Jinli in the fall and winter of 2005–6. Indeed, the film ends with Zhang documenting the destruction of his family home. As with many videos and informal accounts that focus on disputes in the relocation process, *Meishi Street* emphasizes the involuntary nature of eviction, problems related to unfair compensation, corruption, and collusion between developers and district governments, threatening policing, unaffordable or distant alternative housing, loss of community, and lack of legal protocols for appeal.

The film collects a huge amount of visual evidence, bearing witness to long-term and dynamic struggles over speculation, corruption, and enforced modes of inhabiting the city. Of particular interest is Zhang's savvy use of the city street as a medium for articulating both dissent and urban belonging. Roughly half of the film portrays Zhang making and hanging signs protesting the terms of his removal, juxtaposed with scenes documenting the removal

Figures 2.5 and 2.6   Zhang Jinli disputes/records the demolition of his home in *Meishi Street* (2006).

Figures 2.7, 2.8, 2.9, and 2.10
Stills from *Meishi Street* demonstrate the importance of city surfaces and camcorders in contemporary political society. Mr. Zhang's signs (Figure 2.8) respond to government banners: "We petition the government to treat the common people with fairness and justice."

of his posters by area police. Figures 2.7–2.10, for instance, capture the dialogue between the red-and-white banners posted by district governments—"Relocating people in strict accordance with the law, promoting preservation of neighborhood features"—and printed or handmade signs voicing Zhang's refusal to accept the unfair terms of relocation. On the left of Zhang's doorway, just above the word for *demolish*, the characters read: "*Niu Yuru where are you?*"—a plea for aid from a communist leader commemorated by Hu Jintao for his honesty and for helping impoverished communities in Inner Mongolia.[31]

The juxtaposition of government banners and ephemeral signs of protest also brings into relief the important cohabitation of new and old media forms in struggles over urban space. Traditional calligraphy, handmade signs, and street-level demonstrations—Zhang sings and argues, makes and hangs posters, produces legal evidence of his rights—are arrested and amplified by the camcorder, the hard drive, the mobile phone, the internet, and so on. Interestingly, as we have seen with recent protests elsewhere, the handwritten sign remains a critical tool for projecting one's voice into a broader mediascape. These interventions can be recorded and rebroadcast across various online and offline networks, fostering new political affinities and buoying an infrastructure of dissensus. Such low-fi practices are crucial to digital urbanism and to how those erased by planning's inhuman visuality reclaim and repopulate the (image of the) city.

On July 15, 2008, just weeks before the opening of the Beijing Olympic Games, the Dazhalan Project website announced that "After struggling for nearly three years, Zhang Jinli finally got his relocation housing in Daqijia Hutong with the same area and value as his original house at No. 117 on Meishi Street. This is a victory for a civilian."[32] Zhang's exceptional case and legal victory over developers and the city government demonstrates the contours of what I am calling piratical citizenship. To get fair compensation and remain in his neighborhood, Zhang is forced to operate within political society—that is, to create pressure through illegal activism, extralegal negotiations, and witnessed moral legitimacy. This pressure relies on media technologies to document his case, show official corruption and illegal acts, and transmit his claims to a local and international audience. Importantly, these complaints are not made directly to Chinese media—official print and TV rarely cover his or similar cases on their own terms—rather, his dispute enters popular debates from the margins: in the form of hand-painted signs or leaflets, conversations and protests, bystander videos, text messages, pirate DVDs, informal screenings, memes about dispossession, even games like *The Big Battle*.[33]

While many studies have discussed resistance to chaiqian, with *Meishi Street* as a frequent example, I want to draw out a distinctive aspect of this political action—namely the relationship between media distribution and social volatility. This includes new modes of participatory filmmaking and social engagement that rely not only on audience reception, but also on dynamic social assemblages of filmmakers, activists, scholars, and residents like Mr. Zhang. The Dazhalan Project is exemplary of this nexus.[34] The project combines research, documentation, and community action to examine and contest the effects of monumental urbanization on impoverished communities like Dazhalan. In addition to the documentary film, the group manages a bilingual website that collects historical and legal scholarship, archives sounds and video, reprints stories from the Chinese and international press about Dazhalan redevelopment, publishes critical essays, and promotes screenings and workshops in Beijing, Shenzhen, and Hong Kong, as well as at universities and galleries across the world.

Zhang's street-level activism is powerfully mobile, jumping media infrastructures and addressing both local and distant audiences. After its release in 2006, *Meishi Street* could be purchased nearby from street DVD vendors and was widely shared on discs and thumb drives by students, filmmakers, and activists. The film was also screened at galleries and other venues across Beijing, like Three Shadows, the Long March, or the Ullens Center (where I first saw the film), as well as cine clubs at bars, cafés, and universities. Additionally, these sites existed in conjunction with regularizing if always harassed festivals—or exhibitions (*zhanlan* 展览), to use the necessary language that avoided government censorship—in Beijing/Songzhuang, Shanghai, Chongqing, Nanjing, and Dali, among other locales (see chapter 3). Finally, it remains available for download on torrent sites, for streaming on Tudou, Tencent, and YouTube (trailers, clips, etc.), is officially distributed by dGenerate films (via Icarus) outside of China, and can even be viewed on e-commerce megaplatforms like Amazon. It is this mottled and expansive distribution footprint—from a hastily made sign hung in a doorway to Amazon Prime—that interests me here.

What the documentary documents is the transformation of Meishi Street itself into a technology of dissensus.[35] This works both at the level of content—the moving story and images of Zhang's eviction grabbed the attention of people in Beijing and around the world—and also at the level of infrastructure and distribution. The latter leads me to reflect upon the idea of the "documentary impulse," which scholars like Yomi Braester and Zhang Zhen have productively used to analyze a variety of filmmaking modes in contemporary China, and ultimately, film's ability to function as a visual record.³⁶ I want to build on this notion and consider not only documentation and remembrance, but distribution—the *distribution impulse*. In addition to the obsessive cataloguing and archiving of social space that defines the urban cinema's preservational aesthetics, this draws our attention to the public production and distribution of images—the competition over surfaces—that has defined media urbanism in the millennial Olympic era.

What I want to draw attention to here is how distribution matters beyond the circulation or reception of texts (like the sounds, images, and characters of Zhang's displacement). While the latter are clearly important, I also want to consider what Thomas Lamarre, drawing on Gilles Deleuze and Félix Guattari, has called the *production of distribution*.³⁷ The production of distribution points to the historically rooted tendency for distribution channels to outpace production.³⁸ But, more importantly, it signals the fact that distribution is itself productive: it "produces a complex set of social functions."³⁹ Lamarre has in mind the role that media infrastructures and technologies have in shoring up social intimacy or what he terms "affective media geographies." These technological conditions—and not only content and formal address—play a critical role in generating affinity and potentiality. For example, Lamarre shows how the construction of regional television in East Asia—such as the transnational and transmedial success of *Boys over Flowers* (Hana yori dango)—cannot be understood as the simple result of shared cultural or linguistic history, national proximity, or even the effect of coproductions. Instead, it also results from the routes, repetitions, and circuits enabled by long-standing media infrastructures, like TV/media networks. The proliferation of digital infrastructures has only thickened this *productivity*.

The affective significance and volatility of distribution can be extended to the mundane and illegal infrastructures that enable contentious communications on Meishi Street, among many other examples—like the façade of a house, hand-painted signs, singing and talking, amateur photography and video, and so on. As opposed to official media channels, which have largely failed to amplify subaltern and popular claims on the social, piratical infrastructure sustains the individuals and communities neglected by official protocols. What this distribution produces, in other words, is the potential for social emergence and political action—constituting an *infrastructure of dissensus*. By dissensus I mean to invoke both widespread dissent—and thus a kind of consensus among those acting from positions beyond rights, norms, and laws—as well as, following Jacques Rancière, a fracture or "gap of the sensible itself" that is crucial to political action. As Rancière puts it, "political demonstration makes visible that which had no reason to be seen; it places one

Figure 2.11   Traces of residents' protests, such as these painted characters proclaiming "illegal destruction," are common in Beijing's hutong, from *A Disappearance Foretold* (2008).

world in another."⁴⁰ The disruption and occupation of official infrastructures, epistemologies, and institutions is the ground of politics itself. In this way the distribution impulse carves out a set of social capacities that both are entangled with and exceed documentary's record-making function—that is, the aspect of media that is often presumed to be politically meaningful. Piratical citizenship recycles and invents social and cultural infrastructures, fostering new and portable capacities for inhabiting the city.

The Image(s) on the Wall

As a result of increasingly visible and mediated dissent, the Olympic era is also marked by municipal and state projects to reassert control over urban surfaces and informal publicities. Olivier Meys and Zhang Yaxuan's collaborative 2008 film *A Disappearance Foretold* gives particular attention to this dynamic. The film observes everyday life in Qianmen, a long-standing commercial district adjacent to Dazhalan. Because the Qianmen Demolition and Reconstruction Project planned to convert the main north–south artery into a pedestrian-only shopping district—which opened in time to welcome Olympic tourists—seven new streets had to be built to carry traffic. Before the project could

Figures 2.12 and 2.13   A large separation wall, complete with classical scroll painting, is erected to shield demolition and reconstruction of the Qianmen neighborhood in *A Disappearance Foretold* (2008).

commence in the fall of 2005, roughly 80,000 residents had to be relocated and thousands of courtyard houses and other structures, including famous emporia like the Qianxiangyi silk store, had to be demolished. As with *Meishi Street*, *A Disappearance Foretold* explores life between ruins and blueprints, emphasizing the experience of holdouts and the contested relocation process. In addition to the ephemeral street-level image conflicts discussed above, Qianmen focuses our attention on a particularly salient form of urban control in Beijing—the use of large graphic-printed walls to enclose construction sites. These billboard-like fences or structural wraps act to separate, beautify, and make safe spaces of construction, projecting uninterrupted views of urban space and functioning as the (im)material architectures of transition.

A sequence midway through the film depicts the walling in of the Qianmen neighborhood, including images of workers hanging vinyl graphics displaying a traditional skyline reminiscent of scroll paintings like *Along the River during the Qingming Festival* (see figures 2.12 and 2.13). This novel practice both closed off opportunities for sidewalk activism and replaced the blue aluminum fencing that was sometimes used around construction sites in the capital. Given the scale of demolition and reconstruction in cities like Beijing, large graphic landscapes saturated many parts of the city in the 2000s—at times filling the sidewalks of entire neighborhoods. In particular, the colorful walls appeared in heavy-traffic and high-profile areas around infrastructure projects like the new subway lines or Olympic stadia, in heritage zones and surrounding the preservation (often meaning the demolition and then reconstruction) of historic neighborhoods such as Qianmen, and around cultural developments such as shopping centers and leisure areas. My examples here emphasize municipal imagery, though, of course, advertising and commercial billboards are also widespread in certain areas—such as those surrounding new hotel projects in Sanlitun or the central business district. Crucially, the walls also act to stamp out sidewalk documentation and distribution—or at the very least, to significantly alter its techniques. Colorful walls like those shown in figures 2.14–2.17 not only disappear demolition sites behind the Photoshop aesthetics of new and old Beijing, they also demonstrate the agility of district governments and developers, alongside residents and activists, in using media technologies to manage urban visuality.

In the lead-up to the Games, Beijing was home to dozens of print shops whose business it was to reproduce vinyl tableaus for the city's sidewalks. And like the revolution in digital video, these copy shops utilized a range of newly affordable technologies, including wide-bed printers, computers, and design software. The expansive graphic walls emerged to meet new municipal regulations

Figure 2.14 Lush forests fill construction-site panels around the National Museum in Tiananmen Square. Photo by Graham Bury. Courtesy of Pam and John Bury.

requiring optimistic landscapes to beautify and manage the ubiquitous construction. One Beijing project manager remarked that it was largely up to the construction team to choose the specific images used at a given site—though advertisements, not including public service announcements, are forbidden on public projects.[41] The control over such images, however, clearly follows a set of implicit guidelines as specific visions mark particular locations, while other sites have no images at all. Two dominant pictures overwhelm the city: images of China's techno-verdant future or images recalling its imperial past. What's more, at key moments the whole of the city's civic billboard space can be made to come together to strike a single visual chord. The 2006 Sino-African Summit—projecting images of the Chinese imagination of Africa coupled with development slogans—and the 2008 Olympic Games are good examples of this orchestrated address.

In addition to beautifying Beijing's construction sites, these surface architectures are also part of intense debates surrounding commercialization in the capital. For example, the proliferation of billboard advertisements, particularly those ads highlighting the growing gap between rich and poor, came under attack by the early 2000s. In 2004, an earlier ban on commercial billboards in Tiananmen Square was expanded to include a host of other cultural

Figure 2.15 Construction-site fences emerged as a contentious field within Beijing visual culture in the first decade of the millennium. Courtesy of the author.

and political sites.⁴² And by 2007, Beijing Mayor Wang Qishan launched a broad attack against billboard excess. The assault was related to both billboard luxury and Olympic branding rights. As one 2007 report put it:

> in the course of the past decade, high-end boutiques sprang up along the avenues, German sedans started prowling the streets, and billboards have appeared flaunting "ultra-exclusive" "luxury" goods fit for "tycoons." INDULGE IN A SMALL VILLA, read one; BECOME A FOREIGN DIPLOMAT'S LANDLORD, exclaimed another.
>
> In an interview, Mayor Wang complained that the opulent signs "encourage luxury and self-indulgence which are beyond the reach of low-income groups, and [are] therefore not conducive to harmony in the capital."⁴³

As a result, hundreds of billboards throughout the city—including some "90-odd" signs along the airport expressway—were dismantled and new licenses suspended through the Olympic Games. The goal, according to one city official at the time, was to "reorder the urban landscape."⁴⁴

Figure 2.16   Detail from Qianmen beautification billboards project the area's future as a shopping district, complete with fashionable visitors and nostalgic consumption.

The contentious surfaces bring into view the importance of controlling how the city functions as a visual sign and as a medium for communication. The state's ability to dismantle certain forms of visuality (like billboards or Zhang's street-level irruptions) and proliferate others is a good illustration of this tension. But even as graphic landscapes delimit street-level dissent, new modes of publicity and protest emerge. This includes the New Documentary Cinema, communities organized around making and screening videos, as well as a wide range of media urban forms. Most salient to the example here, construction-site walls were often used as canvases for protest or veiled communiqués. This is in part a result of the fact that migrant workers often live in prefabricated housing within or alongside construction sites. In figure 2.17, a palm tree–lined landscape enclosing a construction site on the Third Ring Road is repurposed as a makeshift bulletin board for migrants and others. Its location on a major artery makes it a mass medium. The wall displays traces of graffiti, phone numbers, and other messages signaling the informal practices whereby workers buy forged documents, look for new jobs, or access other services denied to floating populations (*liudong renkou* 流动人口). Because migrant workers do

DIGITAL URBANISM   83

Figure 2.17 Palm trees cover a construction site and worker housing, displaying traces of graffiti and phone numbers connecting migrants to jobs and forged papers. Photo by Graham Bury. Courtesy of Pam and John Bury.

not possess the necessary urban registration (*hukou* 户口) to access municipal services, these walls, alongside other technologies like mobile phones, create important avenues for finding people, opportunities, and care.

Such messages and graffiti, if not co-opted by the industrial chic of the city's art districts (e.g., "798," Caochangdi, Songzhuang Arts Village, or even gentrified hutong like Nanluoguxiang), are quickly painted over. Similarly, handmade or printed banners expressing resident protest are taken down as soon as they appear—not unlike the water-dipped brushes, whose wet characters quickly evaporate in the sun, used by old men to practice calligraphy or lodge complaints on the sidewalk. Other traces of collective agency or everyday occupation—unregistered food vendors, illegal three-wheel taxis (so-called *bengbengs*), informal cinemas, pirate book and disc vendors, street gamblers, even entire alleyways of informal commerce—can disappear at a moment's notice. These ubiquitous practices are at once tentative and have a way of hiding in plain sight. It is because of this illicit persistence that digital documentation and distribution projects are significant: they capture and reanimate forms of life that often exist below the threshold of recognition, folding them back into the social practices and the aggregate knowledge of urban belonging.

Seepage and the Fake City

As I have argued, digital urbanism captures both the agility of the state as well as new capacities in public culture. More than a game of call and response, this process can be understood through the transformative logic of *seepage*. I borrow "seepage" from the RAQS Media Collective to describe how official blueprints, policies, or projects become porous or contaminated, enabling variations and fostering new alignments of the social. As RAQS asserts, seepage describes "the action of many currents of fluid material leaching onto a stable structure, entering and spreading though it by way of pores, until it becomes a part of the structure, both in terms of surface, and at the same time continues to act on its core, to gradually disaggregate its solidity."[45] Seepage helps us to imagine the push and pull, or the generation of pressure, that drives piratical citizenship and processes of underglobalization. It both relies on official structures to "become what it is" and, at the same time, renders them fragile, generating new potentialities.[46]

My interest here is to consider a range of projects that take up official design protocols to enter into the model city. Rather than recalling illegitimate inhabitations or counterfeit publics, these dissensual designs draw on the very basic idea, repeated endlessly in and about the city, that social forms are mutable and can be reengineered to work and feel differently. Put differently, faking the city is itself a way of claiming the social. Examples range from brazen proposals by architects to artist-designed cities to micro interventions—like Mr. Zhang's handmade signs. Consider Beijing-based architecture firm MAD's proposal, *Beijing 2050*, first exhibited at the 2006 Venice Architecture Biennale. The exhibition projects three visions for the future of Beijing: a lush park in Tiananmen Square, floating islands above the central business district, and hutong bubbles—small-scale interventions into life in Beijing's alleys. The plan asserts that "Beijing has a history of short-term futures." It traces a series of shortsighted scenarios from the Ten Great Buildings of 1959 to the intense construction of the Olympic era.[47] In contrast to instant designs, the year 2050 suggests a turn away from the short-term planning that has defined several generations of socialist and postsocialist urban projects. Instead, it explores the city's present *after* the future—an inversion of the future logic employed by official redevelopment. The design of a "People's Park" around Tiananmen Square is a good example of seeping into official strategies. Here the political address of Mao's portrait and state monuments is disappeared into a green future that uncannily resembles many official projections and landscapes—pushing the masterplan's environmental lip service to the extreme. MAD's

Figure 2.18 *Beijing 2050* proposes to turn the concrete expanse of Tiananmen Square into a forest. MAD Architecture, 2005. Courtesy of MAD.

design resists both the performativity of the state and the speculative logic of urbanization, carving out a new imaginative commons.

In addition to challenging both the rhetoric and the reality of the new Beijing, *Beijing 2050* criticizes recent visions of modernization as a mode of self-colonization. Floating islands above the CBD are thus conceptual projections whose aim is to explode a certain developmental rut. MAD's proposal claims: "Yet, as China begins to leapfrog the west in terms of development, this vision is increasingly irrelevant. Instead of simply imitating western downtowns, we need to create a city centre for a new post-western, post-industrial society. In the midst of segregated and competing glass boxes, we propose a floating island above the city, where digital studios, restaurants, multi-media business centres and government functions are horizontally linked. The floating island emphasizes the economic trends of tomorrow: connectivity and interdependence."[48] MAD's future city—presented in models, renderings, and perspective diagrams—enters contemporary debates and visual cultures through the very design strategies that constitute the official city. In this way it also draws our attention to the ambivalent relationship between state capitalism and cognitive capitalism. MAD's Beijing is, on the one hand, a familiar rendering of the technologized city and the problematic ambitions of the knowledge economy and, at the same time, pushes against the failures of official and technocratic interventions to address basic political concerns in the capital: air pollution, potable water, green space, freedom of assembly, the commons, and so on. In this way *Beijing 2050* does not mark a radical departure but instead utilizes the porosity of digital urbanism. Here alternative visions seep into recognizable strategies, taking up their idioms, pressuring their solidity.

Photographer Xing Danwen also takes up planning's visual address to squat urban designs. In *Urban Fiction* (*Dushi yanyi* 都市演绎), an ongoing project that began in 2004, the artist photographs models and maquettes used to promote real estate developments and reedits them, creating new narratives. In fact, many of the models that she photographed are now completed structures. Xing's work comes in postproduction, where she transforms the miniatures into stories about model living, including digitally manipulated images of herself occupying future structures. The scenes range from the mundane—residents putting on makeup, talking on the phone, floating in the pool, playing tennis, and shopping—to the extraordinary. Figure 2.20, for example, shows Xing standing on the edge of a high-rise. Other fictions depict a lovers' quarrel involving a butcher knife, car accidents, and scenes of intense isolation. She asserts: "The models of these new living spaces are perfect, clean and beautiful but they are also so empty and detached of human drama. When you take these models and begin to add real life—even a single drop of it—so much changes."[49]

Xing's works, among other projects like Cao Fei's *RMB City* (2008), Shi Guorui's *New Beijing CBD* (2007), Song Dong's *Eating the City* (2006), Zhan Wang's *Urban Landscape—New Beijing* (2003–7), Feng Mengbo's *Into the City* (2004), Ai Weiwei's many architectural designs, Yin Xiuzhen's *Portable Cities* series (2002–3), and Lu Hao's *Beijing Welcomes You* (2000) suggest how experimental and counter-planning discourses enter the urban sensorium. Critical to many such projects is the process of redeploying the materials and aesthetic strategies of official planning discourse in order to make sense of the cultural and political potentialities of the model. Xing's *Urban Fiction*, for example, relies solely on existing models and digital manipulation to investigate what it *feels* like to inhabit a blueprint. Her miniatures are haunted by human presence, an inversion that draws attention to the lifelessness of planning's visual culture.

Most famously, perhaps, Cao Fei has borrowed from planning's audiovisual register in order to reformulate current designs of and on the city (see figure 2.21). Her project, *RMB City: A Second Life City Planning*, is a "condensed incarnation of the contemporary Chinese city" that intermixes real and virtual urban elements and exists across a variety of platforms in first and *Second Life*. Its audiovisual form is a composite of postsocialist symbolism—panda bears, statues, megastructures, building cranes, trains, and blue skies and oceans—

Figure 2.19 Xing Danwen's *Urban Fictions* (2004–present). Courtesy of Xing Danwen & Danwen Studio.

Figure 2.20 Detail from Xing Danwen's *Urban Fictions*. Courtesy of Xing Danwen & Danwen Studio.

Figure 2.21   Videos showcasing the construction of Cao Fei's *RMB City*, before the project was launched in *Second Life*, capture the complex temporality of the model city.

that displays a mastery of planning's visual rhetoric. Of particular interest is the project's intense focus on its own process of development and construction. Before opening in *Second Life*, numerous videos, interviews, and exhibitions explored the process of designing and building this virtual city, including models, drawings, plans, animations, and weekly construction-site videos. Video clips documenting the construction process draw on the iconography and sounds of actual building sites, demonstrating the importance of such runes to the experience of the global city.[50]

In an interview about the project, Cao asserts: "I don't think that building my own city is an expression of individualism. I feel it is precisely an acknowledgment and belief in the practice of democracy. I think this project will lead to the foundation on which to experiment with utopian practices."[51] Her project links up with a thick field of media urban practices that take up and seep into the technologized city as a way of making claims on the present. Importantly, Cao's utopian experimentation in *RMB City* must also be understood as basically related to her collaboration on *Meishi Street*, among other projects—where building one's own city is tied up with the project of building democratic potentialities across communities of (non)citizens. This latter aspect is, I think, what gives planning experiments across contemporary

Chinese cultural production particular significance. It signals the recognition that equitable and livable futures are not looked after by state-commercial enterprises, but rather emerge from the social projects and legitimacies carved out by precarious and illegal forms of life.

Coda: Citizen-Alien

A final example is the work of the anonymous microblogger, E2MAN, who was active in and around Beijing from 2011 to 2015—and is since presumed to have adopted a new identity. Dressed in the silvery pop costume of an extraterrestrial, E2MAN photographed himself at a wide range of sites across Beijing, posting images tinted with vintage filters and accompanied by comments in an unrecognizable language. In 2011, his Sina Weibo account had over 22,000 followers and his activity could also be tracked on Douban, among other services. One online story covering E2MAN's rise opened: "How would an alien comprehend everyday life in Beijing?"[52] Another netizen interprets his foray as an attempt "to better understand Earth culture."[53] While speculation as to the blogger's identity and purpose ran wild in the comments section—noting everything from performance art to activism to stealth marketing—the images of E2MAN also directly engaged the uncertain politics of inhabiting the city at issue here.

E2MAN's Weibo posts capture an alien figure walking through demolition sites, at the dump, in an abandoned amusement park, shopping in trendy boutiques, seated in a McDonald's window, at a tourist site, and posing in front of an unfinished skyscraper. Another shows him, in relative close-up, pointing to listings in the window of a real estate office, presumably confused or angry about skyrocketing housing prices. As with the examples above, E2MAN's urban forays insist not only on traumatic changes in the material world, but also on how these shifts transform even local and longtime inhabitants into aliens, outsiders, peasants, migrants, illegals, and other subjects to be improved, surveilled, or disciplined. Thus, the question is not only how an alien would understand Beijing, but also how the city regards, creates, and even requires alien life. The figure of the citizen-alien, both as a visual cue and a form of iconic difference, flips the relation between the foreground and background that predominates in images of the future city. Instead of looking at the city as subject—its famous structures or beautifully rendered panoramas—the eye keys in on the alien body gazing out from the photograph. Such scenes, like figure 2.22, consider both the peculiar space generated by official forms or commands, and trace the everyday movements and inhabitations of urban subjects that the masterplan has designed away. In this way the

Figure 2.22 E2MAN passes by Beijing's National Centre for the Performing Arts, opened in 2007. His extraterrestrial attire is peculiarly at home in this space.

citizen-alien gives further depth to the proliferation of illegal life forms—and thus the self-organized capacities and dissent—that animate Beijing's digital urbanism.

From Grandma Gao to E2MAN, these widely circulated examples refuse the logic of the empty, deferred, or pedagogical city. While such examples can be subaltern, avant-garde, or even firmly entrenched in local/global art markets, and are perhaps not widely recognizable to ordinary Chinese citizens, the innovations they have introduced and the emergence of design as a multimodal social capacity are widespread and have everyday implications. In particular, these projects and practices ask what it means to inhabit a projection, plan, or model. Just as Chinese visual culture in the 1990s and into the 2000s was concerned with the problems of living in a city of ruins, and of maintaining cognitive maps of spaces that disappear at the speed of a shutter, so too cultural production in the first decades of the twenty-first century turns to examine the politics of transitional spaces, including the many newly erected buildings, neighborhoods, and facilities that have yet to be made into meaningful and livable sites. These material and imaginary practices challenge the binary telos of the past or future city—demonstrating that it is only by occupying the present that models become worlds.

In bringing together these aspects of Beijing's digital urbanism circa 2008, this chapter has sought to create a snapshot of the city's media sensorium at a crucial moment of transition. One of my chief claims is that occupying the developmental city has transformed (non)citizenship practices. These can be reduced neither to the command logic of (post)socialist management, nor to the democratic reforms associated with the rule of law and the Chinese constitution. Instead, what I have called piratical citizenship jostles across this spectrum—appealing to paternal state care, the promise of constitutional rights, and locally rooted protests or illegal legitimacies. Further, the field of piratical citizenship and political society is basically entangled with media urbanism—including the forms of belonging brought about by media technologies and publicities. A crucial aspect of mediated dissensus is the volatility of distribution infrastructures, including the affective and ideological intimacies they enable. Entangled with the aesthetic textures of popular and political media—street-level interventions, documentary video, digital art and design—distribution organizes social life and consolidates world building projects. The next two chapters extend this analysis by examining two contentious forms of belonging to the technologized city: the explosion of theatrical cinemas and ambient television.

Bricks and Media
Cinema's Technologized Spatiality

3

A 2011 lifestyle piece in the *China Daily*, "Movie Magic," describes changes in the experience of moviegoing since the 1980s. The story centers on China's booming movie theater business, emphasizing box office growth, new theaters, and shifting modes of watching, eating, and leisure. Consider the opening illustration comparing 1980s auditoriums to the contemporary cineplex:

> Twenty-nine-year-old Shao Yan's earliest memory of a cinema is a hall filled with hundreds of people. In 1980s China, a cinema had just one auditorium. Sitting on wooden chairs, viewers would talk and laugh and leave a thick layer of sunflower seed hulls on the ground.
>
> Now Shao works in Beijing, a city with more than 80 cineplexes, often located in big shopping malls. Popcorn and cola have replaced sunflower seeds even as the auditoriums have become smaller and more comfortable. Going to the cinema is now just part of the whole shopping and eating-out experience, with two hours in a theater rounding off a day's outing.¹

The juxtaposition underscores a host of striking changes associated with contemporary film exhibition in the PRC. It emphasizes shifts from rural to urban sites, collective to individualized viewing, communal to commercial exchange, sunflower seeds and wooden chairs to squishy stadium seating and branded snacks, as well as the transition of cinema going from *the* thing to do, to *a* thing to do—part of a "day's outing." The example further suggests the way that urban consumer lifestyles have reshaped encounters between the state and (non)citizens. No longer didactic or leitmotif films in official settings—the work unit, the factory, mobile tent, and so on—cinema now takes on a state-blockbuster spatiality.

Interestingly, this anecdotal history of exhibition and spectatorship finds its earliest memory in the 1980s and the emerging logics of China's market socialism. Regardless of the historical accuracy of the pairing of theaters then and now—which both suggests important aspects of transformation and elides a much more varied history of exhibition—the sentiments capture a certain telos through which cinema, as a social space and ritual, is currently understood. This includes a spatial aesthetics that links particular sites of viewing (e.g., the cineplex, outdoor theater, art house, informal screens) to specific social imaginaries and conditions of possibility. Building on the previous chapters' examination of planning's visual culture, and struggles over occupying the model city, this chapter extends these concerns to the built space of cinema. It focuses on the social infrastructures associated with contemporary modes of cinema-going. These distinct modes draw our attention not only to clashes over (il)legitimacy and (il)legality, but also to the crucial role of movie theaters as sites of cultural and political production.

Technologized Spatiality

In her 1995 book *Primitive Passions*, Rey Chow locates the emergence of China's "technologized visuality" in a transformative cinematic encounter experienced by the writer Lu Xun—a figure hailed as the father of modern Chinese literature. Chow offers a critical rereading of Lu's well-known experience watching lantern slides and films while a student at Sendai Medical School in Japan circa 1904-6. What she draws to our attention is that Lu "discovers what it means to 'be Chinese' in the modern world by watching film."[2] Of this formative encounter, Lu writes:

> I do not know what advanced methods are now used to teach microbiology, but at that time lantern slides were used to show the microbes; and if the lecture ended early, the instructor might show slides of natural scenery or news to fill up the time. This was during the Russo-Japanese War, so there were many war films, and I had to join in the clapping and cheering in the lecture hall along with the other students. It was a long time since I had seen any compatriots, but one day I saw a film showing some Chinese, one of whom was bound, while many others stood around him. They were all strong fellows but appeared completely apathetic. According to the commentary, the one with his hands bound was a spy working for the Russians, who was to have his head cut off by the Japanese military as

public demonstration, while the Chinese beside him had come to *appreciate the spectacular event*.[3]

Lu's attempt to make sense of the violent spectacle and its meanings for his executed countryman, the onscreen witnesses, his own disjunctive position in a foreign classroom, and the imbricated jostling of national bodies, famously led him to abandon medical school and turn to writing, shifting from the care of individuals to the spirit of the social—that is, Lu perceived China's malady to be distinct from biological symptoms. He continues: "the people of a weak and backward country, however strong and healthy they may be, can only serve to be made materials or onlookers of such meaningless public exposures; and it doesn't matter how many of them die of illness."[4]

The lecture hall scene animates a dense layering of watching and watched that amplifies the cinema's forceful role as an agent of external modernity—akin to the blow of the execution itself. As Chow argues, Lu Xun is witness not only to the violence of the execution or the passivity of his countrymen, but to emergent configurations of visuality and power that construct China and the postcolonial non-West as a powerless mass "mesmerized in spectatorship."[5] By foregrounding the critical, and critically neglected, role that visuality occupies in the encounter, Chow transforms the story of how a major writer began to write into a flickering map of geopolitical aesthetics.

This flickering map that Lu Xun first illuminated in the early twentieth century still casts shadows on the broader textures of what might be termed, following Chow, a *technologized spatiality*. Such a reorientation shifts our focus to the vital role that cinema's spatial practice plays in contemporary China.[6] Further, it allows us to extend notions of "cinematic space" to include a range of extratextual practices: urban planning and the construction of new cinemas, film festivals and video publics, and the everyday lifeworlds animated by making, circulating, and watching movies. Approaching contemporary Chinese cinema from the perspective of a technologized spatiality locates the vibrating dynamics of the technosensual in and through the competing social spaces and imaginaries where they operate. For instance, while a good deal has been written about how contemporary Chinese cinema—the Urban Generation, the New Documentary Movement, ecocinema—records and represents postsocialist transformation, relatively little has been said about the material practice of watching films or about how the cinematic encounter *takes place*.[7]

It is instructive that Lu's visual clash, as a foundational moment in the history of Chinese film spectatorship, did not take place in a movie house or similar site. Nor is his the tale of a naïve bumpkin's first encounter with

Figures 3.1 and 3.2   Xiao Jiang's 2004 film *Electric Shadows* compares moviegoing in contemporary Beijing, top, with Cultural Revolution–era Ningxia, bottom.

the strange magic of a newly invented technology, as captured in films like *Shadow Magic* (Hu, 2000) or descriptions of early cinema audiences running from onscreen locomotives. On the contrary, it is a scene of instruction, a scientific space, and an arena for the international exchange of techniques, ideas, and images. Lu's encounter projects an important spatial genealogy that both opens up the limited discourse that treats film exhibition as a history of commercial screenings—or as only a subaltern resistance to official cultures— and demonstrates the importance that watching movies has in situating and organizing the social body.

More than one hundred years on, how are we to understand the fabric of the cinematic encounter in China? What do current spectators discover about being in the "modern" world by going to the movies? And how do disparate technologized sites animate these relations and Beijing's larger project of digital urbanism? In the present context, for instance, China is no longer a mere spectator—as were Lu Xun and his onscreen countrymen at the scene of an execution. Instead, China is increasingly a world historical agent, perhaps *the* agent, and is, equally, an object of global fascination. It is not simply visuality that is once again remade by Olympic-era development; rather, it is the very textures of the cinematic encounter as a site for creating and managing political subjectivity. By examining specific sites of exhibition in contemporary Beijing, this chapter aims to bring into relief the crucial role that cinematic spaces or atmospheres play in constructing competing social legitimacies.

China's Box Office Explosion

Lu's horrific recognition, a century ago, that his country "can only serve to be made materials or onlookers" is, in the present context, reconfigured as pleasure, pride, and power by emerging media forms and practices. From official mandates driving the cultural creative industries to mega-media-urbanism and global networks for cultural soft power, China's emergence is imbricated into a project to harness and reanimate, through spatial practice, the spectacle of looking *and* of being watched. Namely, this is the pleasure of experiencing oneself watch oneself be taken in or consumed (e.g., the Olympics, the Expo, etc.)—a relationship that goes beyond returning the gaze, beyond visuality, to create new technologized sites and modes of performativity that function as forms of emergence and control.

According to recent figures, China is the second largest film market by box office revenue after the United States, moving up from as low as fifth just a few years ago, and is third in terms of the number of films produced, following India and the US.[8] Statistics show the rapid construction of new

Table 3.1 Domestic Feature Film Production, 2000–2016

YEAR	NUMBER OF FILMS PRODUCED	DOMESTIC BOX OFFICE (RMB BILLION)
2000	83	0.96
2001	71	0.80
2002	100	0.90
2003	140	1.0
2004	212	1.57
2005	260	2.0
2006	330	2.62
2007	402	3.33
2008	406	2.56
2009	456	6.02
2010	526	10.17
2011	711	13.0
2012	745	17.07
2013	638	21.76
2014	618	29.0
2015	686	44.1
2016	772	45.7

Ten billion RMB (*renminbi*) is roughly US$1.5 billion.

Source: *China Film Yearbook* [*Zhongguo dianying nianjian*], 2001–12; 2012–16 statistics rely on State Administration of Radio, Film, and Television (SARFT) and the *China Daily*.*

* One recent report in English is "China's 2015 Box Office Soars to $6.8b, Up 48.7%," *China Daily*, January 1, 2016, accessed January 15, 2016, http://europe.chinadaily.com.cn/business/2016-01/01/content_22894484.htm.

cinemas across cities, with about ten new screens added daily nationwide in recent years.⁹ The number of screens increased from roughly 1,500 in 2002 to over 13,000 by 2013. In 2016 alone, China added more than 1,600 new cinemas, bringing its total number of screens to an estimated 41,179—topping the United States.¹⁰ Such phenomenal growth, despite a slowdown in box-office receipts in 2016, exceeded the 2013 prediction from China Film Group Corporation's co-chairman, Han Sanping, that "China's film industry will generate 30 billion Yuan in box office revenues within five years, with the number of screens reaching 30,000."¹¹ This increase has shifted China's theatrical market saturation from one screen for every 220,000 people in 2013 to one screen for every 33,000 in 2017 (as compared with one for every 9,000 in the United States).¹² Competition over screen access, including quotas for foreign releases, has meant that as few as 42 percent of feature films produced reached the big screen in 2012, a trend that has continued in recent years. Productions are further pressured by the preferential access of state-sponsored films, which often squeeze out other national and international fare, regardless of box office performance.¹³

Box office revenues have grown at least 25 percent each year since 2003, and more than 35 percent over the past five years, excluding 2016, bolstering theater construction and the success of emerging theater circuits. The top-grossing theater chains include Wanda Cinemas, Guangdong Dadi, Shanghai United Cinema, and China Film Stellar, with Guangdong Province and the municipalities of Beijing and Shanghai making up the largest markets. Additionally, investments by the China Film Group Corporation, the Huayi Brothers, Dadi Century Films, Ultimate Movie Experience (UME), Hong Kong's Broadway Cinema, Korean CGV Cinema and Megabox, and Canada-based IMAX, among many others, are also driving expansion and forging new partnerships in the face of strict regulation of foreign theater ownership. Such regulations, for instance, drove Warner Brothers out of China's theater market in 2006 after a policy flip-flop decreased foreign stakes in joint ventures from 75 to 49 percent and continues to dominate US coverage of China's theatrical explosion.¹⁴ This anxiety is most concretely captured by the May 2012 announcement that Wanda Cinemas had acquired AMC Entertainment, the second largest theater chain in the United States.¹⁵

China's 40,000-plus screens earned over 45 billion RMB, roughly US$6.7 billion, in 2016 (see table 3.1). While the domestic film industry had struggled in previous years to compete with foreign films, which are limited by quota and subject to intermittent "blackouts,"¹⁶ as well as widespread street and internet piracy, the recent box office earnings for films like *The Mermaid* (Chow, 2016),

Table 3.2 Top Ten Feature Films at the Chinese Box Office in 2015

FILM TITLE (DIRECTOR)	COUNTRY	BOX OFFICE (RMB)
Monster Hunt (Raman Hui)	China/HK	2,439,970,000
Fast & Furious 7 (James Wan)	USA/Japan	2,426,580,000
Lost in Hong Kong (Zheng Xu)	China	1,613,540,000
Avengers: Age of Ultron (Joss Whedon)	USA	1,464,390,000
Goodbye Mr. Loser (Da-Mo Peng, Fei Yan)	China	1,441,600,000
Jurassic World (Colin Trevorrow)	USA	1,420,700,000
Mojin: The Lost Legend	China/HK	1,373,910,000
Jian Bing Man (Ershan Wu)	China	1,160,310,000
The Man from Macau II (Jing Wong, Aman Chang)	China/HK	974,850,000
Monkey King: Hero is Back (Xiaopeng Tian)	China	956,430,000

Source: China box office numbers from EntGroup.*

* Estimated annual box office statistics for each film vary across sources, but here are based on China annual box office data from the Entgroup Inc., http://www.cbooo.cn/year?year=2015/ (accessed December 29, 2018).

Monster Hunt (Hui, 2015), *Journey to the West: Conquering the Demons* (Chow and Kwok, 2013), *Painted Skin 2* (Wu, 2012), *Flowers of War* (Zhang, 2011), *Aftershock* (Feng, 2010), *Let the Bullets Fly* (Jiang, 2010), *Silver Medalist* (Ning, 2009), *The Founding of a Republic* (Han and Huang, 2009), *If You Are the One* (Feng 2008), *Red Cliff* (Woo, 2008), *The Warlords* (Chan, 2007), and *Assembly* (Feng 2007), among others, point to a changing climate for both production and exhibition. Since 2010, roughly half of the ten top-grossing films at the domestic box office were Chinese productions. The recent success of both popular and art films like *The Mermaid* (Chow, 2016), *Monster Hunt* (Hui, 2015), *Lost in Hong Kong* (Xu, 2015), and *The Grandmaster* (Wong, 2013), among many others, signal the increasing draw of local productions.

Enclosures and Apertures: A Spectrum of Cinematic Encounters

At the centenary of Chinese cinema in 2005, the *Guinness Book of World Records* acknowledged Daguanlou or Grand Shadowplay Theater, located in Beijing's Qianmen neighborhood, as the oldest continuously running movie theater

Figure 3.3 China's oldest movie theater, Daguanlou, continues to attract large audiences for films like Peter Chan's *Wu Xia* (2011). Courtesy of the author.

worldwide. Numerous reports on television and in print have celebrated the achievement over the past decade, staking out new terrain for Chinese cinema as a global phenomenon.[17] For example, a February 2011 report on *CCTV News* commemorated "Daguanlou's 100 Years of Light and Shadow." The story highlights the theater's location at the heart of the new "old Beijing," touring the 105-year-old cinema's lobby museum, and emphasizing the continuity of film-going in China. Daguanlou was established by Ren Qingtai (aka Ren Jingfeng) in 1903. Ren is perhaps best known for making the operatic film *Conquering Ding Jun Mountain* (1905), China's first short film, which premiered at Daguanlou in 1905. Today, Daguanlou remains a relatively small two-story theater with three auditoriums—for twenty, fifty, and four hundred persons, including digital projection and 3D—as well as a café and film museum presenting posters, film projectors, and other relics from Chinese film history. A ticket sells for 35–50 RMB (about $5–8), nearly half as much as a trip to the multiplex.

The celebration of the historic Daguanlou points to an increasing emphasis on Chinese film exhibition as a social, economic, and political space. Such theaters at once build on the marketization of film production since the 1980s, establishing an infrastructure to consolidate the rapid growth and influence of China's tightly controlled film industry, and also remake exhibition sites alongside broader patterns of urban and social redevelopment. For example, the recent renovations of Daguanlou are also part of the controversial demolition and reconstruction of Dashilan'r Street—including the relocation of thousands of neighborhood residents—and its subsequent reconstruction into a historical theme park cum shopping district for the capital's many tourists. As such, the theater is now a key attraction in the Qianmen shopping district alongside some of Beijing's most well known brands and chain stores, including Quanjude's famous Peking duck and Zhangyiyuan tea shop.[18] Such development projects have been widely criticized, not only for the slapdash commodification of Beijing cultural products and the Disneyfication of once-vibrant neighborhoods, but also for how demolition and relocation processes have been carried out, including illegal evictions, corruption, and a lack of opportunities to appeal district decisions. Indeed, the demolition and relocation of the old Qianmen neighborhoods has been the focus of the documentary films *Meishi Street* (Ou, 2006) and *A Disappearance Foretold* (Zhang and Meys, 2008), discussed in chapter 2, which were shot in the rapidly transforming zone and widely projected across Beijing's alternative exhibition venues.

The point is not simply to critique the proliferation of state-commercial developments in Beijing—such projects are mundane and hardly unique to China—but rather to emphasize the contested nature of city space and ways of life at the heart of such encounters. In other words, the desire and capacity to transform Beijing into a global capital is not itself noteworthy; what is crucial is how this transformation operates as *a spatial politics* that remains overwhelmingly top-down, closing off challenges, criticism, and both formal political claims and the informal mechanisms of political society. My interest here is not merely to reiterate familiar critiques about authoritarian China failing to live up to the democratic "West"—the North Atlantic states have their own mundane mechanisms of control—but rather to focus on the particular ways that the Chinese state(s) expresses itself in spatial practice. As scholars like Wang Jing have argued, the state's "discovery of culture as a site where new ruling technologies can be deployed and converted simultaneously into economic capital constitutes one of its most innovative strategies of statecraft since the founding of the 'People's Republic.'"[9] With this process in view, the

Figure 3.4 Looking down onto the lobby of the Jinyi International Cinema, located on the lower level of the New Zhongguancun Shopping Center. Courtesy of the author.

Figure 3.5 Patrons choose between sweet or salty popcorn at the China Film Archive Cinema. Courtesy of the author.

Figure 3.6 Beijing's Ultimate Movie Experience (UME) theater, Haidian District, boasts IMAX screens and VIP member services.

remainder of this section outlines a spectrum of cinematic spatialities and encounters in Beijing.

Formal Sites of Exhibition

The China Film Group Corporation (CFGC) is linked to Daguanlou through its own investments in the China Film Stellar theater circuit (*yuanxian* 院线), among others. Under the supervision of the State Administration of Radio, Film, and Television (SARFT), the CFGC is a vast conglomeration of state film resources, including production, distribution, and exhibition channels. China Film Group owns fourteen fully funded subsidiary companies, thirty-four major holdings and joint stock enterprises, and the country's only movie channel, CCTV 6, and boasts a net worth of 2.8 billion RMB.[20] Importantly, CFGC is also the primary importer of foreign films for theatrical release, as well as a major exporter of Chinese films abroad. In addition to distributing over one hundred feature films annually, CFGC has formed seven cinema circuits and contracts with over four hundred movie theaters. This vast organization is also in the process of establishing its own proprietary cinema circuit with the aim of running one hundred cineplexes throughout the country.[21] Such relationships give the Group a 40 percent share of the

Table 3.3 2016 Domestic Theater Chain Performance

THEATER CHAIN	TOTAL ATTENDANCE	2016 BOX OFFICE (RMB)
Wanda Cinemas	160,624,657	6,088,168,555
Guangdong Dadi	121,777,394	3,668,680,638
China Film Stellar	100,102,134	3,568,801,941
Shanghai United Cinema	98,970,039	3,568,801,941
China Film South	96,347,093	3,236,492,242

Source: *Dangdai Dianying* [*Contemporary Cinema* 当代电影], March 2017.*

* Liu Hanwen, "An Analysis Report of Chinese Film Enterprise in 2016," *Contemporary Cinema* [Dangdai dianying] 3 (2017): 18–24.

domestic box office and significant control of feature film distribution and exhibition nationwide.

CFGC embodies the objective of market socialism to use state enterprises to oversee privatization. Regarding the China Film Group, Davis and Yeh argue that this model of marketization reveals the persistence of "ideological safeguards and economic protectionism" that defines China's screen industries.[22] I want to suggest here that beyond the control of film scripts and images—what can be onscreen—managing how and where films are viewed, the social space of spectatorship itself, is increasingly important to official designs on the social body. Just as theater chains provide the infrastructure to consolidate China's burgeoning film production and ensure its market share, so too does this infrastructure, a state-blockbuster spatiality, consolidate modes of collective reception around particular technological sites and ways of life.

China Film Stellar and Shanghai United Cinema earned over 3.5 billion RMB at the domestic box office in 2016, the market leader Wanda Cinemas earned over 6 billion RMB (table 3.3). China Film Stellar coordinates 188 member theaters and 1,043 screens nationwide.[23] In Beijing alone, the company has stakes in at least eighteen theaters, including Ng See-Yuan's UME (Ultimate Movie Experience) venues. One such site is the UME Huaxing International Cineplex in Haidian district. The massive theater occupies a 4,000-square-meter commercial space, with seven screening halls and over 1,300 seats. A far cry from the simple auditorium of the 1980s, the multistory glass and neon structure boasts VIP rooms, lush carpets and gleaming tile, puffy couches and armchairs, chandeliers, illuminated film posters, parking

Figure 3.7 The state-of-the-art Megabox theater in Sanlitun Village mall attracts crowds with its membership promotions and hip design. Courtesy of the author.

lots, loaded concession stands, and crowds of viewers for domestic and imported action films, costume dramas, romantic comedies, and the like. The largest hall also holds a 430-square-meter IMAX screen. IMAX is one of the fastest-growing sectors of Chinese film exhibition, with ninety screens in operation and, according to CEO Richard Gelfond, a total of 450 screens planned for the market.[24] In 2012, UME Huaxing earned over 67 million RMB, making it the fifth highest grossing theater in the country.[25]

South Korea's Megabox chain also runs two popular Beijing cineplexes. Megabox was the first foreign theater to enter the Beijing market in 2007—following Korea's CGV and MK Pictures' Shanghai partnerships. The Megabox Sanlitun Village branch opened for business in 2008 and is a major attraction in the newly remodeled shopping plaza (figure 3.7). The village houses dozens of stores and restaurants including a giant Apple Store, Juicy Couture, Levi's, UNIQLO, Starbucks, and Versace. Theater publicity touts its modern décor, comfortable lobby and screening rooms, state-of-the-art projection and audio equipment, and quality customer service—aspects that make Megabox Beijing's "most fashionable" international cineplex.[26] The multiplex attracts

Figure 3.8 Ticket office and billboard for *Blind Detective* outside Beijing Haidian Theater, July 2013.

large crowds to fill its eight screening halls and 1,600 seats by offering discounts for members (a 20 RMB membership card will get you 50 percent off tickets Monday through Thursday), online ticketing, screenings in both Chinese and English, parking, refunds for dissatisfied customers, and a range of shopping and dining activities just outside the door. The basement theater also bleeds into the village's main courtyard. Its large outdoor display projects film times and promos, alongside advertisements and other location-specific fare.

Daguanlou, UME, and Megabox are just three examples of dozens of such theaters in the capital that signal the importance of new cinematic spaces to larger discourses related to Beijing's history and development. This connects, first, to the increasing importance that theaters play as museums and monuments to China's film history. From Daguanlou to China's National Film Museum, opened in 2005, such sites locate China's film history in the urban fabric and disrupt comfortable narratives about world cinema. The National Film Museum, for example, deems itself to be the world's largest dedicated museum of national cinema. Located in Beijing's northeastern suburbs, the immense facility houses a substantial exhibition celebrating "A Century of Chinese Film." The showcase is laid out over twenty galleries, with themes ranging from the invention of cinema to the cinema of Taiwan, as well as

Figure 3.9 Broadway Cinematheque at the heart Stephen Holl's Linked Hybrid MOMA compound, Beijing. Courtesy of the author.

technological displays exploring areas such as directing, sound recording, and animation. Alongside such expositions, the museum incorporates a large cinema with six screening halls with 1,210 seats for new films, archival screenings, and special events, including an IMAX theater. A trip through the National Film Museum thus literally begins with the Lumière brothers and Daguanlou and ends perched in front of a 567-square-meter IMAX screen.

Second, Beijing's new cinemas link up with official design protocols and embody a particular mode of technologized space. Indeed, these theaters shore up the textures or atmospheres of mediatized space, as well as the ways that mood, tone, or ambience are produced by architecture, marketing, and the state. As such, these technologized sites consolidate a process of social choreography that fuses blockbuster films, urban design, and state policy—a constellation of forces that Achille Mbembe, in a different context, refers to as the "aesthetics of vulgarity." Mbembe is concerned with how state power "*creates*, through administrative and bureaucratic practices, its own world of meanings," and how such codes become "a part of people's 'common sense.'"[27] It is precisely this clustering of coding and commonsense processes, and their enveloping as sociohistorical worlds, that emerging technologized sites like the cinema vivify.

The juxtaposition of the 1980s auditorium and the contemporary cineplex can be understood to do important cultural work by differentiating qualities of life. Perhaps no Beijing cinema demonstrates this developmental instability more clearly than the Broadway Cinematheque. The designer theater is situated at the heart of architect Stephen Holl's "Linked Hybrid" MOMA residential compound. The complex is built to exemplify a porous, mixed-use urbanism that Holl describes as a "cinematic adventure."[28] The cinematheque's walls even project moving pictures into the lavish garden and shopping area—which includes a hotel, designer furniture outlets, and a Montessori school—allowing light and shadow to spill across the pond, vegetation, pathways, and glass in a picture-perfect illustration of the future present.

Broadway Cinemas are part of Hong Kong Edko Films' recent expansion into ten mainland markets. The theaters aim to fill a boutique art film niche that has otherwise been ignored by official screening sites. MOMA's Broadway Cinematheque, also known as the Film Culture Center, houses a library lending film books, magazines, and DVDs, and offers a Kubrick bookstore, a snack bar, and a café. The center also hosts film education events, and offers diverse programming that far exceeds the usual blockbuster offerings. These include international art cinema, free documentary events, in-person visits by directors and actors, as well as popular fare. The range of formal and informal events held at the theater was brought into sharp relief for me during a weekend documentary program that I attended in 2011. The free screening, part of the Film Culture Center's educational programming, drew a large crowd for a Werner Herzog double bill. After a showing of Herzog's *Little Dieter Needs to Fly* (1998), the event had to be cut short because the DVD being used—which appeared to be a pirated copy—lacked Chinese or English subtitles to accompany the German original. This gap between the spectacular new theater and the tactics of the backroom cine club captures the strange position that the theater occupies *in between* formal and alternative film cultures.

What I want to signal here is that there is more at stake in China's theatrical explosion than box-office revenue and industry maturity. In fact, such a statistical obsession obscures the cultural politics fused onto these technologized fields. Instead, to recycle a phrase from a September 2010 news report aired on *Economics Half-Hour*, the rapid emergence of new cinemas in Beijing constitutes an "enclosure movement" (*quandi yundong* 圈地运动). The report charts the recent transformation of movie theaters into a "gold mine" for their financers, offering three keys to the turnaround of the industry. The so-called

Figure 3.10 A migrant worker leisurely watches the big screen atop the Beijing's Worker's Stadium in the lead-up to the 2008 Olympic Games. Photo by Graham Bury. Courtesy of Pam and John Bury.

secrets relate to quick return on theater investments, the restructuring of China's film distribution system by digital projection, which lowers the threshold for smaller theaters to enter the market, and the increasing intersection of multiplex theaters into new commercial real estate projects, which diversify investments and ensure a high volume of customers. The general manager for Poly Theaters, Liu Debin, describes current investments in movie theaters as both reliable and necessary. Such investments, he adds, are much safer than funding film production. Of 456 films produced in 2009, Liu asserts that only 123 of those films reached theaters. The remaining three hundred films went straight to the warehouse shelves. This tendency has

BRICKS AND MEDIA   111

continued in recent years, with as few as 315 of 745 films produced in 2012 reaching the big screen.[29]

While this discussion of new cinemas as an "enclosure movement" is primarily organized around the surprising success of China's film box office, and the cultural industries more generally—a successful harnessing of exhibition's profitability—it also offers a useful, if perhaps accidental, lens through which to consider state-market privatization. The success of sanctioned film exhibition in contemporary China is hinged to a process of enclosure that shuts out residual and emergent cinematic publics. The recent enclosure of the cinema is thus a critical form of social control whereby a multiplicity of screens are disappeared by the atmospherics or common sense of the state. In this context, it is necessary to recognize that beyond the phenomenal growth of box-office revenues and official/commercial cinemas, Beijing still offers a range of alternative cinematic encounters that have not been absorbed by the dominant commercial cum state ventures. Such a relational approach brings into relief the importance of watching films as a mode of communication and, more significantly, the shifting spatial politics of contemporary cinema-going—including the majority of the population, for whom a costly trip to the cinema remains out of reach.

Alternative Cinematic Space

Chris Berry and Lisa Rofel's notion of *alternative* film culture, developed in *The New Chinese Documentary Film Movement* and activist, intellectual, and curator Ou Ning's "Alternative Archive," provide a framework for understanding and locating the politics of technologized spatiality. For Berry and Rofel, alternative culture captures the complex social space constructed by China's market socialism. While this is a space of marketization and pluralization, they argue that it is equally a site where the state exercises control through the market, and where direct forms of opposition are made illegal by the state apparatus. In this context, simplistic understandings of public culture as the absence of the state will not suffice. The concept of alternative, on the other hand, is intended to reenergize cookie-cutter applications of the public sphere (or of independent cinema) by turning to actual social practices. This process is captured by Ou Ning's neologism for the Alternative Archive arts, research, and activism project: *bie guan* (别馆)—a term meaning "side building" and also a homophone for "don't bother me." Understanding alternative culture as a fringe practice or space demonstrates how it exists alongside official structures, engaging them laterally, building on or around, and not engaging head-on.[30]

Cine clubs in Beijing like those observed by Seio Nakajima (Formula 3, Studio Z, Film Movement Society, and Culture Salon) or Chris Berry and Lisa Rofel (Cherry Lane, 22filmcafé, Hart Salon, and Wu Wenguang's Workstation) offer a useful starting point.[31] These old and new spaces for watching films—bars, cafés, artist studios, out-of-the-way spots—exist alongside tensely active screenings organized by Beijing Indie Film Workshop, Iberia Center for Contemporary Art, Ullens Center for Contemporary Art, Think Films, Three Shadows Photography Art Center, the Blue Goat Café, the Li Xianting Film Fund, and universities like the Beijing Film Academy, Peking University, and Beijing Normal University, among many other everyday spaces of art, leisure, and commerce, including ubiquitous handheld devices and even public TV screens. These self-organizing sites respond to the codes and common sense of official spatiality, promoting a range of informal and parasitical practices. From 2007 to 2016 I visited a wide range of such venues, including the four outlined below. These informal exhibition sites continue to operate within the logic of Ou Ning's notion of the "side building," at once proliferating and encountering both stricter censorship and more savvy cultural competition from state-sanctioned cultural industries. But in addition to the notion of alternative cinema, what matters here is how these informal sites bring about social infrastructures and legitimacies.

The Ullens Center for Contemporary Art is located at the heart of Beijing's 798 arts district—a recycled factory zone whose days of youthful artists and lofts have been largely folded into the embrace of the official creative industries. The museum-like center opened in 2007 on the back of Baron Guy and Myriam Ullens's extensive collection of Chinese art, exhibited in 2008 as "Our Future: The Guy & Myriam Ullens Foundation Collection" to coincide with the Olympic Games. While primarily a conventional high art space, it remains relatively unconventional for Beijing. The Ullens Center puts international artists, curators, and intellectuals in dialogue with their Chinese counterparts, opening up a new space for display and discussion. In addition to contemporary art exhibitions—recent shows include Yung Ho Chang, Apichatpong Weerasethakul, Walead Beshty, and Zhan Wang—UCCA also houses a cinematheque and hosts regular film events. From contemporary documentary to international art cinema, the UCCA theater is part of a growing infrastructure showing noncommercial Chinese films to local audiences—for example, a January 2012 event sponsored by the Indie Film Workshop had director Zhang Ciyu in person to present his recent film *Pear* (2010). Beijing Film Academy professor and well-known programmer and film critic Zhang Xianming moderated the discussion.

Figure 3.11   Post-film discussion at Wu Wenguang's Caochangdi Workstation, July 2013. Courtesy of the author.

Think Films (Yingxiang Fangying 影想放映) represents another alternative film venue in Beijing, functioning as a cine club for aspiring filmmakers.[32] The organization emphasizes new films and filmmakers, providing a regular forum for screening, discussion, and networking. Indeed, the group's orientation is professional. It aims to promote film culture so that young directors can find their way into China's bustling media cultures and industries. This includes help finding investors and understanding the international film festival circuit, as well as contact with a wide spectrum of contemporary Chinese films and filmmakers. Their website and blog also serve as a useful resource for information about past and future film events, director bios, and industry news. While not necessarily countercultural in orientation, Think Films is a good example of how many young cinephiles can see the independent Chinese films that never reach China's multiplying theaters.

A third example is Caochangdi Workstation on Beijing's urbanizing rural edge. Caochangdi is the home of filmmaker and theoretician Wu Wenguang, a figure widely credited as the father of the New Documentary Movement. It was founded in 2005 and is composed of Wu's documentary studio, Living Dance Studio, and the Beijing Storm Company. The space is associated with a range of cultural activities including video and performance art, film festivals, as well as the Villager Documentary Project and, more recently, the Memory Project. The Villager project began in 2003 with a grant from the European Union to document village democracy in China. Rather than film the process himself, Wu has reached out to rural communities and provided training and equipment so that villagers can film their own communities. In addition to editing facilities, screening areas, and a film archive, the Workstation also houses a communal kitchen and courtyard, living spaces, offices, as well as an endless flow of visitors, researchers, and collaborators.[33]

Another emblematic self-organized space is the Li Xianting Film Fund and Fanhall Films located in Songzhuang, a quiet cultural village forty minutes outside Beijing. Songzhuang began attracting artists in 1995 after the Beijing police closed down the Yuanming Yuan artist village. Since then, it has become one of the most important bases for independent films in China. Every year, the Li Xianting Film Fund supports two independent film festivals— "exhibition" or film "exchange week" are actually the terms that circumvent the authorities: China Documentary Film Festival (Zhongguo jilupian jiaoliu zhou) in the spring, and Beijing Independent Film Festival (Beijing duli yingzhan) in the autumn. In addition to the Li Xianting Film Fund–supported theater, which seats one hundred, the group distributes independent films, manages a substantial archive of Chinese documentaries, sponsors grants for filmmakers, runs an online discussion forum, and, beginning in 2009, operates the only independent film school in China.

While sites for alternative cinematic encounters are becoming more formal, and some even flourishing, their positions remain tentative. In fact, after a few years of relative growth and stability in the indie scene, independent festivals across China have faced increased governmental scrutiny. One important turning point was the 2012 power outage at Yuanchuang Art Center during a screening of *Egg and Stone* (2012) in Songzhuang. Festivals have been forced to relocate, have been visited by uniformed and plainclothes officers, and have been either physically shut down or forced to regroup by political and financial pressures. Numerous festivals across China—including Yunnan Multicultural Visual Festival (aka Yunfest), the Nanjing-based China Independent Film Festival, the Beijing Queer Film Festival, and the Beijing Independent Film Festival (Songzhuang), among many others—have recently shut down or moved further underground. This includes an uptick in Chinese curators and directors who have emigrated to Europe, Australia, and the United States in recent years.

In particular, government uncertainty and intervention seem to have intensified in the wake of the Arab Spring, leading to the cancellation of the

Figure 3.12 Xianxiang Theater in Songzhuang was a key venue for two of China's most important independent film festivals, held in May and October each year. Courtesy of the author.

Figure 3.13 The screening room at Xianxiang Theater overflows during the 2009 Beijing Independent Film Festival. Courtesy of the author.

2011 China Documentary Film Festival in Songzhuang—and such shutdowns have plagued the festival in each of the subsequent years, though it should be noted that the resilient festivals usually carry on informally through small, word-of-mouth screenings and similar make-do tactics. The tenth Beijing Independent Film Festival, which tried to get underway on August 23, 2013, is a good example of the current negotiated state of affairs. Lydia Wu, in a statement written on behalf of the festival organizers for the independent video portal dgeneratefilms.com, summarizes the event as follows: "On the surface, the opening was different from the scene last year, when policemen in plainclothes showed up to restrict the numbers of attendees and a mysterious power cut disrupted the opening screening, leaving festivalgoers outside waiting for several hours. The opening ceremony went smoothly this year, from the guest registration and opening speech to the gathering of directors and guests. But the opening screening didn't proceed. Under pressure from authorities, the festival couldn't give a clear announcement of what would happen next."³⁴ While the festival's twenty-two fiction films, thirty experimental films, thirty-five documentaries, a special focus "Inside Iran," and a program of Indonesian films seem to have carried on quietly over the next several days, its energy and openness were transformed by government intervention, leading to "weak turnout over the remaining days of the festival."³⁵ Such disruptions and make-do tactics define alternative cinema culture in contemporary China. This dynamic draws our attention not only to the position of festivals and video communities as outside or beside state structures (e.g., bie guan), but also emphasizes their role as a pirate medium and infrastructure—illegal but locally legitimate.

What is more, beginning in 2011, SARFT and the Beijing Municipal Government have staged their own Beijing International Film Festival (BJIFF) to coincide with the festival in Songzhuang. The spectacular gala is held in one of the capital's new megastructures, the National Center for Performing Arts, emphasizing the gloss of the new cinematic space. The first annual festival, held in 2011, was attended by major stars like Fan Bingbing, Feng Xiaogang, John Woo, Jackie Chan, and Zhang Ziyi, commanding much news attention and carving out a new international space for mainland cinema. The BJIFF includes the Beijing Film Panorama, showcasing hundreds of international films, as well as events supporting the Chinese film industry and awards ceremonies. Alongside many other small and large media events, the new festival, now well established, demonstrates how state intervention fosters particular technological intimacies, while attempting to dilute or steamroll others.

Conclusion

Xiao Jiang's wistful *Electric Shadows* (2004)—a film marketed abroad as the Chinese *Cinema Paradiso* (Tornatore, 1988)—projects a history of China and cinema through the experience of moviegoing. Alternating between contemporary Beijing (c. 2002) and Cultural Revolution–era Ningxia (c. 1972), the film returns us to our opening account of "Movie Magic," and to shifting cinematic encounters. A poster for the film suggests time(s) where "dreams can only appear on the silver screen" (*dang mengxiang zhi neng zai yinmushang shixian*). But these cinematic worlds have also endured radical changes, as the collective outdoor cinema of the 1970s gives way, though of course not entirely, to privatized modes of watching associated with the TV and urban movie theater (see figure 3.1). The film opens with a newly urbanized migrant, Mao Dabing (Xia Yu), at the movies in Beijing. He tells us that he spends all his free time in the cinema, because in that space "I can see myself as the movie hero." While a more in-depth discussion of *Electric Shadows*, and other films that go to the movies, is beyond the scope of this chapter, its focus on the transformation of film spectatorship over time underscores the spatial politics considered here.

Contemporary market-socialist development is tethered to a project to reharness film exhibition as a form of spatial practice. This includes collisions between state-market clusters—of which the reach of the China Film Group Corporation is exemplary—and various forms of informal culture that jostle against official structures, projecting disparate social worlds. In this context, the question of scale is crucial. It draws our attention to the cultural work of technologized spatialities across distinct subnational and global constellations. In this international frame, China's reemergence is linked to the new capacity of centers like Beijing to be media capitals and cinema cities—that is, to be onscreen and enfolded into spatial practice across cultural and geographical contexts. This capacity is central to reshaping Lu Xun's experience of visuality and modernity. It transforms a China that is passively "mesmerized in spectatorship" into an active architect of visuality, able to enjoy the pleasure and power of looking, and of watching itself see. A crucial example is China's savvy embrace of global film distribution and exhibition. Even while PRC films struggle to reach broad audiences and to achieve the soft power of its neighbors, such as Cool Japan and the Korean Wave, Chinese ventures have moved to take control of global theater chains—as when Wanda purchased the US chain AMC in 2012.[36] In other words, when blockbusters fail to move global audiences, they are still courted by the *sensational infrastructures* grounding geopolitical distribution and contact. This is important in terms of the politics of the postcolonial and postsocialist non-West and in itself deserves more historical and theoretical attention.

Simultaneously, national and subnational experience also exceeds the power and pride of global emergence. New spatial capacities are also increasingly forms of state power that code experience and shape commonsense space and imaginaries. Cinemas and related technologized sites are tightly entangled in a social context that projects particular subjects, spaces, and ways of life, while limiting or erasing other forms of sociality as fake, illegitimate, or illegal. In this regard, this chapter charts a range of capacities, as well as discourses about them, to take up and utilize space both in the city and *on* or *as* screen. This can be described as an interaction between (il)legitimate and (il)legal practices that get at the core of China's movie theater boom and its relationship to processes of underglobalization.

Beijing en Abyme
Television and
the Unhomely Social

The history of Chinese television since the late 1970s is generally told as a story of commercialization and popularization, emphasizing the relocation of the television set from the collective space of the work unit, factory, and neighborhood committee into the homes of the increasingly affluent urban, and later rural, population. A brief overview of TV in the PRC runs something like this: China's first TV network, Beijing Television, later China Central TV (CCTV), broadcast its inaugural signal on International Labor Day, 1958, to as few as fifty black-and-white sets—the total number of TVs in the capital. By 1960, sixteen of China's twenty-nine provinces had set up TV stations, but few outlasted the severe political and economic crises of the early 1960s, leaving stations in Beijing, Shanghai, and three other sites.[1] As a result, television programming was limited and viewing remained a largely communal affair. In 1966, at the onset of the Cultural Revolution, it is estimated that there were twelve thousand TVs in China, and fewer than a million consoles were manufactured between 1958 and Mao's death in 1976.[2] The introduction of Deng Xiaoping's reforms and "open door" policy in 1978 (*gaige kaifang*), however, brought substantive changes to televisual practices, including the eventual reduction of government subsidies, the establishment of many local and regional stations, and the rapid privatization of the TV set. Roughly three decades on, over 400 million households have a console—making up the world's largest audience.[3]

While current research emphasizes cinema and networked technologies, like the mobile phone, television remains crucial to contemporary media culture and has much to teach us about ongoing technological change. A wave of edited volumes and book-length studies have emerged to address the role of the domestic screen, underscoring questions related to post-reform TV industries, content, audiences, and processes of regionalization and globalization.[4] To supplement this growing body of work, my aim is to trace an alternative history of television *outside* the home. I want to revisit James Lull's oft-quoted claim, in a 1991 study, that the "introduction of television into the homes of Chinese families may be the single most important cultural and political development in the People's Republic since the end of the Cultural Revolution."[5] Instead of insisting on TV's domesticity, and a research model that connects the "market-based party organ"[6] to the stable viewing field of the living room, this chapter pursues television as a spatial practice that extends across media forms and social space. My preliminary argument is that the TV's (re)entry into everyday and public space is one of the most vital cultural and political developments in the Olympic era—reshaping mundane encounters between state and citizens and driving a new technopolitics of legitimacy.

An instructive cue is the Chinese word for television, *dianshi* (电视)—which emphasizes not "remote" vision but "electric" or techno-visuality. As a concept, dianshi provides a way to think about the *technological encounters* that shape the experience of space and time in the first decades of the twenty-first century. I build on the previous chapter's analysis of cinema's technologized spatiality by offering both a prehistory of theatrical explosion as well as an emphasis on the shifting contours of public communication that structure the rise of mobile technologies (like the mobile phone). What follows is a discussion of television's *outsides*, converging around three intermedial contexts: (1) contemporary art and exhibition, (2) nondomestic and *unhomely* space, and (3) contemporary cinema. These disparate assemblages help us to reimagine the space of television and the medium's role as a form of social communication. My primary focus is the intersection of television and the city in articulating the social body *in transition*.

Mise en Abyme

A favorite, if ordinary, exhibition that I visited in Beijing during the winter of 2007–8 was the unheralded *Family Stuff*, hung at a small gallery in the thriving "798" factory-cum-arts district in the city's northeastern corridor (see figure 4.1). The collection of photographs records the travels of artists Huang Qingjun and Ma Hongjie, capturing families outside their homes among their material possessions (sometimes the images are staged for the photograph; in other instances the photos capture urban/economic dislocation). I remain impressed by the portraits' facility in bringing into relief the vibrating relationships among people, objects, and environment. Moreover, this gutting of

Figure 4.1 Untitled photograph by Huang Qingjun captures a family and belongings outside their home in Beijing in 2007. The infamous *chai* character (meaning *demolish*) fills the walls in the background. Courtesy of the artist.

personal space, and subsequent restaging outside, resonates with my interest in contests over interiors and exteriors in Olympic era China. Alongside bedding, cooking wares, basic gear, and furniture, the only other "stuff" that coexists across these contextually distinct compositions is the television set—a reminder, as TV historian Anna McCarthy has argued, that "slipperiness" is part of television's medium specificity, a "a characteristic of its peculiar adaptability as a media object in social space."[7]

The scenes of *Family Stuff* at once index the rapid and concentrated movement of the television into private life in the post-reform era and, at the same time, perform a critical maneuver—an *outing*—that I would like to repeat here. I use the word *repeat* very consciously to capture a modality of repetition that is embodied in the figure of the mise en abyme. Beyond the methodological impulse to chart TV sites/sights outside the home and outside of models of medium specificity, these outings provide a useful heuristic for approaching the overlapping residual and emergent folds of the television city. The images stage a process of exteriorization that parallels shifts in postsocialism, accentuating the jostling antagonisms of socialist residues, marketization and globalization, emerging forms of piratical citizenship, as well as structures that exceed Beijing's publics and privates. The latter I develop below as the *unhomely social*: working conditions in electronics factories, illegal e-waste economies, and the politics that partition economic aspirations, such as the division between rural and urban lifeworlds.[8]

So-called postsocialism combines complex and idiosyncratic political, economic, and cultural modalities, including the turn to market-driven cultural production and mass consumer society *and* the continued rule of the communist government with its promise to "use capitalism to develop socialism."[9] The PRC shares a great deal with other postcommunist societies—rising unemployment, crises of value and identity, rural–urban disparities, a resurgence of nationalism, socialist nostalgia, and "similar cultural and ideological" legacies[10]—but it is also distinct in shape and influence. China's phenomenal "growth" and coastal urbanization remains tethered to a shrinking but substantial state-owned portion of the economy, exemplified by the Special Economic Zone (SEZ). In this uneven socialist market terrain—what Aihwa Ong has dubbed "neoliberalism as exception"—(post)socialist and (non)capitalist politics congeal and crumble in all sorts of unanticipated ways.[11] This is to reiterate a point made elsewhere in this book: rather than relying on either idealized bourgeois or socialist conceptions of the political sphere—the former pretending the absence of the state or market in civic interactions, and the latter pretending that public-ness is coterminous with the state—my aim is to trace television as a public practice and a mode of performativity.

The figure of the mise en abyme is instructive here. It describes the situation where an object is placed in an infinite sequence of relationships with itself. The object under scrutiny here is the media capital—Beijing. The concept concentrates our gaze on the proliferation of what I am problematizing as *outside* TV—including nondomestic screens, art exhibitions, cinema, and sites of electronics production—and puts into play a series of relations between the TV and the city that are vital to struggles over time and space, and the larger condition of underglobalization. I attempt to draw this out in two ways. First, I argue that the televisual mise en abyme reframes historically rooted strategies for connecting the people and the state around the image of Beijing, emphasizing the screen's role as a spatial practice with distinct uses, protocols, and legitimacies. Second, this recursivity—the repetition of relationships between the screen and the city—produces the rationality that naturalizes modernization, eliding the human and environmental costs of development, and, at the same time, is an important resource for enacting alternative presents and futures.

Ah Gan's 2006 *Big Movie* (*Da Dianying* 大电影) offers an initial illustration of this technological mise en abyme. The film is a spoof comedy that both mocks and celebrates popular media productions such as *In the Mood for Love* (Wong, 2000), *The House of Flying Daggers* (Zhang, 2004), *The Matrix* (Wachowski brothers, 1999) and *Forrest Gump* (Zemeckis, 1994), among many others, while telling the story of a real estate scam bilking naïve home buyers. It focuses on the rise of urban middle-class investors who, excited by the opportunity to own a home and build personal wealth, are easily duped by crooked developers. In hyperbolic fashion, the flashy condo development pictured in the film is built on toxic land, next to a shooting range, near a power plant, and so on. Interestingly, the film's political critique and playfulness rely on television's plasticity both to understand corruption, and to cognitively render and to organize families against fraudulent real estate speculation. Figure 4.2 depicts one defrauded investor, Luo Qian's (Yao Chen), intervention. After learning the truth about the development, she breaks into a real estate showroom's control booth and covertly broadcasts herself to potential buyers, alerting them to the corrupt scheme. An onlooker records the event and soon it is rebroadcast throughout the city. The scandal leads to a confrontation between the duped Mr. Anderson (Eric Tsang) and a B-list celebrity real estate promoter (Huang Bo) on a political talk show. As the controversy is aired, the sequence, anchored by the continuous soundtrack, shifts across multiple urban screens and across media: a closed-circuit monitor in a real estate showroom, a countertop television at a restaurant, a close-up of the screen, an architectural display, and the film itself. Such fantasies of speed, coverage, and circulation are crucial to Beijing's televisual urbanism and to struggles over the repetitions and sites that ground public legitimacy.

Watching the State

In his analysis of the role of the TV set in contemporary art, Wu Hung observes that "if a 'contemporary art of network TV' is absent in China, the television has played manifold roles in contemporary Chinese art as icon, metaphor, concept and instrument." While primarily interested in art practice, Wu's analysis also illustrates the important role of television as a material technology for public communication that exceeds the routine emphasis on

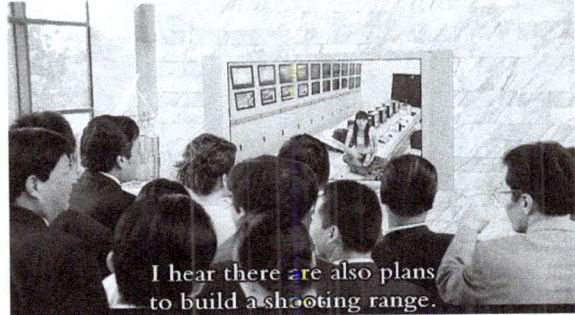

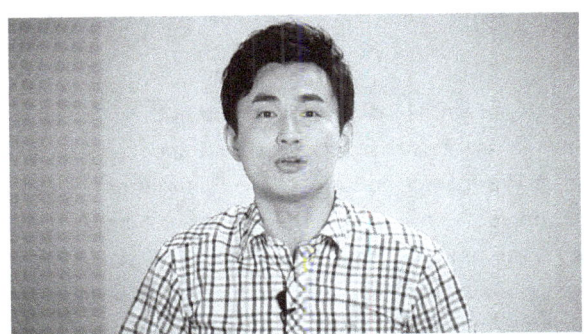

Figures 4.2, 4.3, 4.4, and 4.5 *Big Movie* (Ah Gan, 2006) signals the plasticity of the TV screen in Olympic-era China.

Figure 4.6   Zhang Peili's *Document on Hygiene No. 3* captures both the history of communal viewing and the intensity of political address that informs Chinese TV. Courtesy of the artist.

the screen as a domestic party organ. His discussion examines the particularities of China's art and media histories that make the contemporary engagement with TV meaningful. Wu focuses on how Mao-era communal viewing and collective memory inform the use of the TV set in 1990s artworks by Zhang Peili, Qiu Zhijie, Wang Jin, and Liu Wei, reminding his readers that the screen has a long history of outdoor and public circulation in socialist and now postsocialist China.[12] For instance, Zhang Peili's 1991 installation *Document on Hygiene No. 3*, the first domestic video exhibition in China, can only be made sense of in relation to the memory of such collective activities. The video is installed with ninety-nine brick seats facing four looping TV screens, recalling an alternative history of TV spectatorship. Onscreen, the video stages a Cultural Revolution–esque "hygiene campaign," where a member of a "Model Hygiene Neighborhood" compulsively washes a live chicken until it is exhausted or dead.[13]

Another notable example is Wang Lang and Liu Xinhua's 2007 exhibition, *Implemental Photography*. The exhibition displays thematic compilations of images gleaned from advertisements and periodicals that, when arranged as a group, make visible certain heralding strategies. One key cluster of images from the show includes multiple pictures of people watching CCTV's newscast of the party congress. Taken together, these images of TV viewing—as an encounter between the people and Beijing—draw our attention to the startling formal similarities of photographs from different periods and places. In each instance, the left portion of the frame is composed of TV viewers facing a television in the right third of the frame, their uniform responses clearly marking them as "citizens of the state."[14] We are immediately struck by the awkward composition of several photos where the diegetic audience members stare intently at the television, but the television is turned toward the imagined observer of the photograph, for example—as in figure 4.8—showing President Jiang Zemin addressing a conference of party leaders in Beijing. Wu points to the illogical nature of such images, suggesting that they have most certainly been "doctored" to clearly present separate viewing spaces and broadcast images in a single frame. Why, he continues, have such strange compositions become the "norm"?

The answer lies in the history of propaganda art, and in particular the "persistent quest for formulas to represent a symbolic 'meeting' between the leader and the people."[15] Wu identifies an entire field of image-making—beginning with Dong Xiwen's 1952 oil painting, *The Founding of the Nation*[16]—whose primary aim is to represent the harmonious encounter of the people and the iconic personages that embody the state. Notwithstanding various tactics to alter perspective through manipulation, composition, and montage, Wu asserts that many such nationalist representations fail to represent the leader and the people as "interacting parties," and ultimately betray the separation of the individual leaders from the mass of people.[17]

The use of the television brings new possibilities for projecting the state-citizen encounter by using the TV screen itself as a picture within a picture in real time and space, emphasizing the interaction of the two parties in ritual communication, and the importance of television as an apparatus of legitimacy.[18] In what follows, I want to add to Wu's lineage a range of televisual techniques—both official and informal—for shaping interactions between the leader and the people. Consider, for example, a screening of *The Founding of the Republic* (2009) that I observed on a mobile display outside the railway station in Chongqing—with bored travelers, workers, and migrants huddled around the screen in near-perfect imitation of Dong's original image. The screen's capacity to function as a mise en abyme is thus key to its role as a governmental technology—a form that reaches far beyond Wu's interest in representational tactics and gallery space. In the context of Beijing TV, these examples point to

Figure 4.7 Students from China's Central University of Minorities watch CCTV coverage of the party congress from Beijing. From Liu Xinhua's 2007 exhibit *Implemental Photography*. Courtesy of the artist.

Figure 4.8 Communist Party members watch CCTV coverage of the party congress from Beijing. From Liu Xinhua's 2007 exhibit *Implemental Photography*. Courtesy of the artist.

Figure 4.10 (*Opposite*) Sidewalk TVs in the "old" Beijing—a hair salon. Photo by Graham Bury. Courtesy of Pam and John Bury.

Figure 4.9 Sidewalk TVs in the "old" Beijing—a hardware store. Photo by Graham Bury. Courtesy of Pam and John Bury.

the spiraling ways in which the capital/state may be embedded on the screen, and the TV may be embedded elsewhere—for instance, on the street, at an exhibition, or in a film.

Outside in Beijing: Television as Public Culture

The pervasive use of the screen outside the home and across the plastic arts does more than recall socialist sonic and visual culture; rather, the screen as a public and multimodal media object is a critical, if underexplored, texture in contemporary media urban space. An instructive historical analogue is the wired loudspeaker that dominated the Mao-era mediascape. In 1960, for example, 70 million loudspeakers were set up across China, creating an atmosphere of ceaseless political address. Broadcasting scholars Huang Yu and Yu Xu give us a sense of that space: "To ensure the whole nation listened to one voice, the Communist Party . . . installed loudspeakers in such public places as school playgrounds, factories, rice paddies, and in rural villages and urban areas. Anyone who visited China during those years would find a common sight—large loudspeakers hanging on telephone poles, building roofs and treetops."[19] While the loudspeaker has not entirely disappeared from commercial, informational, and political settings, its omnipresence has been supplanted by the manifold roles of the screen interface. The task is thus to consider the changing terms of technological encounter in the current economic, political, and cultural milieu.

China's current emphasis on the "cultural creative industries" (*wenhua chuangyi chanye* 文化创意产业) constitutes an important policy context for thinking about innovations in TV and urban space. Media scholar Michael Keane defines the creative industries as a "set of interlocking segments of the economy focused on extending and exploiting symbolic cultural products." An integral aspect of the creative industries is the establishment of urban "creative clusters" or districts organized around film, television, animation, gaming, software, and advertising.[20] Importantly, these cultural industries connect state and market sectors around national efforts to remake media, technology, and the arts—and to expand China's symbolic and financial capital. In this way the creative industries—and the project to transform the "made in China" image—suggest a larger horizon for thinking about contemporary screen cultures, including, to take examples from Beijing, the Zhongguancun high-tech zone, the Dashanzi 798 arts district, animation hubs in suburban Tongzhou, and the relocation of CCTV, Beijing TV, and Phoenix TV to the center of the city.

A forceful example of this transition is the changing role of the screen in everyday street life.[21] Figures 4.9–4.15 show how informal TV sets are replaced

Figure 4.11 "New Beijing": Closed-circuit TV, Sanlitun area. Photo by Graham Bury. Courtesy of Pam and John Bury.

by new commercial or municipal displays, making up an important part of the city's remaking. This fact was brought home to me as I discussed my research with neighbors and shop owners on the streets of Beijing. They wondered why I was interested in old TVs, kiosks, and decaying alleyways. These routine objects and sites are perceived to be residues from the early days of reform or even markers of poverty. Put differently, they demonstrate a developmental logic whereby particular technologies, locations, and practices are linked to specific points in the modernization process (figures 4.9 and 4.13 clearly marking "old" Beijing, and figures 4.14 and 4.15 the "modern" city). Such narratives of transition, from communal courtyards, factories, and sidewalk TV sets to mobile phones and large-format video displays on building façades, are intricately tied into emerging ways of experiencing—and being addressed by—the city and the nation in the Olympic era.

In this context, the screen indexes both changes in economic modes and the reorganization of the public space (e.g., the shift from work unit TVs to mom-and-pop sets to state/commercial displays). Importantly, as I develop below, this transformation can be understood as part of an effort by the state to reshape televisual address, outside the home, at a time when TVs are vital to social space and political life. Independently administered "public" screens are part of a luminous media field that emerged in the 1980s and 1990s with the decentralization of TV production, the explosion of console manufacturing, and the atomization of party-organized living and viewing. Collective spectatorship, however, did not disappear with the onset of economic reforms and the breakdown of many, but by no means all, state-sponsored collectivities. Instead, outdoor and public screen cultures multiplied as the TV set entered the routine space of everyday life—both outside the home and outside the oversight of the party. The more recent image of Beijingers fingering their smartphones on the subway, while advertisements are projected onto tunnel walls and closed-circuit screens flicker above their heads, is a case in point.[22]

What I want to signal here is the vitality of outside TV as a social practice in contemporary China. My aim is to challenge simplistic understandings of television as a one-dimensional party apparatus or a residual apparatus that is out of place in new media culture. Instead, television's plasticity draws our attention not only to struggles over real and fake information, like official propaganda, but also to the forms of social legitimacy lived out alongside the console(s). What matters here is thus not only the programs onscreen and their presumed significance for audiences—though it's worth noting that TV production and content are more varied and complex than is often acknowledged—but the political life of dianshi outside of the canned address. Currently, little data or analysis exists to describe screens, spectators, and consumption/production patterns in nondomestic contexts, as both the industry and TV scholars have neglected what Zhang Tongdao has dubbed the "fluid" viewing field.[23] From TVs in outdoor markets, restaurants, salons, and video stores to screens on buses and elevators, or large-format displays in parks and malls, these everyday sites are crucial contexts for thinking about TV and urban or national belonging.

Take, for example, the middle-aged man at my neighborhood bodega near the northwest corner of Beijing's Second Ring Road who routinely watched news, sports, and TV dramas, both alone and with neighbors and customers; the DVD store staff who played and/or watched movies all day; or the young women who pressed dumplings at the back of the Fujian-style café, the screen positioned for their consumption of dynastic dramas. Among many possible examples, these contexts differ from home viewing and are far from temporary. In fact, many workers occupy these spaces six or seven days a week for the entire workday—the position of the screen, volume levels, "reserved" staff seating, and the remote control clearly indicating that the TV is only tangentially for the establishment's fluctuating clientele. And still other locations double as living rooms and sleeping quarters for proprietors and their families, making the TV's operations plastic, a continuum of practices throughout the day.

For the purposes here, the idea of the "fluid" viewing field helps us to think about the ways urbanites wade through and attach themselves to TV's signals as they negotiate the city. Zhang's useful approach, however, gives short shrift to how audiences themselves organize the signals arriving in and departing from these spaces. It is crucial to recognize that there are important differences between the *informal publics* (routine, user-generated) briefly discussed above, and the *formal publics* (state-organized) of TVs in public squares, on public transit, and on a host of other closed-circuit screens in government buildings, banks, universities, department and grocery stores, and hotels. These screen sites display significantly different structures of address, control, and social interaction. And while each may be called "public," they also demonstrate the clumsiness of the term. Instead, these screen constellations suggest "a particular sense of the relationship between public and private," and the state.[24] Such a method moves us beyond simplistic notions of privatization, including the console's movement into the home and the capitalization of the longtime state-run industries, to consider the field where state, market, and (non)citizen actors collide.

It is precisely this undulating relationship between the informal and piratical on the one hand, and the official or state-sanctioned on the other hand, that is reconfigured in Beijing and across China in the 2000s. Without artificially celebrating ubiquitous forms of informal TV culture, I want to stress the importance of these sites as nondomestic conjunctures that are organized outside the direct control of the state—even if TV sets and content are largely produced and transmitted by market-government ventures. As such, they have distinct uses, protocols, and scope. Unlike the fixed location and address of state media–controlled screens in elevators, projected onto subway tunnels or on building façades, these everyday screens are installed, positioned, decorated, turned on and off, channel surfed, or watched intently, used to play VCDs/DVDs or downloaded torrents, used as background noise and lighting for sidewalk gambling, positioned toward the street for evening shows for migrant workers, and more, by the owners, workers, and users of the sites. Of course, myriad subtleties exist across locations, but generally speaking these public and routine spaces are qualitatively and quantitatively different from state-designed forms of collective spectatorship.

What I describe here has to do not only with the social capacity to make meaning through reception—which remains vital—but also with individual and group capacities to organize and reshape the terms of the technological

Figures 4.12 and 4.13 Neighborhood TV viewing, Xicheng District, Beijing. Photos by Graham Bury. Courtesy of Pam and John Bury.

Figure 4.14 Official TV site/sight on the Beijing subway platform. Photo by Graham Bury. Courtesy of Pam and John Bury.

encounter (dianshi) through spatial practice. Critical to this engagement is reworking the "mobile privatization" thesis that remains influential in many studies of TV culture in post-reform China. Coined by Raymond Williams, the concept of mobile privatization has been picked up by numerous media scholars to explore the paradox of both increased mobility and home-centered (interior) living.[25] In the hands of most critics, mobile privatization assumes that TV viewing occurs in the home, its real and imagined contours are chiefly personal, and its mobilities are virtual. As Shaun Moores asserts, mobile privatization is about "simultaneously staying home and, imaginatively at least, going places."[26] What if, however, television spectatorship is understood as taking place outside the home? As a collective and public act? And as associated not only with imaginative journeys but with everyday forms of movement and inhabitation?

City TV

It is in this context of widespread and everyday outside TV use and the changing claims on public space that the emergence of state-administered nondomestic TV stations and screens in the 2000s, such as those operated by Beijing All Media and Culture Group (BAMC, *Beijing guangbo yingshi jituan*), must be viewed. If, as I suggest, user- and state-generated screen space embody substantially different modes of publicity, then the imbrication of socialist-market forces to remake social spaces around governmental screen address is critical. New screen technologies not only emblematize the economic promise of postsocialist modernity; they also demonstrate the enduring role of the TV as a "citizen machine."[27]

Established in 2001, Beijing All Media and Culture Group is the most important nondomestic urban media outlet in Beijing (in this period) and a vital national interest. BAMC is a constellation of media holdings—including digital and cable broadcasting, film and TV production, and outdoor media subsidiaries—and is led by the Beijing Municipal Party Committee's Publicity Department.[28] Relevant to my interest here are BAMC's Beijing City TV (*chengshi dianshi*), Metro TV (*ditie dianshi*) and Mobile TV (*yidong dianshi*), described in turn.

Beijing City TV is an "outdoor video media platform" that operates more than forty large-format LCD displays in high-traffic areas across the city—including parks, heritage sites, the central business district, and shopping districts like Xidan and Wangfujing. Additionally, City TV is the only video medium permitted in state-owned enterprises, with more than ten thousand closed-circuit screens in government buildings, hospitals, banks, Olympic hotels, and entertainment areas. In 2008 the network presented fifteen hours of programming each day using a TV magazine format that focuses on news, fashion, current affairs, public service announcements, special reports, and advertisements, and in the run-up to the Olympic Games was the only closed-circuit media agency authorized to broadcast Olympic content and the popular *Fuwa* (Beijing Olympic mascot) cartoon series. Further, according to the City TV profile, the urban network is organized to connect with media outlets in Shanghai, Guangzhou, and Shenzhen, with the aim of establishing "an alliance of state-owned new media in China."[29]

Beijing Metro TV Co., Ltd, founded in 2007, broadcasts to subway platform and subway carriage screens. Metro TV expanded rapidly in the period leading up to the Olympics, outfitting terminals and subway cars throughout the city—including the newly opened subway lines 4, 5, 8, and 10. Metro TV offers programming options similar to those of City TV, with a particular focus on "daily life guidance" programs—including social education campaigns geared toward littering, line etiquette, spitting, and other social behaviors.[30]

Unlike the closed-circuit systems just discussed, Beijing Mobile TV operates wirelessly as a "digital TV trial project," broadcasting signals from four digital transmitting stations to buses, taxis, and other vehicles within the city's Sixth Ring Road. The wireless network broadcasts eighteen hours daily to a mobile audience of 10 million. It is estimated that by the 2008 Olympic

Figure 4.15   City TV picturing the "Bird's Nest," Wangfujing. Photo by author.

Figure 4.16   Mobile TV. Photo by author.

Figure 4.17 Beijing Metro TV, subway line 5. Photo by Graham Bury. Courtesy of Pam and John Bury.

Games, fifty thousand digital receivers were in operation throughout the capital. Programming roughly corresponds to the above and is as follows: news (30 percent), entertainment (17 percent), public service announcements (6 percent), special reports (21 percent), weather and traffic information (6 percent), and advertisements (20 percent).[31] As I argue elsewhere, this thick televisual footprint plays a crucial role in articulating the "seamless social"—where TV signals accompany urbanites as they navigate the city.[32] It attempts both to reclaim control over informal TV publics and to create a mobile mediascape for China's massive migratory population—that is, the 200 million-plus workers who are not home for the nightly news.

In contrast to the image of Chinese TV history that opens this chapter—a small crowd huddled around the work unit console—the television now appears to huddle around viewers. The density of the media urban field recalls the atmospherics of the Mao-era loudspeakers, an enduring form of address that grasps at bodies as they commute to work, eat lunch, and shop. This tendency, originating with plastic displays, has only intensified with the proliferation of handheld devices fueled by satellite, wireless internet, and Bluetooth connectivities. As citizen-spectators move through the urban space, they increasingly engage in a process we might call *interlacing*—from the term de-

Figure 4.18 The 250-meter LED Sky Screen in Beijing's Chaoyang District has become a tourist attraction in its own right. Courtesy of the author.

scribing the alternation of scan lines to create a video image. Just as interlacing scan lines use two fields to create a single frame, interlacing describes the multiple audiovisual modes associated with the repetitive encounters with the televisual city. This might include a corner store clerk shifting between the diegesis of a soap opera and, at the counter, a customer bugging her or him for a pack of cigarettes. Or, alternatively, the concept might involve a bus passenger watching projections of Beijing's Olympic Green on TV, only to look out the window at a dusty construction site or, after the Games, an unspectacular and often dormant district—both a far cry from the architectural projections. In the context of Beijing's massive remaking, where much of the urban fabric is under construction or newly remodeled, interlacing becomes a tactic for everyday navigation.

This is also to give another meaning to the notion of *pirate* TV. Rather than pointing to illegal broadcasts from stations without licenses, it recalls the everyday redeployments and claims upon TV and its presumed legitimacies. If television remains the government apparatus par excellence—heavily regulated, marked by official rhythms and address, filled up by state aesthetics—

then such mundane practices are also part of what I have termed *piratical citizenship* in this book. That is, the normalized and illicit forms of belonging brought about (non)citizens' claims on media technologies and infrastructures, like the social life of TV.

Screen Postsocialism

André Jansson and Amanda Lagerkvist, writing about the social circulations of urban vistas, note the way New York City's skyline became the "symbolic blueprint for *the modern city* and represented 'the future' throughout the world" in the twentieth century. City panoramas, they argue, are *"constituted as emotive geographies"* that, when turned into visual signs, are imbricated in political projects that "activate a future gaze."[33] Their analysis centers on Expo-era Montreal (1967) and Shanghai (2010), working toward a theorization of what Nigel Thrift refers to as the "politics of encountering city spaces."[34] What I want to emphasize here is the relationship between outside television practices and the politics of encountering Beijing—in particular, the regularized encounter with Beijing onscreen in the city. This proliferation illustrates the repetitive rendering of Beijing as a model—that is, a rationale that connects lived experience with the promise of modernization.

The importance of television to postsocialist transformation was made explicit as early as the Eleventh Chinese Radio and Television Conference, held in 1983. The conference concluded that:

> Radio and television are the most powerful modern tools in encouraging the people of the nation to strive to create a socialist civilization that is both materially and culturally rich.
>
> Radio and television are the most effective connections between the Chinese Communist Party, the Chinese Government and the Chinese people. The international and domestic situations demand the acceleration of the development of the Chinese television system.[35]

These basic tenets form the backbone of the TV's role as a mechanism for development and a site/sight-specific form of social communication. This logic has led to the emergence (and reemergence) of television as a spatial practice that constitutes a *screen postsocialism*.

Screen postsocialism describes the role of TV as a social capacity that, like Benedict Anderson's "print capitalism," articulates new perceptions of time and space around variegated imaginaries, including the city and the nation.[36] This includes new forms of *simultaneity* that intensify Anderson's assertion that the novel and newspaper provided "the technical means for 'representing' the *kind* of imagined community that is the nation," actions that he understood to take place "in the lair of the skull." Instead, as I argue, the contemporary Chinese mediascape is made up of a dense field of surfaces that not only are "visibly rooted in everyday life," but project the audiovisual data necessary to sufficiently render the experience of place.[37] It is precisely this repetitive mechanism that makes television such a critical technology in/as public space. If print culture, according to Anderson, is the axiomatic medium enabling populations of strangers to think the nation in the eighteenth and nineteenth centuries, then screen postsocialism makes possible—and perpetuates—the imagination of the social body *in transition*.

The Unhomely Social

A normal working day is 8am and 5.30pm but many people work till 8pm. The night shift starts at 8pm and ends at 8am. After work we go for a walk, we get online, sometimes we go together outside the supermarket to watch TV on a big screen. Life here is OK.

—ANONYMOUS FOXCONN WORKER

To summarize, I have been arguing that the Olympic era consolidates a transformational imaginary around *outside television*.[38] This emphasis on a particular technology of reception, moreover, acts to screen out the broader textures of cultural and economic production. This is to say that examining television's spatial practice and the refiguring of public–private socialities in China produces a missing term: the *unhomely*. The unhomely constitutes a nexus of nondomestic, subaltern, and sub-urban zones and designates a variety of sites and practices that cannot be properly described as public or bourgeois private spheres. The image of workers gathered around a big-screen TV at the factory supermarket signals the politics of the largely invisible sites of electronics production outside Beijing, and connects the address of screen postsocialism to broader economic manifestations.

In this context, the notion of the unhomely is a critical tool for thinking about political society in its nonpublic and nonprivate configurations as well as the forms of piratical citizenship endemic to popular politics in China (and much of the world). Partha Chatterjee's engagement with political society is interested in how members bracketed out of formal relations mobilize and "succeed in applying the right pressure at the right places in the governmental machinery."[39] He focuses, for instance, on organized squatter communities that manage to wrestle electricity, water, garbage, education, and other services from the state—even though they have no "legal" claims to these public goods. Similarly, the unhomely acts as a critical wedge, opening up the closed (mise en abyme) structure of the social body, and highlighting the spectral infrastructures elided by the prescriptive and ideological discourses on screen.

Critically, it is only at moments of crisis that labor conditions and environmental risk in China's electronics factories, mines, and e-waste industries surface.[40] Suicides at Foxconn's electronics plants in southern China, resulting in fourteen deaths in 2010, bring the larger textures of this technological encounter into focus. The company's "town within a town plant" in Shenzhen employs more than 400,000 workers earning roughly $1 an hour assembling and packaging mobile phones, game consoles, personal computers, and other screen technologies. While Foxconn executives defend the company's labor practices, activists and workers describe loneliness, mandatory overtime, toxic exposure, assembly lines that "move too fast," and managers who "enforce military-style discipline." Workers are even forbidden to speak.[41] Foxconn, of course, is not exceptional—such conditions are the norm in many low-wage, low-profit-margin, export manufacturing zones—but its hypervisibility is an important aperture for understanding the real sites of risk and abandonment that animate processes of underglobalization.

Political fallout over the suicides of these young workers—they were all under twenty-four years of age—led Foxconn to announce a 66 percent pay increase as well as initiatives targeting suicide prevention and leisure activities. The October 2010 announcement promised to bring salaries up to 2,000 yuan per month (approximately $300) in Shenzhen and caused many US publications to worry about rising electronics prices.[42] More cynically still, several reports indicate that such wage increases will never materialize; Foxconn has since built new factories at inland locales in Henan, Hubei, Sichuan, and Shanxi Provinces, where cheaper labor conditions, policy incentives, and access to new markets keep prices down and workers out of view.[43] I will return to this unhomely context in chapter 5.

Television in Contemporary Cinema

To rephrase James Lull, quoted at the beginning of this chapter, the persistent movement of the television outside the home and across media forms "may be the single most important cultural and political development" in millennial public culture. The common metaphors of the TV as a "mouthpiece" or "receiver," rooted in the home, fail to describe the screen's spatial plasticity—and its capacity to both pick up and transmit sounds and images. Precisely because of the medium's long-standing function as an instrument and icon of the Chinese state, it has surfaced as a volatile technology for projecting subaltern

Figure 4.19 Reedited newscasts from Wang Wo's 2010 documentary *Zheteng* (dir. Wang Wo, 2010), Copyright Wang Wo. Courtesy of Wang Wo.

and popular struggles. As Wang Wo's selective editing of "blind" leaders and reporters suggests in his 2010 documentary film *Zheteng*, the television is also an archive and an instrument that is ripe for resignification.

Contemporary cinema's obsession with TV sets parallels the shifts in televisual/electronics practice surveyed above. Just as state-market clusters have clashed with informal publics around the organization of screen address, the use of television in cinema, among other media, has emerged as a contentious field for social communication. As above, this includes overlapping official, popular, and informal engagements with the screen. For instance, *Dream Weavers: Beijing 2008*, a host of promotional films leading up to the Olympic Games, and made-for-DVD television events like the sixtieth anniversary of the PRC exemplify official interactions with the intermedial and political screen. Other widely exhibited filmic examples include Zhang Yimou's *Not One Less* (*Yi ge dou bu neng shao*, 1999), Feng Xiaogang's *Big Shot's Funeral* (*Da wan'r*, 2001), Ning Hao's *Mongolian Ping Pong* (*Lü cao di*, 2006), and the films of Jia Zhangke, among many other examples.

In contrast to the extension of official techno-visuality in films like *Not One Less* and *Dream Weavers: Beijing 2008* is the use of the TV in the blockbuster comedy *Big Shot's Funeral*. While the material console itself plays only a small part in the movie, the film's mise en abyme structure centers on the intersection of film, television, and the media event. *Big Shot* is a satire about the spectacular comic funeral of Hollywood bigwig Don Tyler (Donald Sutherland) in the Forbidden City—Tyler had been in Beijing to remake Bernardo Bertolucci's *The Last Emperor* (1987). Regarding the film's structure, Jason McGrath notes that the film "accumulates so many layers that the audience cannot be sure whether the story they are watching is the real film or another film-within-the-film."[44] Alternatively, I want to suggest that what the viewers of *Big Shot's Funeral* are watching is TV. Not only is Yoyo's (Ge You) "behind-the-scenes" documentary of Don Tyler's remake made for television, but the film's central farce—Yoyo organizing a comic funeral for the famous director Don Tyler—satirizes the commercialization of the TV city, not to mention the state-market convergence around the Olympic Games.

A large portion of the film is taken up with handling branding rights and product placement for the televised spectacle. In the film, the Forbidden City setting becomes so saturated with advertising, which even covers the corpse, that a gang storms the set demanding that Yoyo and promoter Louis Wang (TV personality Ying Da) make room for their copycat bottled water, Le Ha-Ha. Many critics have commented on the film's reflexive play with consumerism and its own commodity form, but its reflexive play with television has been largely overlooked. What the film draws our attention to is the way in which TV, like the iconic logos of real and imagined products in the film, functions as an object of affective investment. Here I follow Bishnupriya Ghosh's discussion of the popular redeploying of the Coca-Cola logo in water rights disputes in India. Ghosh argues that "it is precisely because of their encoding as a signifier of something global, representing a global force, that icons like Coca-Cola become contentious objects for local actors."[45] Similarly, *Big Shot* plays on the semiotic import of the TV as a metonym of the state, and thus a charged instrument for social communication in China.

This iconic congruence between the TV and the state fuels cinema's engagement with the television. Most notably, Jia Zhangke's body of work is a

Figure 4.20   Olympic celebration and malaise in Jia Zhangke's *Unknown Pleasures* (2002).

rigorous meditation on China's changing media environments. Jia's 2002 feature *Unknown Pleasures* (*Ren Xiao Yao*), like *Xiao Wu* (1997) before it, displays a keen awareness of the centrality of the television set to everyday life and, in particular, its capacity to connect to outside locales. A particularly poignant scene from the film depicts the central characters, Bin Bin (Zhao Weiwei) and Xiao Ji (Wu Qiong), leaving a dance club skirmish and stumbling into an outdoor broadcast of Beijing's successful Olympic bid in 2001 (see figure 4.20). In the context of the work's despairing narrative, emphasizing the lives of those left behind by China's economic progress, the placement of the TV—and, in particular, of Beijing—is critical. It indicates a larger trend in independent and popular productions to use the television to reframe Olympic-era development. Though many filmmakers do double duty as freelancers at TV stations, the general lack of access to TV production has resulted in a cinema of televisual urbanism interested not only in documenting changes in the social body, but in producing its own television—in signaling back. This *pirate television*, which inaugurates an alternative mode of transmedial broadcast, is an important aspect of the technologies' capacity to (re)organize political action and encounters.

Unknown Pleasures is set in the director's hometown of Fenyang and is structured around a series of encounters with the ambient television. In addition to the anticlimactic Olympic announcement, routine transmissions connect the diegetic world to provincial and national narratives. In these scenes one is acutely aware of one's distance from Beijing. Broadcasts of Falun Gong

Figure 4.21 Watching TV at the salon. The new freeway project linking Datong to Beijing seems worlds away. From *Unknown Pleasures*.

protests, the 2001 US spy plane incident, and the bombing of a local textile mill are interwoven with Olympic news and coverage of a new highway infrastructure project—the Beijing–Datong Expressway—linking Fenyang to the capital. Such retransmissions of actual news footage give the film an ambient verisimilitude. But more than indexing postsocialist media space, the convergence of cinema and TV adds a new layer to historically rooted modes of social encounter.

Figure 4.21 depicts Xiao Ji at the hair salon discussing a news report about a massive new highway project with his hairdresser. This sequence, among others in the film, recalls similar compositions of minority students and party members watching CCTV's broadcast of the party congress (see figures 4.7 and 4.8). Above, we observed that such images were part of a long-standing tradition that sought to represent the state–society encounter in real time and space. The liveness and reach of the televisual image thus provide new possibilities for social communication, a fact made tangible by the recent explosion of state-administered TV screens in nondomestic space. In contrast, *Unknown Pleasures* reframes the television's iconic function, calling attention to TV viewing as a site-specific event. The same news footage, for example, would play quite differently outside the home, in Beijing. A second example shows a series of TV reports describing massive sabotage at a textile mill within earshot of the TV screen in Bin Bin's home—a sequence that connects the story world to, among others, the actual March 16, 2001, bombings in Shijiazhuang,

Figure 4.22 Connecting Suining County to spectacular Beijing in Zhang Zanbo's *Falling from the Sky* (2009).

capital of Hebei Province, three hundred miles from Beijing, which resulted in two hundred deaths.

Unknown Pleasures is but one example of a large body of popular and independent productions that have siphoned from the state the TV's capacity to function as a mise en abyme. Other key examples include Jia's *Xiao Wu* (1997) and *The World* (2004), as well as Zhao Liang's 2008 documentary *Petition* (*Shangfeng*), Du Haibin's *Under the Skyscrapers* (2002), and He Jianjun's *Pirated Copy* (*Manyan*, 2004), among many other works. It matters, of course, that films like Jia's are largely not officially distributed in China and thus are only seen on personal TVs and in informal screenings. This fact only intensifies the impact of this *cinematic broadcasting*, among other piratical and high-tech interventions, which both link up with other struggles and prefigure the interactive logic of web 2.0 and tube video sites. As with various nondomestic TV practices discussed above, formal and informal publics seize the screen as a critical technology for articulating disparate visions of modernization, making their own claims on the here and now.

A final example from China's New Documentary Movement is Zhang Zanbo's 2009 *Falling from the Sky* (*Tianjiang*). *Falling* captures the atmospheric tensions of life in Suining County, Hunan Province, during the summer and fall of 2008. Disconnected from the economic progress of China's eastern belt, Suining is connected to the national and global economy by falling rocket debris from the Xichang satellite launch center in Sichuan. Set against a backdrop of out-migration, failing agriculture, harmful milk powder, and the Olympic Games, Zhang explores the often horrific footprint of international communication satellites and China's space program. The film follows residents as they clamber to locate fallen debris, lingers over damaged homes and crops, and talks with crying mothers about a bright sixteen-year-old girl decapitated by a fragment from a satellite launch. One mother asks: "Debris always falls down here. Why? Our nation is so wide!"

This is precisely the question Zhang seeks to answer as he explores the ideological rift that leaves the mountainous community in danger and poverty, even while many residents of the former revolutionary base remain loyal to the party. Powerful scenes of villagers installing satellite dishes and watching live satellite broadcasts of the Olympics via Chinasat 9—whose debris assaulted the area—bring this gap and the developmental rhetoric of sacrifice in contemporary China to the foreground. The scenes, among many others in contemporary cinema, link Beijing to the interior, emphasizing the changing contours of public space and the TV's significance as a political technology that far exceeds ideas about party rhetoric and home viewing.

Conclusion

At stake here is the type of change that is posed by official discourses about Olympic-era redevelopment. Intellectual historian Wang Hui has noted that the concept of "transition" itself undergirds contemporary thinking about Chinese society, adding, "it presupposes a necessary connection between the process of current inequality and an ultimate ideal."[46] With this in mind, it is useful to remember that historian Arif Dirlik coined the concept "postsocialism" in 1989, before both the Tiananmen Square massacre and the dissolution of the USSR. For Dirlik, the concept both drew on the postmodernist loss of faith in socialism as a meta-narrative, and was charged with potential. "Postsocialism," he noted, "rather than signaling the end of socialism, offers the possibility in the midst of a crisis in socialism of rethinking socialism in new, more creative ways."[47] While that coinage is perhaps far from our current intellectual-political moment, it remains an important claim upon historical difference and democratic futures: globalization can be otherwise.

What I call screen postsocialism in this chapter aims to salvage some of the spirit of Dirlik's three-decade-old musing. To this end, I have sketched the conjunctural media fields where various actors—artists and filmmakers, audiences and residents, officials and state media—broadcast Beijing, and in doing so make claims on the everyday life and the organization of society. A key element in this politics of the public is the unhomely social. The unhomely describes a form of life that is pushed underground by hegemonic underdevelopment. Always on the edge of emergence, this spectral labor is what drives the postsocialist political economy and is driven out of view by the audiovisuality of development. The unhomely social thus emerges as a critical if submerged part of the transforming social body, connecting with other nondomestic, subaltern, and sub-urban assemblages. As such, these *outsides* are emblematic of the condition of political society and the practice of piratical citizenship at the center of this study—bringing into relief both state-led models of repetition and techno-legitimacy, and the forms of illegal life and unhomeliness required by creative capitalism. As such, they offer a basis for theorizing (post)socialist and (non)capitalist forms and capacities in the long Olympic era.

Videation

Technological Intimacy and the Politics of Global Connection

> What composes a human social world may be anything but proximate to it, let alone human.
> —ELIZABETH POVINELLI

> Part of your life had waned and waned, but to whom do you beautifully belong?
> —MY FUTURE IS NOT A DREAM (FACTORY BAND)

An unnamed worker at a Wintek subsidiary in Suzhou, China, that assembles touch screen interfaces describes the repetitive task of finishing iPhones: "I used my left hand to hold the iPhone screen when it came down the work line, and with my right hand I used a cotton cloth dipped in hexane to wipe the screen."[1] N-hexane has since been linked to neurological damage, causing sweats, dizziness, and paralysis in hundreds of workers. The shockingly mundane scandal, acknowledged by corporations like Apple in a 2011 *Supplier Responsibility Progress Report*, signals the crucial role of emerging interface intimacies—interfaces that sit at the edge of aspiration and exposure, life and death.[2] Emblematic of these contact zones are the much-reported eighteen attempted suicides—resulting in fourteen deaths—at Foxconn's southern China plants in 2010 alone.[3] The Foxconn suicides have emerged as an index of globalization's violently uneven sway, capturing what scholars like Elizabeth Povinelli have termed "economies of abandonment," or,

Figure 5.1 A worker leaps from a factory dormitory in the final chapter of Jia Zhangke's 2014 film *A Touch of Sin*.

alternatively, the peculiar "freedoms" that undergird life in so-called Special Economic Zones.[4] The tensely mundane textures of factory living—and, in particular, "dormitory labor regimes" and long hours on the factory line—animate new and old forms of risk, incessant labor protests, and shifting conditions of (il)legality, (im)mobility, and (non)citizenship that are at the very heart of the just-in-time economy and its entangled imaginaries of connectivity.[5]

Beyond the spectacular image of workers leaping from dormitory balconies, or the antisuicide netting that surrounds factory buildings, assembly-line production is entangled with other forms of technological cohabitation and "technomobility."[6] Numerous recent ethnographic studies and journalistic accounts describe the ways such media forms seep into the everyday life of factory migrants, among so many others, animating routine labor, clandestine activities on the line, and the habits and intimacies that take place after clocking out.[7] These workers/residents spend long hours in internet cafés, public TV rooms, and on personal mobile devices, chatting, texting, browsing, gaming, watching. They use screens to find new jobs; learn about evening courses; organize walkouts and protests; date and maintain personal connections; watch music videos, TV dramas, and movies; and take their own photos and videos, including the many viral music video covers featuring migrants or a 2015 scandal broadcast on Guangdong Public TV describing factory workers disciplined for taking pictures and videos of middle school girls at a school outside their dormitory windows.[8]

As such, forms of technological production and consumption do not simply exist side by side but are woven together to constitute the fabric of the everyday—from the touch of screen assembly or the synesthesia of sound on the factory line to the intimate hours passed *with* videos and entangled screen media. This interlacing of making and using, hazard and hope, brings into view new forms of social subjectivity that the anthropologist Lisa Rofel dubs "desiring China"—a pun that refers to both the importance of desire to becoming a transnational citizen-subject, and the multiple fascinations with or desires for China that drive such affective economies. As Rofel argues, new "hopes, needs, and passions" are at the center of postsocialist political experiments, social allegories, and understandings of what it means to be a human being.[9]

This chapter builds on the discussion of the *unhomely social* in chapter 4, and considers occluded relationships between urban centers like Beijing and the migrant factory workers who make the technologies that make up the technologized city. In particular, it offers some speculations about contemporary forms of technological or screen intimacy—and how these interfaces discriminate valuable and superfluous bodies. I refer to these forms of material and imaginary proximity as *videation*—signaling video culture's unique *mediations*, as well as its overlooked actions, habits, or results (as indicated by the suffix *-ation*). In this sense, videation shores up a thick field of "new" media practices that are consistently occluded in understandings of digital modernity and global emergence. It builds on conventional understandings of video as a format of capture, copy, and playback, and emphasizes intimate practices and infrastructures beyond content. In particular, I focus on those instances or actions of screen economies that are limited neither to "productive labor" in the economic sense, nor to the often valorized acts of "producing consumers" associated with fans or other popular cultural practices. Touch and screen intimacy are linked to media consumption and to those users who purchase and use authentic products in the global metropolis—rendering the close, tactile, and detailed habits of labor, and of living laborers, illegible.

Anna Tsing's theorization of the fricative shuffle of commodities offers one useful entry point into this analysis of technological production. Tsing writes: "Commodities seem so familiar that we imagine them ready made for us throughout every stage of production and distribution, as they pass from hand to hand until they arrive at the consumer. *Yet the closer we look at the commodity chain, the more every step—even transportation—can be seen as an arena of cultural production.* Global capitalism is made in the friction in these chains as divergent cultural economies are linked, often awkwardly. Yet the commodity must emerge as if untouched by friction."[10] This friction, the passing from hand to hand, signals the important economic and social world building that takes place within domains bracketed as imitative, unskilled, and low value by dominant forms of faking globalization. Against such circumscriptions, this chapter understands factory labor and living as cultural production. It asks how making interfaces joins up with making them intimate, how such notions constitute an alternate sphere of engagement and desire, and how this alternative geopolitical framing might open up beyond self-referential guilt narratives or melodramatic discourses where modernity always arrives "too late," among other failures grafted onto the forms of precarity required by the global system.[11]

Neoliberalism and "Remaindered Life-Times"

This shift in perspective allows us to recalibrate influential notions like the "social factory," "cognitive capitalism," and the 24/7 economy—concepts that are integral to interpreting digital modernities across the Global North (even when the North is South). Such notions emphasize how "work processes have shifted from the factory to society,"[12] transforming basic understandings of labor, time, and self-regulation, or what Donna Haraway, in her manifesto on cyborgs, presciently termed an "informatics of domination."[13] These critiques tell us a great deal about the sorts of general patterning—or the new *dominant*—associated with processes like globalization, financialization, and the information age.[14] But such techno-global discourses too often take on a prescriptive character that represses lifeworlds across the South in favor of frenzied and familiar cultures of clicking, and the fetishization of knowledge sectors and the creative industries. Interestingly, they also mirror anxieties in North America and Europe over "outsourcing" (itself a unidirectional imaginary)—where service work, unemployment, and never-ending reeducation replaces jobs at the factory, port, and similar bastions of industrialism. New digital habits like those required by high-bandwidth internet cultures, mobile devices, and social media, as well as the shifting forms of precarity tied to the much-touted tech and design sectors, are no doubt significant. But this diffusion of tasks and touching offers only a single vision of the textures of contemporary information societies. This is to say: it is out of sync with emergent media cultures in much of the world. Indeed, rigid frameworks for understanding technomodernity, largely derived from idealized Western metropolitan practices, are unable to account for on-the-ground practices elsewhere (including the heart of northern capitals). In China alone, the migratory population exceeds 250 million people. A large percentage of these rural-to-urban migrants exist outside the household registration system (hukou), in a state of perpetual migration for factory work and related heavy labor jobs, constituting a massive and mobile "floating population" (*liudong renkou* 流动人口)—with, I would add, their own "floating" media and cultures of legitimacy.[15]

This divisive gap between North and South—often articulated as a gap between West and East—is also tied to new disposabilities engendered by global neoliberalism(s). Drawing on Michel Foucault's *The Birth of Biopolitics*, among other texts, numerous theorists have taken up the wager that under neoliberalism market rationality is generalized throughout the social body, inaugurating an entrepreneurial subject: "an entrepreneur of himself . . . being for himself his own capital, being for himself his own producer."[16] An extreme iteration of privatization and the Protestant ethic, this new *Homo economicus* relies on the assumption that labor as human capital is a kind of (potentially risky) investment—configuring a subject that bears the burden of that risk and therefore has to be both self-innovative and self-responsible. In this context, the state exists to ensure the "freedom" of the market as a playing field and as an algorithm managing the population as such.[17]

Angling such debates toward the non-West, the anthropologist Aihwa Ong has theorized this relationship as one that shores up tensions between "neoliberalism as exception" and "exceptions to neoliberalism"—a connection that hinges upon what the assumed normative order is at a given site. Ong focuses on East Asian and Southeast Asian locales where neoliberalism is not the normative mode and is thus an exception to governing as usual. In this context, she argues, neoliberalism is a technology of government that is a "profoundly active way of rationalizing governing and self-interest," and can also be "invoked, in political decisions, to exclude populations and places from neoliberal calculations and choices," such as erasing safety nets, political rights, subsidized housing, or the standards of living and opportunity associated with new economic policies like Special Economic Zones.[18] In other words, the play of "exceptions" describes the insides and outsides of market-driven criteria where individuals and groups not only struggle for legibility, for the right to play, but also against residual, often highly centralized and paternalistic, forms of statecraft. This fact also reminds us of the continued importance of the national within this economy of global connection. Thus, in addition to Maurizio Lazzarato's assertion that neoliberalism establishes "a threshold, a vital minimum, above which the individual can become an 'enterprise,'"[19] we must add that neoliberalism is a malleable or "mobile technology" that can be adopted and adapted by different political regimes for different ends.[20] This, of course, includes asking—as do Ong and Li Zhang—

how marginalized actors take up neoliberal techniques within their own social projects.[21]

Emblematic of such exceptions to/as neoliberalism, not to mention the crucial role of the nation-state, is the emergence of new "dormitory labor regimes." These regimes embrace modes of social organization that are central to the management and profitability of global factories. Sociologist Pun Ngai argues that dormitory labor regimes in contemporary China produce a more or less permanent reserve army of migrant workers by utilizing the socialist-era hukou (household registration 户口) system—which strictly divides rural and urban registration, and leaves millions as aliens in their own country.[22] The household registration system limits peasant access to the city as well as to basic amenities like education, health care, and housing, creating liminal forms of citizenship that both entice workers with economic opportunity and can be revoked at any time. As Pun Ngai and Jenny Chan argue: "In this political economy, employers need not pay a living wage because they provide workers with minimal necessities of life within the enclosed world of factory complexes. Maintaining dormitories, in which a dozen young people may share a single room jammed with bunk beds only a few feet apart, costs the employer far less than wages necessary for workers to find their own housing. The same goes for the notoriously low-quality food provided in employee cafeterias. Employers reduce their costs even more by deducting food and housing from worker's wages."[23] With factory compounds like those operated by Foxconn and its subsidiaries employing between 50,000 and 400,000 workers at different sites, the social fabric of such labor regimes is crucial. It shapes the structurally constrained pathways open to China's floating population, as well as the textures of everyday life for the millions who migrate to the city and enter the factory gates—giving a new meaning to "gated community."[24]

In her essay "Life-Times of Disposability within Global Neoliberalism," Neferti Tadiar sums up this biopolitical turn as a shift from discourses of rights and property to one of risk and security—a move that is understood to have basically altered "lived subjectivities and feelings and transformed modalities of social experience and imagination."[25] It is, in other words, a shift that is basically related to burgeoning forms of fake citizenship and illegal life. Tadiar draws on a range of theorists, including Foucault, Lazzarato, Wendy Brown, and Melinda Cooper, in order to examine how the financial logic of personhood shapes a new distribution of the social. Crucial here are the "new temporal protocols" engendered by neoliberal philosophies of the self. Such protocols ask: "Which individuals inhabit and qualify for the investor model of subjectivity and its structure of temporal experience?" And which fall away as non-subjects—as bad investments?[26]

In her analysis of the gap between "risk capable" and "at risk" populations, Tadiar suggests a useful critique of certain tendencies in the literature on human capital and inhuman disposability. She argues that this influential model of subjectivity qua speculation—which relies on the "colonization of the future as a mean of present realization"—confines itself to only the most "advanced" and familiar forms of capitalism, itself constituting a *threshold of intelligibility*. These now-routine frameworks elide an "entire arena of production processes" wrongly presumed to have been supplanted by a shift from industrial to postindustrial capitalism and related modes of accumulation.[27] What are occluded are those "remaindered life-times" tangential to the modalities of everyday production under neoliberalism, including its exceptions. She writes: "Such life-times consist of a diverse array of acts, capacities, associations, aspirations in practice, experiential modes, and sensibilities that people engage in, draw upon, and invent in the struggle to make and remake social life under conditions of their own superfluity or disposability."[28] Tadiar turns our attention to a thicket of practices and modes of social existence that are blocked by the dominant discourse—but are integral to the formation of the contemporary world.

Memes

The 2008 "iPhone girl" meme captures instances of Anna Tsing's "every stage" of production, as well as "superfluous" capacities, and an intertwined politics of victimization and guilt that buttresses dominant notions of global connectivity, and especially links to Asia.[29] The meme spread widely on the internet in the fall of 2008 after a user in the United Kingdom found several images of a young female factory worker on a newly purchased handset. Pictures of the smiling young woman provided a rare glimpse of Hon Hai Precision Industrial Company (Foxconn Technology Group's parent company) assembly lines—including her soft pink uniform, rubber-tipped gloves, and seemingly relaxed, even creative, work space and colleagues. Originally posted to macrumors.com on August 20, 2008—in the midst of the final days of the 2008 summer Olympics in Beijing—the user "markm49uk" writes: "Not sure if this is or is not the 'norm' but I just received my brand new iPhone here in the UK and once it had been activated on iTunes I found that the home screen (the screen you can personalise with a photo) already had a photo set against it!! It would appear that someone on the production line was having a bit of fun—has anyone else found this?"[30]

Figures 5.2 and 5.3 Images of the iPhone Girl "found" on a handset by a user in the UK became an international sensation in the fall of 2008.

The thread quickly generated thousands of responses and was recirculated across both English and Chinese print, broadcast, and web media, including thousands of Google and Baidu search results, and a call by netizens for a "human flesh search engine" to locate the real iPhone girl.[31] Numerous bloggers even labeled the event a promotional hoax, suggesting that it was manufactured to draw attention to Apple's new iPhone 3G, then unreleased in China, highlighting the camera and video functions and, for consumers, a guilt-free supply chain. The Chinese/English blog 东南西北 (EastSouthWest-North) suggestively referred to the contagious pictures as the latest "Internet fairy tale"—signaling the Cinderella-like entrance of a marginalized young woman into global visual registers.[32] Similarly, a short piece in *Wired* hyperbolically states: "Following the footsteps of YouTube's Lonelygirl15 and Chris Crocker, the next self-made viral super star is shaping up to be a mysterious Chinese factory worker people are calling 'iPhone Girl.'"[33]

Regardless of the story's veracity, the iPhone Girl's "selfie" shores up the everyday and intimate uses of screen technologies by factory workers. From the repetitive acts of assembly to the care of quality control and even, perhaps, the playful testing of cameras, the pictures challenge the routine invisibility of laboring bodies in understandings of media politics and economies—bodies with complex and multisited technological intimacies. While creative labor and design rhetoric figure centrally in discourses about Apple products—and high-tech in general—the repetitive, menial, and fragmented tasks of technolabor are generally viewed as insignificant—merely the mindless execution of a particular action (like the example of wiping a glass screen with which I began). This discourse does significant political work by differentiating valuable sites of creativity and low-value imitative tasks, a fact captured by Apple's "designed in California" ethos and underscored by understandings of China as a site of *assembly* for components that are designed and built elsewhere—its role as a menial middle (wo)man. Mirroring debates about intellectual property and rip/mix/burn culture, the aspects of this supply chain not understood to creatively "add value" through their productive capacities are of little individual or specific value, but rather function as a *dividual* mass of potential labor to be slotted in or out of production as necessary. What I want to stress here is that it is the laboring body's presumed insignificance that renders it disposable. Indeed, this stereotypical view consolidates notions of "mindless labor," which themselves reaffirm routine disposability and are, in part, what the memes counter.

In the mainstream US context, Leslie Chang, journalist and author of the bestselling ethnography *Factory Girls*, offers a useful if limited description of this split and, in particular, of exploited laborers.[34] Chang argues that Euro-American understandings of factory labor are rooted in a guilt narrative, and based on the assumption that Asian factories are oppressive and that it is the Western desire for goods that makes them so. It is a simple narrative that connects Western demand to Chinese/Asian suffering. It is, moreover, a narrative, she observes, that smacks of self-obsession.[35] Chang suggests that "by focusing so much on ourselves and our gadgets," "we" have rendered workers' actions and desires "as menial and replaceable as the parts in the screens they make."[36] Such discourses have the added effect of erasing diverse local specificities and the world-making capacities of the non-West—or at the very least, making them visible only in relation to hegemonic national and global projects. In other words, this self-referential logic ascribes different geopolitical locations and time zones to the assembly and consumption of media hardware (where technological objects are made in one place and used in another). Such dominant logics subsume larger questions of who can be a desiring and technological subject.

Echoing legal activist Lawrence Liang's critiques of piracy discourse—which, in one variation, he describes as relying on a model of piety and the "'poor third world' figure, and fundamentally dependent on . . . 'catching up with the West' accounts of global relations"—the image of the iPhone girl also asks us to reconsider the common distinctions between sentient and menial labor.[37] The former signifies creativity, design, and the knowledge economy, and the latter is imitative, mindless, and highly replaceable; the former is the savior of the global economy, the latter the modern-day pirate. Instead, what does it mean to place factory labor and living, among myriad everyday and informal media cultures, at the center of critical studies of global emergent media? How are understandings of the cultural and creative industries, and the growing fields invested in production cultures, transformed by taking the habits and intimacies of penumbral users and makers as capacities in reshaping technology and sociality? The basic contours of the narrative of the "poor third world figure"—or in the national frame, the "low-end population"—is crucial because it animates a familiar imaginary through which the politics and ethics of national and global relationships are understood and lived out.[38] Challenging familiar relationships, this chapter reconsiders the routine thresholds through which we understand social capacity—Northern creativity on one side, Southern imitation on the other. It critiques the role that the migrant or the "third world figure" is made to do in buttressing the good economy and the benevolent North—whether that North is China's capital

(*Beijing* literally translates as "northern capital") or the centers of the so-called developed world.

Technological Intimacy

Debates about industrial labor and alienation or dehumanization are hardly new. Crucial to such discourses is the Marxist idea of labor processes as a kind of alienation from the physical knowledge and capacity to make things. In the vulgar reading, technology is understood to materialize the interests of capital by maintaining control over labor and wages, turning workers into mindless bodies.[39] As Fordist assembly lines spread transnationally (e.g., across Asia and Latin America) and incorporated women into the workforce in new ways, a new generation of feminist scholars sought to make gender crucial to understandings of labor processes.[40] One influential area of research, for example, centered on the relationship between labor, imperialism, and patriarchy, capturing the imposition of "first world" technology on "third world" subjects, especially women.[41] This work inaugurated crucial new areas of research, activism, and policy. But critics also worried about its determinism: factories materialize social relations, and both work and women workers recede from view. Put otherwise, such discourse very often consolidates understandings of women as "sites" of struggle, rather than contesting "subjects." Writing of similar gender slippages in postcolonial studies, Ania Loomba argues that while such issues capture the role of gender itself as a kind of political currency, as well as how women are subordinated by discourses "about" them, "such a formulation also implies that gender politics is only a metaphor for the articulation of other issues."[42]

Extending this productive debate—where gender is shown to be integral to labor processes—feminist scholars of Asia like Aihwa Ong, and more recently Pun Ngai and Ching Kwan Lee, have continued to recalibrate prevalent discourses of technical instrumentality by focusing on the resistance of women workers on the factory line.[43] Ong's influential examination of microelectronics factories in Malaysia's export manufacturing zones, in particular, is seen as a corrective to accounts where "machines subordinated an essentialized category 'women' to the interests of transnational capital."[44] Her work illustrates how the microelectronics assembly line acted to "disassemble" and "reassemble" gender, serving as a contested space where technology is both a form of power and a site of excess. Ong describes women workers who intentionally jam machines or suffer spirit attacks as "expressions of both fear and resistance."[45]

While Pun Ngai's 2005 study, *Made in China*, emphasizes how factories in Shenzhen function as disciplinary machines designed to turn workers into "mindless bodies," she too observes how young female workers—*dagonmei*—act to resist the speed of the assembly through coordinated slow-downs and collective illness. I mention these two well-known accounts here in order explore an alternative framing of "technological intimacy" developed by the anthropologist Jamie Cross in his factory work in one of India's special economic zones. Cross extends and critiques the valuable contributions of Ong, Ngai, and others, pointing out that these important ethnographies continue to rely on a theory of *technology as power*—one-way and deterministic—and further, that present technology as a "stable external force." As Cross puts it: "In [such] cases resistance is formulated *in spite of* and not *through* technology: acts of resistance all involve cutting, limiting or severing ties with tools and machines, either by turning them off, slowing them down, or walking away from them. In accounts like these, technology remains materially and symbolically unchanged through use."

Complicating the technology-as-power model, Cross draws on science and technology studies to advance an alternate account of technolabor. He notes that if researchers have given short shrift to embodied relationships with technology, it is precisely because the global factory worker is "rarely conceived of as a sentient, practicing, tool wielding body"—and further, we can add, a body with her own dreams and desires. Cross argues that to gain proficiency at a particular repetitive task is to become intimate with "tools and machines, a kind of 'carnal knowledge' or 'material consciousness.'"[46] In this context, even the most mundane assembly line actions are "constantly attentive, perceptual engagement with the material environment involving qualities of care, judgment, and dexterity."[47] Put otherwise: technological intimacy—in contrast to the menial/innovative binary—is transformative. This shift in perspective accentuates human–machine intimacies as a technological performance that works on the materiality of the workspace, the body, and social relationships.

The distinction between sentient and robotic bodies is also consolidated by influential discourses describing the new global economy and the ascendency of *affective labor*. One variant of so-called immaterial labor, affective labor is defined by human contact and interaction, such as "in-person services or services of proximity," and the production of affects like ease, well-being, satisfaction, passion, community, and so on.[48] Michael Hardt argues that this "affective face" of immaterial labor is perhaps best understood by returning to what "feminist analyses of 'women's work' have called labor in the bodily mode." This labor is at once corporeal or somatic, but its affects are nonetheless "immaterial." As with a mother's love, Hardt adds, affective labor animates "processes whereby our laboring practices produce collective subjectivities, produce sociality, and ultimately produce society itself."[49]

Hardt describes changes in the nature of labor processes as a result of the dominance of the information economy. What is new in the creative economy is that affects are capitalized and constitute new logics of "biopolitical production" that are generalized throughout the economy.[50] Or, as Lazzarato puts it, it is about a shift in understanding whereby "capitalism is not only a mode of production but a *production of worlds*."[51]

My interest here is to critique a certain tendency in affective labor's world picture. To limit affective labor to only certain kinds of human proximities and services, and to emphasize its immaterial transmission en route to certain consumers, is merely to reproduce dominant geopolitical cartographies.[52] But what of the technological intimacies of factory life, among many entangled zones? By this I mean both the crucial relationship between human and nonhuman actors (such as a worker and an iPhone), as well as the affective exchange among workers and multiple publics. Indeed, what top-down views of immaterial labor make apparent is the crucial role it plays in shoring up Apple's brand (viz. Apple showrooms and how the brand signifies the creative economy itself)—that is, precisely in disappearing the iPhone's material assemblage. As Helen Grace puts it, "That the object . . . cannot be made without being made of material and by a process involving manual labor—is disavowed in the language of magic which characterizes the marketing process, where the empty shell of the generic product gains the fullness of the brand's meaning."[53] In contrast to this delimited affective scenario, how might social and political theories take seriously the affective and sensuous activities bracketed as machinic, laborious, or imitative? How might we understand the "affective face" of the screen as it is conveyed hand to hand, down the line, as culturally and politically transformative? This modest twist, I think, opens up useful registers for what Hardt terms "biopower from below"—registers sensitive to the "remaindered life-times" and technological subjects foregrounded by the "social factory" of the factory itself.

Floating Media

To this point I have argued that approaches to video cultures and related media assemblages have neglected a range of intimate and haptic technological habits—like those associated with the workers who literally produce (assemble, test, package, ship, etc.) global electronics. Such workers spend their days and nights with screen technologies—and in ways not accounted for by the limited imaginations of digital culture as articulated by high-tech convergence and high-bandwidth networks. This separation is consolidated by discourses of immaterial labor and creativity as well as an orientalizing fascination with global supply chains—chains that move things in a single direction and keep everyone in their place. Put otherwise, this elision is epistemological and categorical, and does not reflect the actual existing practices in China and in much of the world. Opening up understandings of the *transformative subject*, of who gets to be a producer/produser, is not only to recalibrate frames of creativity and the creative economy, but to challenge the projects and policies that rely upon the presumed insignificance of menial labor to justify its exploitation. This is an important task for numerous reasons, not the least of which is the mundane point that China is no longer merely a site for export processing en route to the metropole. Instead, Apple's China stores, like the five massive stores now open in Beijing, are the tech giant's most profitable outlets globally—recasting the idea of a West–East–West supply chain.

I want to add texture to this discussion by turning to what we might call *floating media*—after the forms of videation that encapsulate and are carved out by migratory media practices. Floating refers to the masses of people unmoored by postsocialist cum neoliberal economies, as well as diverse technologies and practices that constitute digital cultures in such contexts. Video is a key form and platform within this floating media assemblage. It draws our attention to the crucial role played not only by content but also by distribution—that distribution itself *produces something*. What it produces, Thomas Lamarre argues in a parallel context, are "affective media geographies."[54] Thus, alongside and in contrast to clouds, data centers, and the fiber optic sublime of contemporary media infrastructures, floating media are animated by their capacity to *jump* formal and informal infrastructures—making up technological and affective networks among the presumably disconnected (hence the importance of DVDs, SD cards and hard drives, Bluetooth and the mobile phone). I am particularly interested in the savvy of workers and their social partners (workmates, friends, families, activists, journalists, artists/filmmakers, sectors of political society) in using micro and mainstream technologies and infrastructures to project their dreams and desires and to make claims on the future of the social. Outside coverage of factory workers and marginal media cultures emphasize *giving voice* or forms of petitioning and policymaking *on their behalf*. In contrast, we also encounter myriad and sophisticated uses of media by floating populations to advance personal and political projects that exceed state-corporate channels.

The iPhone girl "selfie" captures such creative sophistication and attentiveness to the currency of contemporary visual forms and infrastructures by workers and other illegible populations. The images can be understood as not merely unerased but as *created*—the clever employment of a prepackaged handset as a form of projected virality. Such small, personal, even poor visualities drive micro and local communications, suggesting crucial forms of transmission and contact. These connectivities rely upon and reanimate the technological intimacies left out of factory lifeworlds: routine care and dexterity of assembly and quality control, the furtive use of screens on the factory line or in bathrooms, as well as more familiar texting, chat, and short-form messaging like QQ or Weibo, photo and video posts, and other proliferations across the city (as video has become the ambient medium par excellence). Much more than an accident or intractability, the iPhone girl meme instead captures an emergent *performativity* that is crucial to video media's specificity.[55]

The idea of the technologized and (im)mobile self has been explored by numerous recent ethnographic studies of migrant media practices. Critically, such work remains to be digested by "mainstream" media studies, with its tendency to label them as exceptions—even when such practices constitute technomodernity in much of the world. We have a lot to learn from popular ethnographies like Chang's *Factory Girls* as well as academic studies of mobile migrants and technologies in factories, retail, construction, call centers, tourism, and the sex industry. Such work offers up crucial specificities and descriptions that refashion our very understandings of video culture, China, and the global.

Cara Wallis's 2013 monograph *Technomobility in China: Young Migrant Women and Mobile Phones* is a good example of the explosion of research on mobile telephony and migrant workers, among other entangled practices. Phones serve as a crucial object precisely because of their personal nature and what Wallis terms "necessary convergence."[56] That is, rather than the convergence of phones, tablets, laptops, desktops, and TV/cinema screens, for many these contents and practices converge on a single device—the mobile phone—out of economic necessity. While not explicitly focused on the factory, Wallis's account delineates the important vectors shaping contemporary "technomobility" for economic migrants in a wide range of jobs. In particular, she argues that mobile devices animate new forms of "immobile mobility." She defines this as "a socio-techno means of surpassing spatial, temporal, physical, and structural boundaries."[57] Technomobility drives both new forms of control within spaces like the factory (such as the ability for workers to be constantly tracked by their bosses) and marginal capacities or emergences within the limits of postsocialist cum neoliberal modernity. In this sense, "floating media" signals variability and fluctuation on the one hand, and states of suspension or endurance (e.g., as floating on the surface of water) on the other.

Coda

Discourses of robotic workers and media incapacity are not only a way for the global to manage the national (as in North Atlantic anxieties over China's "rise"), but are also an important part of national and subnational developmental regimes in China and beyond. It points to the vibrating forms of overlapping legitimacy at the center of this book, as well elite-subaltern relations that exceed international contact zones. A key example in this context is the proliferation of discourses around the suzhi (or quality 素质) of populations in post-reform China. The idea of suzhi has taken on a range of new meanings in recent years, especially as it becomes linked to the idea of the population (*renkou* 人口) and prolonged economic reforms. As Ann Anagnost argues, the idea shifted from its early project of educating beleaguered peasants and managing births to a project pitched at the population as a whole—a shift from an emphasis on quantity to quality.[58] Suzhi thus signals the specificities of biopolitical mechanisms in Olympic-era China. This recalibrated focus on the quality of the population drives a range of new imaginaries about the transfer of value—eerily reminiscent of fears over counterfeit purses or fake DVDs—especially investments in education, training, etiquette, and the like. The power of suzhi as an ideological formation signals a shift from a model of surplus extraction to a model of investment, where bodies, like things, must be improved and reutilized—and where recouped investments drive ever-harsher forms of exposure and abandonment.[59]

What I want to tease apart in this coda are the disparate politics of aspiration and desire—and their relation to floating video—that are conflated by such visions of the corpus and its qualities. Here we can return to Lisa Rofel's argument about the role of *desire* in the construction of new human beings in China—a logic, she points out, that at once captures aspects of neoliberal transformation *and* shores up the unruliness of desire itself—the difficulty of channeling it in a particular direction. Following Bhaskar Sarkar, I want to pressure Rofel's somewhat loose configuration of aspirational politics to suggest an important analytical distinction between *desire* and *aspiration* (even if these impulses cannot be isolated in practice).[60] Here, we can understand *aspiration* as the official modalities of ambition and development, including explicit targets for transformation, ranging from education and city plans to anti-spitting campaigns and middle-class consumption. Desire, while basically

Figure 5.4 Worker dances in the factory as part of Cao Fei's 2006 collaborative documentary *Whose Utopia.*

entangled with aspiration—and this, indeed, is part of the point of neoliberal self-regulation—suggests modes of experience and a repertoire of actions that necessarily exceed postsocialist cum neoliberal blueprints. Desire is what spills over from aspirational politics, including the "sensibilities that people engage in, draw upon, and invent in the struggle" to remake themselves and inhabit the present.⁶¹ Because such habits and imaginaries are largely incommensurate with aspirational targets, they drive forms of life that are both occluded and devalued by sanctioned modes of personhood, development, and global timeliness—not to mention the disciplinary concerns and categories of media and cultural studies research.

As a final example, I want to look at the Beijing-based visual artist Cao Fei's 2006 video project *Whose Utopia*. *Whose Utopia* is a partnership with workers at the Osram China Lighting factory in Guangdong—including six months of filming, interviews, and collaborative projects with factory workers. Divided into three parts, the video explores the intimate and mechanized tasks labor (part I, "Imagination of Product"), includes performances with workers in costumes and street clothes (part II, "Factory Fairytale"), and a final section pairing the music of a factory band, My Future Is Not a Dream, with video portraits of workers at their posts and staring directly into the camera. A catalogue description of the project describes it as follows: "The poetic, dreamlike vision of individualism within the constraints of industrialization illuminates

Figure 5.5 A young worker looks through the camera in the final section, "My Future Is Not a Dream," of *Whose Utopia*.

the otherwise invisible emotions, desires, and dreams that permeate the lives of an entire populace in contemporary Chinese society."[62]

What I find particularly striking about the video is its engagement with forms of technological intimacy. In a range of performances—scenes exploring the cohabitation of workers and machines, choreographed dance and movement, and a musical sequence that directly addresses the viewer—*Whose Utopia* takes seriously the material consciousness and social performativity of factory life. As Cross describes it, above, it is about a process of action and world-making that comes into being *through*, rather than *in spite of*, everyday occupations. When a middle-aged dancer, dressed in a black Osram uniform, methodically edges across a warehouse with movements that mimic the rhythm of machines and the erect posture of workers, or a gowned dancer twirls amid tall storage shelves, the space is transformed into the setting for a very different kind of tale. And while the video's "fairytale" intertitle suggests such actions are beyond normal life, it also refuses the notion that these people are merely cogs in a machine. At stake is the relationship between marginalized subjects and political subjectivity. It is one thing to trace structural exploitation and the limited pathways open to aspirational subjects, but it is quite another to turn those limitations or segregations into attributes of precarious subjectivity. Judith Butler makes this point sharply in her reworking of Hannah Arendt's *space of appearance*. She argues that if we accept that the "destitute are outside of politics—reduced to depoliticized forms of being—then we implicitly accept as right the dominant ways of establishing the limits of the political."[63] Against this division, the collaborative video performance both captures and generates its own political agency and volatility.

Promising to capture invisible "emotions, dreams, and desires," the video thus suggests a peculiar form of affective ethnography. Beyond recording and staging intimate acts of factory life, and listening to young men and women explain their motivations, *Whose Utopia* illustrates how various actors utilize video to project themselves and claim political subjectivity. This points to yet another form of technomobility—from the factory floor, local exhibitions, and international galleries to DVDs, film festivals, news coverage, and viral videos (such as the easily accessible mp4 file I downloaded to watch the video)—whose affective circulations seek to rework the limits of political space. Importantly, the audiovisual field inaugurated by such interactions is not limited to the videographer and spectator, but rather suggests a space of political relations that includes the look and aims of the videographed subject. This is also to challenge web 2.0's limited understanding of participation as the capacity to alter media content. Figure 5.5, among many such images, instead signals an alternate mode of interactivity. It registers the insistent refusal to accept the disposability or fractured citizenship assigned by the state (and its corporate and civil partners). Such forms of videation, following Ariella Azoulay's delineation of the civil contract of photography, expresses a "demand for participation in a sphere of political relations in which claims can be heard and acknowledged."[64] What is crucial about such videos is how they constitute, alongside a range of new and old media, a *remaindered* media assemblage. Put otherwise: video *floats*. It drifts across analog and digital forms, social classes, and global space times—enabling penumbral capacities that are disappeared by dominant epistemological horizons and discourses of global emergence.

People as Media Infrastructure

Illicit Culture and the Pornographies of Globalization

Discussing an infrastructure is a categorical act. It is a moment of tearing into those heterogeneous networks to define which aspect of which network is to be discussed and which parts will be ignored. It recognizes that infrastructures operate on differing levels simultaneously, generating multiple forms of address, and that any particular set of intellectual questions will have to select which of these levels to examine. Infrastructures are not, in any positivist sense, simply "out there."[1]

—BRIAN LARKIN

If the people are constituted through a complex interplay of performance, image, acoustics, and all the various technologies engaged in those productions, then "media" is not just reporting who the people claim to be, but media has entered the very definition of the people.[2]

—JUDITH BUTLER

The 2004 film *Manyan* 蔓延 (directed by He Jianjun, translated as *Pirated Copy*), a global classic in piracy and intellectual property (IP) circles, captures and sensationalizes the social life of informal media in Beijing (c. 2004). It weaves together stories about people who come into contact through the exchange of pirated movies, focusing on street vendors, a film professor who relies on pirate video shops and delivery for her teaching, a bar hostess paid for sex in DVDs, an HIV-positive collector who buys but does not watch films, and a migrant couple abandoned by the new economy and obsessed with acting out scenes from *Pulp Fiction* (Tarantino, 1994). The film's title, which translates as *to spread*, describes the complex social forms and desires brought into being by the hand-to-hand exchange of discs as well as a certain ambivalence signaled by its usage in describing the spread of other social contagions like violence, drugs, or disease. What interests me about this cult film—which both depicts a kind of pirate sociality and relies on such infrastructures for its own production, narrative, and circulation—is how it opens onto social entanglements beyond the industry paradigms or technological materialities that overwhelm attention to media infrastructures.

Manyan enlivens and theorizes a world of pirate bodies and volatile distribution that cannot be reduced to hackneyed discussions of legality, security, or access. In this chapter, I consider an alternative genealogy of the handheld and of social media—theorizing the optical disc cultures of the 2000s as a way to resituate attention to more recent digital media practices like mobile phones, *kuaidi* (express delivery 快递), and video platforms, among others. Tracing lineages of hand-to-hand delivery and of embodied networks challenges what constitutes socially valuable production and interactivity. It replaces the hoopla surrounding users and the creative industries with an eco-ethic of bodies, contact, and assembly. It is this latter arena that opens onto what might rightfully be termed "social media," or what Judith Butler, in a different context, terms "the social network of hands" to describe the importance of social interdependency and infrastructural supports to creating livable communities and nurturing life itself.³ Building on Butler's claim that "media has entered the very definition of the people," and on AbdouMaliq Simone's formulation of "people as infrastructure," this chapter extends the notion of *media* infrastructure to the everyday habits and itineraries that constitute urban belonging.⁴

The *Saohuang Dafei* Campaigns, 1989—

The recurrent *saohuang dafei* (扫黄打非) campaigns that seek to "sweep away pornography" and "strike down illegal" publications provide the larger context for this analysis of people as media infrastructure and, what I term below, the *pornographies of globalization*. Established at the Fourth Plenum of the Thirteenth Central Committee in 1989, the saohuang dafei movement has emerged as a semipermanent campaign against a broadly defined array of

Figure 6.1 Leaders theatrically announce plans to destroy/burn (*xiaohui*) illegal and pirated materials at a 2016 conference in Beijing.

"illegal publications," including, as IP scholar Andrew Mertha asserts, "those deemed 'anti-government' or 'anti-Party,'" but also encompassing "illegally produced (i.e., copyright-violating) published works."[5] Administered by the National Anti-Pornography and Anti-Piracy Office (Quanguo saohuang dafei gongzuo xiaozhu bangongshi) and an equally ad hoc bundle of government institutions and resources, the campaigns first emerged after the US trade representative placed China on the Priority Watch List in 1989.[6] According to Shujen Wang, the institution was originally referred to as the National Anti-Pornography Working Committee, and only in February of 2000, before joining the WTO, was "Anti-Piracy" added to its official name. At that time, it was devised as the main antipiracy office in China, including fifteen participating institutions from the communication, transportation, cultural, and informational branches of government.[7]

The "Sweeping Away Pornography, Striking Down Illegals" campaigns pool numerous governmental bodies and resources to police copyright issues in relation to a broad range of political objectives. As Mertha notes, such composite governance means that, "in practice, copyright issues are often subsumed to other enforcement goals of the participating government units."[8] Important in terms of its visibility in the press and on the street—not to mention their periodic recurrence over a thirty-year span—the campaigns both

PEOPLE AS MEDIA INFRASTRUCTURE

Figure 6.2 After successful raids, the National Anti-Piracy and Anti-Pornography Office displays its own pornographic imagination by making a spectacle of destroying the confiscated DVDs. One of the many images hosted on the campaign's website: http://www.shdf.gov.cn/cms/html/190/1763/200311/678801.html (accessed April 5, 2011).

boast massive successes in the fight against illicit materials and illustrate a fundamental tension in conceptions of illicit culture.

Headlines such as "Anti-Piracy Fight Posts Remarkable Results,"[9] "Anti-Piracy Campaign on Scenic Spots, Airports in Holiday,"[10] "China Gets Tough on Porn and Piracy," and "Porn Dealer Jailed for 12 Years in China's Piracy, Pornography Crackdown"[11] are common in Chinese- and English-language media, and tend to reach frenzy level around major holidays like National Week, mega-events like the Olympic Games, economic summits, or the anniversary of the Tiananmen Square massacre. They demonstrate the Chinese government's willingness to fulfill WTO-related IPR protections and create a mediascape where the illegality of copyright piracy is clearly marked. However, as numerous observers have indicated, and *Pirated Copy* explores, media piracy in the PRC remains entrenched—even in internationally surveilled sites like Beijing, Shanghai, and the Pearl River Delta. Further, copyright violations—a relatively clear legal category—are more than tolerated, and when policed receive far lighter punishment than do violations of the much more plastic category of pornography.

While targeting copyright violations, it is also clear that this is not an explicit antipiracy movement—though that is certainly how it addresses international media, among other contexts. Mertha explains the rationale for the motley combination of antipornography and antipiracy as follows:

> The logic behind such reasoning is that because the sale of pornographic and antigovernment works is illegal in China, it is by definition an infringement of copyright (or represents, in theory at least, the illegal licensing of the pornographer's copyright). However, although one can liberally interpret the sale of pornography and antigovernment works as an infringement of copyright, most copyright piracy in China (one official placed it at 80 percent) is *not* pornographic or antigovernment in nature. The majority of copyright infringement in China is politically neutral: computer application software, compact disks, VCDs, DVDs, technical books, journals, and other publications.[12]

Put simply, policing copyright piracy alongside pornography and other antigovernment violations works at cross purposes—playing very differently at distinct scales and to different audiences. As a result, Mertha adds, even when "such 'apolitical' and 'nonpornographic'" material is confiscated, the pirates typically receive fines. Those violating the shifting saohuang aims, on the other hand, are jailed or even executed.

The National Anti-Pornography and Anti-Piracy Office draws our attention to a governmental assemblage marked by confusion, aggressive policing, and performative publicity. This includes the strategic legal clustering of pornography and piracy by state sectors managing distinct forms of illegality. The local and national campaigns pose important questions about the operations of illicit culture in the contemporary PRC: Why are pornographic targets and copyright violations linked together in legal discourse, popular media, and urban governance? How do such practices both disrupt and enact new categories of (il)legitimacy by disparate actors and at different scales? And what does this imbrication—at once strange and familiar—tell us about contests over legality and legitimacy under globalization?

Piracy

A critical aspect of piracy, among other forms of illegality, is its emergence within and alongside a particular set of political, technological, and economic conditions. This is not to say that piracy itself is a novel practice—it is not—but that its irruptions are historically specific.[13] In China, contemporary piracy is an outgrowth of the economic reforms begun under Deng Xiaoping in the late 1970s. The process of reform and opening led to the gradual integration of China into the global economy and the shift from a mostly socialized to a mostly marketized mode of (cultural) production. This transformation involves the continued significance of state management and intervention, new pressures for China to uphold neoliberal understandings of property, including adopting global intellectual property and copyright norms, as when China joined the World Trade Organization (WTO) in 2001, as well as massive new projects within China to develop manufacturing capacity and, subsequently, to transform itself into a creative economy.[14]

But, as Adrian Johns argues, it would be a mistake to see piracy as a mere by-product of changes to legal regimes, marketization, and the like. On the contrary, Johns notes that piracy often outpaces economic shifts and intellectual property, among other legal regimes. He writes: "to assume that piracy merely derives from legal doctrines is to get the history—and therefore the politics, and much else besides—back to front."[15] One of the aims of this chapter, indeed of this book, is to contribute to this reorientation, and to take seriously the ordinary ways that public culture operates as a piratical zone.

The transition from a discrete centralized economy to an integrated socialist-market economy also coincides with substantial technological changes across the globe. Indeed, China's (re)entry into the global was not only through capitalism, but also through new technological networks and logistical infrastructures that reterritorialize prior processes of locality, driving a knowledge-innovation economy that has in turn been described as the "space of flows," "flexible production," a network of "global cities," "venture labor," and "cognitive capitalism," and, at the same time, is marked by massive and intensifying inequality.[16] As Wang notes, the very same technological developments that made it possible for China to plug into global trade and financial networks at the end of the last century (e.g., the WTO, spectacles like the 2008 Olympic Games) also enabled pirates to "copy, distribute, and profit with exceptional quality, speed, and reach."[17] This imbrication recalls a basic aspect of piracy: piracy networks often rely on official institutions and infrastructures to work, and yet they bring about their own infrastructures and social worlds.

Let me outline a spectrum of responses to piracy that are germane to this discussion. First, a common response to piracy advocated by copyright exporting nations like the United States is that piracy is theft. Such responses are rooted in narratives that construct producer nations of hardworking artists, innovators, and businessmen and, alternatively, pirate nations of premoderns, cheaters, and those lacking in the creative spirit. A favorite strategy of Euro-American governments and organizations like the Motion Picture

Association of America (MPAA) is to link copyright infringement to organized crime, human traffickers, and terrorist groups.[18] As Nitin Govil argues, conflating IP piracy and terrorism has been a key theme for watchdogs, policymakers, and pop culture since 9/11. Writing in the same year as *Manyan* was released, Govil notes: "British detectives claim that Pakistani DVDs account for 40% of anti-piracy confiscations in the UK, and that profits from pirated versions of *Love, Actually* and *Master and Commander* funnel back to the coffers of Pakistan-based Al Qaeda operatives."[19]

Such rhetoric of threat and evil recalls Roman law and Marcus Tullius Cicero's 2,000-year-old proclamation that pirates, because they operate outside of territorial sovereignty and ordinary jurisdiction, are the "enemy of all" (hostis humani generis).[20] Historically, their role as universal enemy results from an "antagonism" that, as Daniel Heller-Roazen observes, "cannot be defined as that of one individual with respect to another" individual or political entity. In other words, the pirate constitutes a crucial third term—besides individuals and states—within international law. It consolidates a state of exception, or rather statelessness, that legitimizes the "enemy of all" as those persons that can be killed by anyone.[21] This universal antagonism is crucial to the pirate's role in confusing formal and felt categories of legitimacy, including "the collapse of the distinction between the criminal and the political."[22] Recent years have seen the extension of this vulnerable enemy to include diverse piratical forms—the figures of the terrorist, other nonstate actors like immigrants and refugees, as well as sexual, religious, and racial minorities, among many others.[23] What matters here is that this third realm—the realm of the illegal subject who stands against and is endangered by all other subjects, legal regimes, and structures of governance—is proliferating and demands new political-theoretical frameworks.

A second approach to piracy is tied to emergent understandings of intellectual property, the cultural commons, the creative industries, and so on. Kavita Philip's critique of such discourses, in her essay "What Is a Technological Author?" is an instructive starting point. She focuses on the work of Lawrence Lessig and Lawrence Liang—two theorists of piracy writing from very different geopolitical locations.[24] These two positions, it turns out, make a world of difference. Lessig, a legal scholar at Harvard University, is widely perceived as the major theorist of the *free culture* movements in the United States. His work relies on how transformations brought about by digital technologies can reshape how we use and share culture. Against widespread attempts to expand intellectual property law, Lessig's work has celebrated *certain* forms of piracy and a return to the commons—and has thus produced modest gains in areas like creative commons licensing. As Philip points out, however, notions of good piracy and bad piracy undergird his interventions. Good piracy, for Lessig, is brought about by uses that creatively transform copyrighted content or alter the markets where it competes.[25] A key figure here is the teenage hacker or tinkerer who reanimates existing cultural forms by slashing, mashing, or mixing, replaying them in new forms to new audiences.

On the other hand, Lessig describes bad piracy: "All across the world, but especially in Asia and Eastern Europe [later references to this phenomenon drop the European reference and call it simply Asian piracy], there are businesses that do nothing but take other people's copyrighted content, copy it, and sell it. . . . This is piracy plain and simple. Nothing in the argument of this book [*Free Culture*], nor in the argument that most people make when talking about the subject of this book, should draw into doubt this simple point: This piracy is wrong."[26]

Lessig thus turns to Asian piracy to establish a limit case for pirate value and politics. Slashing a vid is creative and good. But making a copy of a vid is "piracy plain and simple," and bad/wrong. Here Lessig's seemingly radical notions of "free culture" emerge as a rather pragmatic, if xenophobic, set of considerations aligned with the marketable innovations of the creative industries. His aim (not unlike the universities or other institutions where many of us labor) is to enable the kinds of creativity that make both savvy producer-consumers and Silicon Valleys. In other words, he does not tackle inequality, pricing gaps, neoliberal abandonment, or the widespread illegality of everyday life. Nor does he attend the local values or social distributions generated by "plain" piracy. Lessig's approach is firmly tethered to existing legal, property, and market relations. In fact, his picture of Asian piracy is meant to illustrate why those relations are so important, and to scare us with the dystopian picture of Asian sameness—an all too familiar sci-fi image of a dark future where Asian languages and technologies of control dot the urban landscape.

In contrast, Lawrence Liang shifts the argument away from the high-bandwidth politics that drive Lessig's concerns about intellectual property and the creative industries to consider the low-cost world of street piracy and make-do modernity: most people in the world do not have regular access to computers, high-speed internet, patent registries, and the like. Liang is clear, in his echoes of Lessig, that *this piracy* too is "transformative piracy."[27] What shifts in the movement from California's Silicon Valley to India's Bangalore is that piracy's value—its goodness or badness—is no longer rooted in legality and the proprietary genius. Philip notes that Lessig's content problem—"with your piracy are you creating something?"—does not apply here. Instead, Liang emphasizes the make-do tactics through which people find "avenues of participation" and ways of entering into and inhabiting the world.[28]

This approach dislodges political theory's reliance on idealized and bourgeois normativities in understandings of the politics of other modernities. The "challenge of having an intercontinental dialogue," Liang asserts, is "really to push the limits of thinking through the problem of understanding the publics which lie outside the assumptions of the liberal public sphere."[29] His claim echoes this study's focus on political society—demanding that we take seriously the conditions of illegality that undergird current political and economic contracts. This is to recognize not only the realities of postcolonial and postsocialist life, but also its entanglement with *postdemocracy*, where everyday life—from housing rights to culture sharing—is increasingly marked by illegal relations and thus the denial of basic rights and legal status to a growing number of people. What this book terms underglobalization is, on the one hand, the recognition that formal democratic practices and aspirations (including the democratic centralism of the Chinese Communist Party[30]) are increasingly impoverished if not violent. On the other hand, it argues that the illegal and piratical forms of life created by democracy's concrete failures are, paradoxically, the grounds upon which equitable social forms might be built.

To get at these constitutive undersides, I want to signal two additional problems in piracy discourse. First, approaches to piracy remain too narrow in focus and are limited by a vague specificity that privileges high-value commodities over other forms of illegality. Put otherwise, they privilege the objects and practices that are central to antipiracy discourse itself. In this context, the high visibility (and financial value) of blockbuster media, designer handbags, and similar counterfeits not only erases proliferating conditions of illegality, but also erases their social, political, and economic significance. It matters that pirate media exists alongside fake medicine; illegal housing; cardboard dumplings; false passports, birth certificates, or urban registration (hukou); siphoned electricity; stolen water; ripped software; copycat Mao statues; reverse-engineered microchips; brandjacking; fake slogans; "black" taxis; bootleg alcohol; counterfeit money; and an endless range of phonies, frauds, and forgeries. My point is not that scholars should avoid studies of film piracy or similar practices. Rather, the overwhelming focus on pirated blockbusters, knock-off luxury goods, or high-tech patents in China and throughout the region reiterates the hegemonic claims of globalization. These discourses not only reproduce violent notions of good and bad piracy but cover over the real condition of underglobalization: the proliferation of illegal citizens, cities, and forms of life. As Philip notes, the question of "who can be a pirate" and "who does not need to be a pirate" requires more attention.[31]

Finally, Shujen Wang's work on piracy and globalization productively turns our attention to problems of scale and sovereignty. Wang demonstrates that current theoretical models are overinvested dichotomies between center and periphery, national and global, East and West, and are insufficient for the analysis of contemporary media technologies and questions of legality and governance. Such dualities, she argues, are tied to understandings of globalization that tend to downplay the role of states and to overemphasize outputs, including the state's ability to oversee those outputs. Instead, Wang is interested in the unevenness of global networks. Drawing on Saskia Sassen, she argues that globalization can be more productively conceived "in terms of a transnational geography of centrality with *multiple linkages* and strategic concentrations of material infrastructure."[32] Wang thus shifts the debate from global control and local resistance to the "overlapping sovereignties" articulated by disparate legal regimes, social and economic aspirations, and technological cohabitations. This includes expanding the network of multiple linkages well beyond the global cities of New York, London, and Tokyo.

Overlapping sovereignties describe the gaps or "in-between spaces" of global and legal intercourse: "between copyright legislation and law enforcement, between global copyright governance and national/local compliance, between global actors and national networks, and among different levels of juridical spaces." While the transnational synchronization associated with the Agreement of Trade-Related Aspects of Intellectual Property (TRIPS)—a key component of the World Trade Organization—shifts conceptions of sovereignty (by "harmonizing" the IP laws of developed and developing countries), at the same time, such legal regimes rely on various local and state institutions to interpret and enforce their laws.[33] States may perform their tough stance on piracy to certain national and global audiences, but other municipal, provincial, and national offices may find the pirate economy to be culturally and economically valuable—creating jobs, incomes, tax revenues, access to culture, skills, and solving social problems, among others. Wang's focus on the spaces in-between policy and implementation underscores the spatial and geographic nature of the law, and thus the instability of sovereignty itself. What I want to emphasize here is the basic relationship between partial sovereignty and mushrooming forms of illegality, on the one hand, and the increasing political significance of legitimacy, on the other hand. In a growing number of contexts legitimacy replaces legal claims as the crucial site of political negotiation. This is both to identify rising tensions between legality and legitimacy within con-

Figure 6.3   DVD title screen of *Pirated Copy* combines a production still with a looping video of one of the film's sex scenes; heavy breathing and the theme music from *In the Mood for Love* (Wong, 1999) fill the soundtrack.

temporary politics, in China and globally, and to observe a shift from overlapping sovereignties to contested and *overlapping legitimacies*.

Pirated Cities

Pirated Copy is rooted in the contested street-level legitimacies of piracy, pornography, and globalization. The film has had moderate play in the international festival and art house circuit—including receiving financial support from Fanhall Films and premiering at the International Film Festival Rotterdam—and achieved a sort of cult status for media copyright scholars. Though unreleased in the PRC, it has circulated widely through the very street piracy practices it represents. I bought my own copy, for instance, at a well-established bookstore/café situated between Peking and Tsinghua Universities in Beijing's Haidian District (and later glimpsed it in stacks of plastic-wrapped discs in the hands of street vendors and in the bootleg corner of more legitimate media outlets across the city). A fixture in the university zone, the shop was one of countless spots across the city that sold pirated (*daoban*) music, videos, books, and other media alongside the real thing,[34] though it is not always so easy to distinguish between them.

While the large-scale communal viewing situations of the past and present—the tea house, work unit, or movie theater—have been reshaped or even replaced by mobile devices and ambient screens, the public circulation of pirated media (on mobile devices, SD cards, Bluetooth sharing, hard drives, streaming) continues in very visible, collective, and routine ways. In fact, as many scholars have noted, it would be a mistake to discount the infrastructures and practices that made up the flourishing and flagrant bootleg industry in first decade of the twenty-first century.[35] Pang Laikwan, for example, has noted the way in which pirate distributors on the mainland successfully branded themselves in the image of legitimate agents, becoming recognizable in their own right. She writes: "Each of these pirate companies has its own editorial direction and image, so that the films or music they choose to pirate are calculated to fit the images of the general brand or specific series. While pirated films are sold mainly on the streets or [in] temporary stores in Hong Kong and Taiwan, where anti-piracy is fierce, the distribution networks on the mainland are so highly developed that each of these established pirate groups has national distribution and retail lines."[36]

In millennial Beijing, pirate video stalls and vendors played the role that rental had assumed in countries like the United States.[37] For example, the shops I regularly visited in Beijing's Haidian, Xicheng, Dongcheng, and Chaoyang Districts boasted large inventories of international film, TV, and music, allowing customers to exchange faulty discs and place special orders, and even provided home delivery. In many cases, the vendors primarily sold legal media, with a few boxes of pirated material discreetly available, while more informal stalls featured only pirated CDs and DVDs.[38] A common organizational logic in larger stores is to conspicuously display legitimate wares and blend in a limited amount of the thinly packaged pirate discs, allowing for both quick removal upon a warning of a raid or, in the case of confiscation, minimal losses. However, allegations of local corruption and industry participation in the business of piracy complicate the issue.[39] Such allegations are shored up by the fact that even in 2017, when many VCD/DVD shops had long been closed, several pirate stores specializing in Hollywood and Bollywood blockbusters, Korean and Japanese TV dramas, and international art cinema remain conspicuously open in heavy traffic areas and near commercial centers and government buildings.

But more than pirate industries, what I want to draw attention to is the importance of informal media networks as a spatial and social practice.

Figure 6.4   Interior of the Blue Goat bookstore and café (*Lan yang*), Haidian District, which specialized in classics and independent cinema.

Figure 6.5   DVD shops selling both authentic and pirated copies dotted Beijing's landscape in the 2000s.

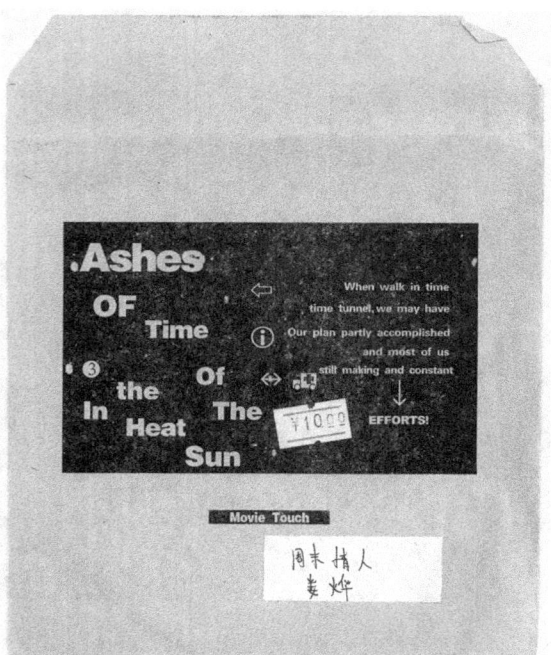

Figure 6.6 Made-to-order DVDs of Chinese independent films were sold in brown sleeves at the Blue Goat, among other Beijing shops. Lou Ye's *Weekend Lovers* (*Zhoumo qingren*, 1993).

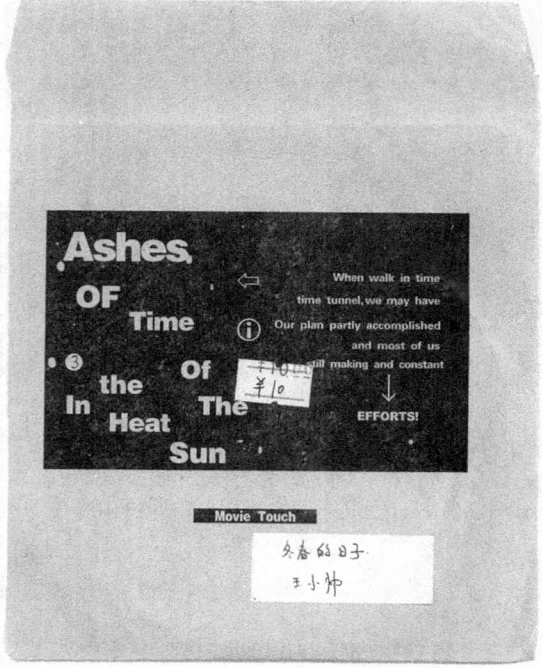

Figure 6.7 Made-to-order DVD of Wang Xiaoshuai's *The Days* (*Dongchun de rizi*, 1993).

These networks prefigure contemporary e-commerce and delivery culture in China—what is now referred to as the Jack Ma economy after the founder of Alibaba—and also constitute a social infrastructure whose significance extends far beyond media circulation.[40] In Olympic era Beijing, street pirates, with duffle bags of DVDs, were a reliable site at metro and bus stops, the entryways to office buildings and supermarkets, as well as a host of regularized itineraries in the city. Perambulatory vendors would offer boxes of DVDs for customers to peruse at bars, restaurants, and even the workplace—often leaving business cards for orders or addresses for established stores and hidden venues. One particularly well known "secret" DVD shop was located near the North Third Ring Road. To enter, patrons first walked through a storefront displaying unfashionable lingerie, then passed through a door in the rear that opened onto a large room filled with thousands of DVDs, organized by country and genre, as well as books and magazines about Chinese independent cinema, among others. This is to make two points. First, these informal networks of people and things expand the domain of the political to include the mundane habits, curiosities, and desires tied to social assemblages—that is, the aspects of exchange that are not taken seriously by instrumental notions of access, value, rights, and so on. Secondly, they enact a foundation for broader actions across political society.

In addition to hand-to-hand exchange, piracy also remakes cultural objects and practices. This includes changes to the materiality and content of DVDs, among other media, as well as changing modes of interactivity, mobility, spectatorship, and sociality. Consider, for example, how informal producers redesigned DVD covers or added bonus features to discs to enhance sales and localize content. A notable practice related to piracy and pornography is the use of erotic images not included in the actual film for disc packaging—a tactic that also seeped into more official productions.[41] Films that lack the traction of the blockbuster or art house film often use pornographic packaging to win the browser's eye, making it difficult to differentiate not only the real from the fake—in many cases the quality, packaging, and holographic seals were indistinguishable—but also pornography from mainstream fare, legal from illegal. In other cases, pirated discs would highlight their illicit status by boasting unofficial subtitles in many languages, and special features or songs not included with even the most expensive official editions. These seemingly minor changes in materiality, circulation, and address help us to reframe ideas about interactivity, among digital buzzwords.

These seemingly minor changes in materiality and address, among similar tactics, demonstrate how pirate infrastructures transform formal structures, creating new forms of participation as well as apertures into a wide range of social, cultural, and political domains. Put differently, they upend familiar ideas about the cognitive economy and creative property by localizing their protocols and directing value toward the people ignored by official industries. What matters here is how "peoples activities in the city," to borrow Simone's formulation, help us to redefine *social media* as an interdependency of people and things—and not simply the exchange of user-generated content.[42] Such infra-structures are created as marginal actors enter and make claims on formal zones (like the sidewalk, legal discourse, or distribution industries) and, at the same time, remake these zones through their use. As such, they draw our attention to the importance of ambient and affective experience, or *aesthesis*, in organizing techno-social worlds. As Brian Larkin notes in his overview of infrastructural thinking, aisthesis looks beyond familiar aesthetic categories, questions of representation, or the mental appreciation of art. Rather it emphasizes how embodied experience and supports shape "the ambient conditions of everyday life: our sense of temperature, speed, florescence, and the ideas we have associated with these conditions."[43] Aisthesis imagines how ordinary experiences of cognition and sensation—the sense of navigating the city, social interactions, and cultural modes—are embodied and infrastructural, as well as how they shape political and social life.

I want to make two related points here in relation to this chapter's wider focus on illicit culture. First, (il)legality increasingly frames the conditions of everyday life in China, and this condition is basically related to the discursive performativity of piracy and pornography. While all pornographic and pirated materials are illegal in China, in practice the situation is more ambiguous. As Dru C. Gladney observes in relation to representations of ethnic minorities, the difference between pornography and erotica in China is defined by "what the state regards as legal and illegal." He writes:

> The point here is not about eroticism in general, it is that in China representations of Han subjects classed by the state as pornographic would not be illegal, and thus only erotic, if the Hans were dressed as minorities. In China, "erotic" is generally glossed as *xing aide*, or that which influences or encourages sexual love; whereas "pornographic" is generally translated as *seqing*, or literally, "colorful sentiment," obliquely referring to the color yellow, which refers specifically to the pornographic press.[44]

Pornification—or *seqinghua* (色情化)—describes both a proliferation and confusion of sexual material, including erotica and hardcore, racial drag and the anthropological gaze, gender and sexual categories, but also *yellow* packaging,

Figure 6.8 A basket of pirated DVDs, sold tableside at a restaurant in Songzhuang artists' village, mixes softcore pornography with global art cinema. Courtesy of the author.

sex education media, bonus features, uncertain copyright, illegal networks, and myriad other issues. Second, it draws our attention to a crucial form of power—the means to differentiate legal from illegal. This administration and enforcement of legality—the power to decide between legal and illegal—produces illegal forms of life and is also refused by everyday experience and practices of urban belonging. This is to say that pirate circulation and hand-to-hand exchange connect to other forms of illicit life and informal solidarity—from sex work and labor disputes to illegal medicine and housing. It is crucial to contemporary forms of political society and what I have termed piratical citizenship—how, that is, social and democratic forms are nurtured by claims on informal infrastructures.

A Scene:

Pirated Copy begins with a low-angle shot of a leafless winter tree, the visuals led by the off-screen voices of a street pirate and a customer haggling over the price of DVDs. The segment lasts several minutes and follows a number of vendors and consumers. Even on this cold winter day in Beijing the routine foot traffic of pirate movie culture is abuzz. "DVDs, sir?" shouts one woman from a bicycle to off-screen passersby. Finally, a man bites: "Got any porn?" (Literally got any *"maopian* [毛片]*,"* a term associated with pubic hair and commonly applied to popular media like porn and TV shows.) "Sure," the woman replies as her infant looks on from the bike's rear seat. "Where from?" he asks. She hands him a stack of DVDs of European and American porn. They haggle over the price, finally settle on 8 RMB (about US$1). The scene continues to other buyers and sellers; some browse for popular Hong Kong films, others for love stories, and one recurring character—the recently laid-off husband—searches for violent films, finally choosing a copy of *Pulp Fiction* (Tarantino, 1994). The opening sequence culminates with a chase: a street pirate is pursued and finally arrested by two policemen for selling discs on the sidewalk. Fade out.

A black screen is paired with the unrecognizable sounds of heavy breathing, struggle, and a dog's barking. It fades to a close-up of a man, Shen Ming (Yu Bo), watching intently. A quick cut reveals a television screen and the previously unsourced sound—from Kieslowski's *A Short Film about Killing* (1988). Similar film snippets are intercut with close-ups. A scene from Hou Hsiao-Hsien's 1983 film *The Boys from Fengkuei* and the ending of Vittorio De Sica's *The Bicycle Thief*: Antonio Ricci chased on the stolen bicycle, little Bruno looking on. A far cry from claims of cultural homogenization or lazy mimicry, the movie suggests the potential, somewhat ironically, of open access to diverse cultural texts and artifacts—a kind of unfettered fecundity.

Next, the film shifts to the interrogation room and the arrested pirate, making a clear linkage between *The Bicycle Thief*'s postwar, neorealist critique, and contemporary piracy. The interrogation focuses on the question of why the man turned to bootlegging—boredom and lack of money, he answers—and the nature of the discs. Here the issue of pornography and its relation to copyright/piracy comes to the foreground. The street vendor is asked if he has ever sold pornographic films, to which he quickly answers no. The police respond: "If we ever found out you had, we could send you to prison." The response underlines the uneven enforcement of illegal media—of which pirated material and pornography are both guilty. The scene continues as the policemen and bootlegger argue over the pornographic content of Nagisa Oshima's *In the Realm of the Senses* (1976). The young policeman asks: "What the hell do you call this?" "It's an art film," the pirate responds.

Manyan continues by exploring the everyday networks that move people and media around the city. New characters are introduced and their lives transformed by the hand-to-hand encounters of pirate DVD circulation. We learn, for example, that Shen Ming is also a street pirate and manager of an

Figure 6.9 A Beijing street vendor sells pirated DVDs in the 2004 film *Pirated Copy*.

underground video store. However, he finds working in the store too boring, and instead spends his time previewing the new discs—the snippets above—and hustling on the street. He prefers the excitement of the street and how DVDs bring him into contact with strangers. It is this stranger sociality—and not the promise of bourgeois inclusion—that engenders meaningful itineraries, knowledges, and interdependency in the city. Indeed the film unfolds by juxtaposing scenes of watching films with people's encounters in the city. After the interrogation scene, we return to Shen Ming's room where he watches scenes from *Sex, Lies, and Videotape* (Soderbergh, 1989), other art house fare, and explicit pornographic films, before again returning to street. In these and similar scenes, all of the characters' lives are shaped by the hand-to-hand exchange of discs—encounters that emphasize the embodied nature of media infrastructures.

The film suggests a sort of hyperrealism where one's imaginative encounter with movies, the materiality of discs, and contact with other people immediately lead to changes in everyday experience. Shen Ming's perambulations, for example, create many new social relations and pathways through the city. This includes practical knowledge of urban byways, claims on public space, business relations, and friendships as well as more sensational contact—such as his sexual encounters with a cinephile bar hostess who charges him in DVDs, and spontaneous sex in the university bathroom with a lonely film professor to whom he delivers Almodóvar films for her university teaching. In each case, it is the raw emotions and bodily desires unleashed by the exchange of DVDs that lead to action in the diegetic real. At times such contagions are explicit, as when a struggling couple watches *Pulp Fiction,* plans a robbery, and then commits murder and suicide. Notwithstanding the film's often exaggerated and ambivalent engagement with piracy, it insists on the transformative potential of DVD circulation and its role as social media.

These passionate irruptions also underscore the stifling mechanisms that manage the illicit. This includes censorship and IPR regulations, which have produced widespread illegality and both legitimate and illegitimate forms of belonging to the city. For instance, one of the chief issues made visible by the film is the way in which copyright law, among other forms of illegality, elides reception rights. In this context, desire and creativity are made illegible by official structures and must seek out their own infrastructures and informal connections. But attention to censure and access also clarify a key objection to *accessibility* as the normative model for understanding piratical practice. Formal models of access, like those associated with information and communication technologies for development (ICT4D), pedagogical at root, emphasize appropriate and pedagogical forms of access—including access to things like medicine, the internet, and directly applicable knowledge. What access arguments ignore are questions of desire, pleasure, curiosity, and joy, not to mention the forms of social creativity and human infrastructures that bring about values for local communities but often fail to generate new profits for global IP portfolios.[45] Part of the film's popular and radical gesture is to insist upon the mundane pleasures and values associated with the feverish spread of DVDs and the social network of hands. These practices, more than unregulated media circulation, drive collective actions that reconfigure the space of the city and create their own social forms.

Mimicry, or the Pornographies of Globalization

Before returning to the question of piracy and pornography, I want to draw an analogy to Bhaskar Sarkar's contention that the experience of globalization is "highly melodramatic."[46] Speaking broadly of melodrama, Sarkar posits a homology between the "too late" logic that drives the genre and the "developmentalist" rationale projected by hegemonic discourses of globalization.[47] His analysis begins with a discussion of "history's 'waiting room,'" and of Dipesh Chakrabarty's important rereading of Marx in "The Two Histories of Capital." Rejecting historicism's narrative of a "putatively single capitalism" that leaves the developing world eternally behind and *waiting,* Chakrabarty argues that capital is composed of two historical modalities. The first, History 1, is the history posited by capital itself as its precondition. The second, History 2, are those pulses that do not belong to capital's life process.[48] History 2s describe a range of practices, including "habitual physical gestures, collective practices, and ways in which people relate to their environment."[49] While not external to capital, this second modality is animated by social practices of assembly that are not easily recuperated into a retrospective history of becoming. Rather, History 2s describe people as infra-structural.

The central point for Sarkar is that the dominant narrative of globalization (History 1) is reiterated by melodrama's deferral of desire, its "too late" logic, and, simultaneously is negated by the "persistence of difference."[50] This double movement—lateness and difference—helps explain the immense popularity of melodramas in the region as well as Bollywood's fraught relationship to Hollywood. In a nuanced analysis of the contemporary Indian film industry, he illustrates that what is pleasurable about Hindi melodramas is how they engage issues of economic, social, and cultural difference. They affectively probe how the contradictory experience of globalization—the *latest* stage of capitalist modernization—is always somehow in the distance. For instance, Sarkar notes that nations like India and China are repetitively perceived as somehow hindering themselves, of not doing globalization right (e.g., they are too repressive, or too protectionist, or indulge in piracy). But these "*unreasonable* detours" in the global game of catch-up can also be understood to suggest a competing logic that interrupts the totalizing gesture of modernization.[51]

The "too late" logic of the melodramatic imitates the pleasures of the detour and difference, and is complicated by the "ambivalent subject position" of the victim or underdog—the aspect of melodrama that moves us.[52] Such forms of moral authority and guilt erase the capacities of bodies that are endlessly arriving *too late*, and are never *on time*. Building on these insights about social timeliness, I consider what we might call the *pornographies of globalization*. In contrast to melodrama's endless deferral and lateness, pornography's temporality is precisely and always *on time*.[53]

Pornography's bodily pleasures refuse "not yet" narratives by investing in the sensate experience and desires of the here and now: they are a tactical exploit that holds onto difference while reaching for timeliness. Pornographic time is enmeshed with the piratical in important ways. If economic inequities mark many commodities, practices, and even public goods or rights as too expensive and too distant, this assemblage signals repertoires of action that enable a living out in the here and now. Like pornography, fakes can be experienced as being *on time*, and not as late or early, by those who use them. Ziauddin Sardar for instance, describes the political economy of the fake in Malaysia as precisely a way of being "*in*-cluded." He writes: "The fake economy, the inability to tell the real from the imitation, enables those with little money to keep themselves in the game of social presentation and fashion permutations. Slight Malay bodies clad in designer jeans, fake T-shirts, wrists adorned with fake designer watches, clutching fake designer bags and cloned mobile phones look as if they have wandered straight out of Beverly Hills for the pittance the get-up cost them. They are *in*-cluded, fashion and fancy, and not *ex*-cluded, marginalized onlookers."54 Sardar's conceptualization helps us to rework common cultural understandings of the pornographic. It draws our attention not just to modes of excess, but to lapses in the relationship between excess and normativity that emphasize social practices and embodied desires. Put otherwise, this is to focus on consumption, not production. By way of contrast, copyright producers and owners incessantly complain that piracy is a mode of circulation that is *too early*—for them, piracy is a horror story.55 It is about objects that leaked *too soon*, traveled *too far*, and possess too little regard for existing property regimes and the ideologies that sustain global modernity.

My interest here is in homologies between piracy, pornographic time, and Homi Bhabha's well-known idea of mimicry. For Bhabha, "mimicry is one of the most elusive and effective strategies of colonial power and knowledge."56 It relies on the promise of progress and the present tense, which is why it endlessly prescribes and prohibits, and, at the same time, inserts a gap between genuine and imitative modes of being that cannot be bridged. That is, the colonial subject must mimic but never attain the subject position of the colonizer. As Bhabha famously claims, it is about *"a difference that is almost the same, but not quite"* (also: *"but not white"*).57 In fact, the entire field of colonial (imperial, global, neoliberal, etc.) power that employs mimicry to both sell and stall globalization is built upon this chasm: *almost . . . but not quite.*

This is perhaps why Ackbar Abbas argues that the fake is not "capable of being politically subversive of the global order."58 For Abbas, the fake—including Sardar's postcolonial recuperation—remains a symptom of development. It is also why at the precise moment that the real and the fake become indistinguishable (e.g., digital copies, real fakes, reverse engineering, corruption), new institutional and discursive formations emerge to legislate and adjudicate between genuine and false products, practices, and worlds.

Abbas's claim that *faking* cannot be subversive, however, misses the potential force of Bhabha's critique of mimicry. This may also be why, not unlike Lessig, he ends his essay, "Faking Globalization," by calling for a turn to new cultures of design (e.g., high-value creative industries) as a way to level the social, cultural, and economic playing field.59 The move to design and create—and to move away from manufacturing for export and the tag "made in China"—is rooted, in my view, in the problematic notion that imitating more completely the global division of labor can dissolve the inequities grafted onto the fake. What makes the fake *fake*, and the real *real*, often has nothing to do with material properties or use values—and everything to do with the performative power of legitimization: "this, not that." Recall that many of the world's best-known commodities are already "made in China"—and yet somehow emerge as untainted originals. Abbas's call to more intensely imitate the protocols of cultural globalization by becoming a designer can at best merely reverse the terms in the North–South relation, for surely this mode of capitalist creativity cannot make everyone a designer: who will assemble the wares?

But commodities themselves are only part of the equation. The performance of legitimacy is a complex process that is entangled with legal regimes, state power, technocultures, branding, desire, and the like. This confusion is at the heart of Pang Laikwan's critique in *Creativity and Its Discontents*. A key example for Pang is the fake Ferrari. On the one hand, the fake Ferrari is instructive because it makes tangible concerns over divisions in production and over piracy: "the West fears China's copying power, while China is concerned that it can only copy."[60] On the other hand, it helps us to understand the relationship between real and counterfeit. Pang notes, for example, that it is difficult to give an exact price to a fake Ferrari. Should it cost more than a fake BMW? "Should it be priced according to its condition and quality (use value), or its brand image (exchange value), or its secondhand market value (surplus value)?"[61]

The answer for Pang lies in the performative nature of branding itself. What matters in this context is not any specific thing, but, as Celia Lury argues, the performativity of the brand image. Lury writes, "Brand innovation need not derive or emerge from innovation in the organization of the production process. Instead, it may be produced in the practices of simulation or behavior modeling"—that is, in consumer lifestyles.[62] Creative investments in this ecology are not realized in a finished product, but are part of a chain of desire and consumption that always leads to yet another commodity. For Pang, this performativity matters because it helps us to understand the strange relationship between brand-name products and their copies: "each carries a metonymical movement that constantly displaces itself."[63] It also recalls, as Pang notes, Michael Taussig's theorization of mimesis as a kind of commodity imperialism where consumerism replaces colonialism as a dominant force in contemporary culture.[64]

Pang's point is well taken, and her interest in the magic or performativity of real and pirated things helps us to grasp a crucial linkage between them—especially the way they remain beholden to the brand. But I want to push this performativity in another direction. Rather than focus on the thing itself, and its relation to brand performance, I want to take seriously piratical performativity in its embodied and social dimensions—as History 2s, everyday habits, human infrastructures. In terms of *Pirated Copy*, this means valuing the practices and encounters of people—and not the content of discs, discrete spectatorship, or media industries—as what matters when we talk about piracy. This is to demystify the commodity by refusing it its central position in debates about authenticity, legitimacy, and legality; by refusing, that is, the self-descriptions of the fetish. Here Bhabha's canonical critique of mimicry still has much to teach us. For Bhabha, mimicry is a *social relation* that "must continually produce its slippage, its excess, its difference" in order to be effective. As such, mimicry always alternates between "resemblance" and "menace."[65] Mimicry's effectiveness relies on its propensity for melodrama, for being perpetually out of reach. At the same time, its menace is related to the possibility that such slippages, excesses, or delays will fail. Pornographic time is a way to name that failure.

To understand this mimetic capacity we need to differentiate "automatic" or "jerk" reactions—that is, the involuntary reactions generated by watching popular genre films, like horror, melodrama, and pornography[66]—from more tactical forms of mimicry, while still taking the involuntary seriously. Mimicry, as Bhabha notes, speaks with a "tongue that is forked, not false." We can identify two tongues or forms of speech in the context of the piratical-pornographic assemblage at issue here. The first might be described as tactical or as an act of camouflage. "Of Mimicry and Man" begins with an epigraph from Jacques Lacan likening mimicry to camouflage: "it is not a question of harmonizing with the background, but against a mottled background, of becoming mottled."[67] Bhabha thus provides a rather different understanding of intersubjectivity or self and other. As he clarifies later in the essay: "What I have called mimicry is not the familiar exercise of *dependent* colonial relations through narcissistic identification so that, as Fanon has observed, the black man stops being an actional person for only the white man can represent his self-esteem. Mimicry conceals no presence or identity behind its mask. . . . The *menace* of mimicry is its *double* vision which in disclosing the ambivalence of colonial discourse also disrupts its authority."[68] Mimicry as a form of colonial/imperial power is virtual or incomplete. It animates a form of *partial presence*, but also the recognition of a limit, injustice, or disavowal within dominant discourse itself. Camouflage is using presence metonymically to defend one's own difference—of entering a mottled relation purposefully.[69] What if, in other words, the desire for the fake is not only the desire for the real, but also a conscious or tactical desire for the fake—an attempt to relocate the creativity folded into the commodity back into the creativity of the social? This desire, I argue, differs from the postmodern fascination with artifice. Instead, it demonstrates a self-consciousness and worldliness that challenges assumptions about agency and prepolitical subjects. If this desire produces pornographic subjects, it is because they become "mottled" in order survive and repurpose the conditions of their own precarity.

If the first layer of mimicry works at the level of resemblance or representation, involuntary mimicry works through reaction and repetition. Here it may be useful to recall Chakrabarty's distinction between History 1 and History 2. The first mode survives and contests authority within authoritative discourse itself: it is camouflage. Involuntary reactions and repetitions, on the other hand, fit within the second historical mode—bodily gestures, relations to the environment, social habits. Such actions are contradictory in that they exceed official frameworks or histories, but also help to make it up. It is no surprise that these involuntary actions are marked as "low" in cultural discourse, assumed to be below the threshold of taste, easily manipulated, and leaky in their corporeality. But these automatic social gestures are also menacing. This is the social obscenity or incivility that I want to recuperate. While repetition can be a form of control, it is also a reservoir for the street-level and resilient habits generated by everyday activities. These involuntary actions, a kind of muscle memory of the social, are critical to political subjectivity and urban belonging, and to how people direct materials, services, and rights toward themselves when legalities fail or render them illegitimate.

The Social Network of Hands

What AbdouMaliq Simone calls *people as infrastructure* describes the "ability of residents to engage complex combinations of objects, spaces, persons, and practices." These activities are part of reproducing life in the city and themselves become an infrastructure.[70] Here it is worth reflecting on the idea of infrastructures and their relation to people and media. The "peculiar ontology" of infrastructure, Larkin observes, relates to the fact that "they are things and also the relation between things." As such, they are both material objects that facilitate the operations of other material objects *and* systems—though we often emphasize the former.[71] This dual function suggests both how people enact forms of circulation, and how this peopled infrastructure carves out a larger social network. Larkin's overview of infrastructure studies, and its import for anthropology, glosses a wide array of such things, networks, and epistemologies—including technologies and systems building, political address and colonial/imperial affect, semiotics, aesthetics, and aisthesis.

This chapter has emphasized people and/as media infrastructure, paying particular attention to pirate sociality and contested legitimacies. Let me sharpen this discussion in relation to the social network of hands, *Pirated Copy*, and some of the chief claims of this book. First is the basic problem of how to understand the politics of pirate infrastructures, including mundane entanglements like the hand-to-hand exchange of DVDs. This is also to return to the problem of illegal subjects and to proliferating conditions of illegality that mark public culture, including citizenship and everyday forms of contact, as pirate relations. The question of media distribution, of *pirated copies*, in this context is particularly thorny: is what matters state censorship/control? massive economic/price inequity? global media industries devaluing Chinese spectators? new postnational hierarchies? the pleasures of piratical exchange? the entanglement of illicit capacities? While piracy is not often understood as self-consciously political (e.g., as organized, programmatic, a counterpublic), and while issues of curiosity, knowledge, pleasure, and joy are dismissed as rights (and thus *doubly* illicit), what matters is understanding how people and communities pushed to the margins of the social organize against their own precarity and extralegality.

This is a complex problem, not least because the actions of marginalized communities may be antiprogressive, violent, and unjust—from widow burning to ethno-nationalists to the mafia. But it would be wrong to dismiss the potentiality of everyday habits and claims—the realm of political society—simply because they are uncertain and antiteleological, just as it would be naïve only to romanticize them. But the stakes of this tension are central to how we understand culture and to how we intervene in the massive inequalities of our time. As Judith Butler puts it, this is the "question of whether the destitute are outside of politics or are in fact living out a specific form of political destitution along with specific forms of political agency and resistance."[72] This claim draws our attention to a crucial epistemological problem. Do our theoretical frames work to understand conditions of inequality, illegitimacy, and illegality—what this book terms underglobalization—or do they inadvertently contribute to the regulation of the political, guarding or disciplining its emergence?

While acknowledging the complexity this issue, I argue against the knee-jerk, and now wildly common, dismissal of cultural studies, postcolonial studies, and related fields. Versions of this critique suggest that scholars merely describe subaltern conditions in order to advance their own careers without in fact changing the underlying conditions. They are, in other words, dismissed as mere romance. But it might be truer to say that this critique has enabled a generation of scholars to retreat into their disciplines, without the burden of the political, and to comfortably answer conservative disciplinary questions as if these were the questions that mattered. This is to reiterate and extend an argument that Bhaskar Sarkar and I have made elsewhere: epistemological frames very often occlude our apprehension and analysis of actually existing practices.[73] It is these practices—how people successfully reproduce themselves in harmful and illegal states—and not dominant social imaginaries, that provide the basis for theorizing present and future social forms.

Here, Butler's reworking of Hannah Arendt's "space of appearance" is valuable. Not only does Butler offer a decidedly infrastructural approach to street politics, but her attention to bodily actions and material supports in the production of social space helps us to understand more mundane forms of assembly—that is, practices that fail to achieve the eventfulness of mass protests or large occupations, which are her focus. For Arendt, the space of appearance is "the organization of the people as it arises out of acting and speaking together, and its true space lies between people living together for this purpose, no matter where they happen to be."[74] What Butler rejects is Arendt's notion that this relational space generates its own location—as if the material or infrastructural underpinning were somehow outside the contested power relationship. This view dismisses how actions are supported and embodied. It also assumes delimited and gendered notions of public and private that foreclose the space of appearance for many. On the other hand, Butler takes up Arendt's claim that freedom and humanity are essentially relational. It makes no sense, as is the neoliberal impulse, to identify or emphasize individual dignity or freedom: to be human is to act together under conditions of equality.[75] This is what Butler takes from Arendt. What she adds to Arendt's formulation is that the space of appearance is "not only spoken or written, but is made precisely when bodies appear together"—when, that is, bodily actions bring about the space of appearance by virtue of their persistence and exposure, which itself calls into question the operations of legitimacy.[76]

This formulation helps us theorize the tension between legality and legitimacy at the heart of this study. First, we can define the condition of illegality and of pirate sociality as zones where social, economic, and political supports fall away—where the space of appearance becomes infrastructurally hard or hostile. This, in part, explains the proliferation of illegal forms, as well as the increasing significance of the politics of legitimacy (e.g., political society), to postsocialist cum neoliberal governance. Put otherwise, the creative logic

PEOPLE AS MEDIA INFRASTRUCTURE 195

inherent to neoliberalism(s) overwhelms or occupies other social and political value—only the economic remains. Subjects not able to entrepreneurialize to a point of self-care, responsibility, and profitability become illegitimate, potentially illegal. Recall the vague and expansive logic of illegality put to work by the Anti-Pornography and Anti-Piracy Office. Here the relationship between legality and legitimacy is intentionally blurred, as certain illicit acts can be comfortably recuperated (nonpornographic piracy), while others must be policed more aggressively still (pornographers are jailed or executed).

The foundational category of the piratical—the *enemy of all*—is no longer an exceptional legal state describing maritime bandits, or a third legal entity beyond states and individuals. It is now quotidian and fractal, akin to the decentered and repetitive cities that Mario Gandelsonas calls "x-urbanism," or what Abbas, riffing on the term, calls the "x-colonial": "colonialism was not where we thought it to be; and where we did not expect it, there we still found it."[77] We might similarly think of the *x-legal* as a way to make sense of the confused or *overlapping legitimacies* associated with global and imperial challenges to traditional sovereignty. Rather than recalling a particular space of withdrawal or unintelligibility—the high seas, wartime, the bandit mountain described by the term *shanzhai*—it shores up the dull, cruddy, slow violence of abandonment that is not only about the sovereign right to kill but the relational politics of "letting die."[78] Put otherwise, the *enemy of all* is now potentially all of us as life itself is remade on the imperial logic of risk and uncertainty.

Second, examining people as (media) infrastructures helps us to understand how bodily assembly and inhabitation not only distribute things, but constitute *a new distribution of the social.* In this way, the social network of hands constitutes a crucial, and crucially ignored, part of digital culture, and is also the arena where social legitimacy, by virtue of its bodily presence and daily habits, is contested and reworked—regardless of the law. It is, in other words, transformative but devalued by dominant notions of transformation. If this chapter is largely conceptual, and has not emphasized ethnographic and material "proof" for its claims, it is because we are not lacking such thick descriptions of political destitution and its hard-won, if ephemeral, agencies. More to the point: it is because the crucial problems of illegality, illegitimacy, and faking globalization already shape the frames of analysis. These frames are, of course, varied—ranging from dismissals of anticolonial thought and pedagogical global civil society discourse, to the political economic logic of creativity and the new hierarchies driving international law, including human rights—but each contributes to a breakdown in recognition and in critique. It is against such political occlusions that I offer the example of pirated copies, social infrastructures, and volatile mimicry.

What matters here is how actors make claims on cities and citizenship from positions that shift between and are often outside the domain of rights, civil society, and the law—how they direct the promises of legitimacy toward themselves. This *becoming legitimate* is what is meaningful about pirate assembly and relations. From the perspective of media infrastructures, hand-to-hand delivery creates offline "bandwidth" in order to animate media worlds where there was none. It enables access but also constitutes a larger social system whose value exceeds banal debates over access to culture, authorship, intellectual property, and similar debates.

While my focus in this chapter is on the social life of media piracy, it should also be clear that such forms are only meaningful in the context of larger illicit assemblages—from the expansive saohuang dafei campaigns to struggles over housing, health, education, water, and other supports required to make life livable. Indeed, one of my arguments is that culture—as History 2s, gestures, assembly, joy, and curiosity—needs to be resituated alongside medicine, housing, education, and related rights as "bad" illegalities. Cultural forms are tied to more properly civil society concerns, but are also crucial to how they are lived out, reimagined, and become volatile. As the larger book has explored, this includes the basic imbrication of pirate sociality and technological infrastructures within political society. These systems—people as media infrastructures—have played and continue to play a central role in distributing, disputing, and re-creatings illegal or illegitimate cities, citizens, and futures. This is also to reiterate one of the chief arguments of this book: It is the enforced imitation and implementation of developmental and legal protocols or norms, and not make-do inhabitations, that constitute the crucial problem of the fake and of underglobalization.

NOTES

Introduction: After Legitimacy

1. Numerous such stories circulated online in 2007. See a summary of the story's lifespan at Danwei.org: Jeremy Goldkorn, "Is the Fake News Story Fake News?" July 20, 2007, accessed April 1, 2011, http://www.danwei.org/media_regulation/fake_news_about_fake_news_abou.php. See also "Meat Buns with Cardboard Fillings in Beijing Is Hoax," *People's Daily*, July 19, 2007, http://en.people.cn/90001/90782/90872/6219458.html.
2. Several online forums debate the plausibility of the cardboard baozi tale. The story traveled at least as far as Japan, where bloggers tried unsuccessfully to replicate the cardboard dumplings based on the original report's recipe. A version of the story is reprinted on the EastSouthWestNorth (东南西北) blog, "Why Do People Think a Fake News Story Is Real?," accessed April 5, 2011, http://www.zonaeuropa.com/20070720_1.htm.
3. See Winnie Wong's discussion of "a draft to be copied" in *Van Gogh on Demand: China and the Readymade* (Chicago: University of Chicago Press, 2013), 17–22.
4. Josephine Ho, "ShanZhai: Economic Cultural Production through the Cracks of Globalization," plenary speech, Crossroads: 2010 Cultural Studies Conference, Hong Kong.
5. Ackbar Abbas, "Faking Globalization," in Nicholas Mirzoeff, ed., *The Visual Culture Reader*, 3rd ed. (New York: Routledge, 2013), 282–95.
6. Abbas, "Faking Globalization," 282.
7. Bhaskar Sarkar, "Postcolonial and Transnational Perspectives," in James Donald and Michael Renov, eds., *The SAGE Handbook of Film Studies* (London: SAGE, 2008), 138–41.
8. This assemblage echoes Homi Bhabha's seminal reading of colonial power as a "subject of difference that is almost the same, but not quite." Homi Bhabha, "Of Mimicry and Man: The Ambivalence of Colonial Discourse" *October* 28 (spring 1984): 126.
9. Edward S. Steinfeld, *Playing Our Game: Why China's Rise Doesn't Threaten the West* (Oxford: Oxford University Press, 2010).
10. Abbas, "Faking Globalization," 282.
11. Abbas, "Faking Globalization," 283.
12. Abbas, "Faking Globalization," 285.
13. Abbas, "Faking Globalization," 285.
14. Abbas, "Faking Globalization," 291. For example, he describes the importance of taste, per Walter Benjamin, during times when consumers are "ignorant" of how objects are actually made.

15　Gregory F. Treverton et al., *Film Piracy, Organized Crime, and Terrorism* (Santa Monica, CA: RAND Corporation, 2009).
16　Abbas, "Faking Globalization," 291.
17　Abbas, "Faking Globalization," 293.
18　Abbas, "Faking Globalization," 293.
19　Abbas, "Faking Globalization," 294–95. That these gestures are both undeveloped and seem to fit comfortably with the global order suggests the severe limits of the design ethos—one that is eerily familiar of the claims of neoliberal innovation industries themselves.
20　Abbas, "Faking Globalization," 295.
21　Bhaskar Sarkar and I develop this epistemic logic as "penumbral" in the introduction to *Asian Video Cultures: In the Penumbra of the Global* (Durham, NC: Duke University Press, 2017), 2, 5–6.
22　Eric Hobsbawm, *Primitive Rebels: Studies in Archaic Forms of Social Movement in the Nineteenth and Twentieth Centuries* (London: W. W. Norton, 1965). For work on counterpublics, see Michael Warner, *Publics and Counterpublics* (Brooklyn, NY: Zone, 2002).
23　Joe Karaganis, ed., *Media Piracy in Emerging Economies* (New York: Social Science Research Council, 2011), i, http://piracy.ssrc.org.
24　Ravi Sundaram, *Pirate Modernity: Delhi's Media Urbanism* (New York: Routledge, 2010), 13.
25　Pang Laikwan, "'China Who Makes and Fakes': A Semiotics of the Counterfeit," *Theory, Culture and Society* 25, no. 6 (2008): 131–32.
26　Three decades of critiques against cultural studies, for instance, have led to a knee-jerk response to engagements with antagonism and resistance. While there is much to be vigilant about, and critical of, in academic work, these critiques very often sustain the business-as-usual conservatism that allows disciplines to motor along. In other words, critiques of work in the resistance genre have failed to produce alternatives. It's as if the critique itself, for many scholars, is the point.
27　Here it is worth remembering that one of the best-known arguments about the creative economy in China directly links the innovation industries to national security. See, for example, Hu Huilin's *The Development of Cultural Industries and National Cultural Security* [Wenhua chanye fazhan yu guojia wenhua anquan] (Guangdong: Guangzhou renmin chubanshe, 2005).
28　Lawrence Liang interviews in *Steal This Film II* (League of Noble Peers, 2007). The abridged interview with Liang, "Piracy and Production," can be viewed at https://www.youtube.com/watch?v=7p0xanXV3u4. *Steal this Film II* can be downloaded at http://www.stealthisfilm.com/Part1/.
29　Neferti X. M. Tadiar, "Life-Times of Disposability within Neoliberalism," *Social Text* 115 (summer 2013): 22.
30　Lawrence Liang, "Piracy, Creativity, and Infrastructure: Rethinking Access to Culture," *Alternative Law Forum*, July 2009, 15, https://papers.ssrn.com/sol3/papers.cfm?abstract_id=1436229.

31 I thank Bhaskar Sarkar for his long-standing engagement with this project and his suggestion to think about piracy in this way. This understanding of piracy as illegal but socially legitimate is also developed in Sarkar's forthcoming work on the pirate humanities.
32 Ho, "ShanZhai."
33 See IDEO's collective intelligence report: Makiko Taniguchi and Eddie Wu, "Shanzhai: Copycat Design as an Open Platform for Innovation," *Patterns*, 2009, patterns.ideo.com.
34 Daniel Heller-Roazen, *The Enemy of All: Piracy and the Law of Nations* (New York: Zone, 2009), 10–11.
35 Deborah Cowen, *The Deadly Life of Logistics* (Minneapolis: University of Minnesota Press, 2014), 137.
36 Heller-Roazen, *The Enemy of All*, 11.
37 This legal imagination has led numerous commentators in academic and popular contexts, including periodicals like *Legal Affairs*, *Foreign Affairs*, and the *Wall Street Journal*, to speculate that the category of piracy holds the key to unlocking the global scourge of terrorism. One such article, entitled "The Dread Pirate bin Laden," argues that piracy provides the legal precedent through which terrorism can be criminalized. See, for instance, Douglas R. Burgess Jr., "The Dread Pirate bin Laden," *Legal Affairs*, July/August 2005, http://www.legalaffairs.org/issues/July-August-2005/feature_burgess_julaug05.msp. See also Bhaskar Sarkar, "Media Piracy and the Terrorist Boogeyman: Speculative Potentiations," *positions* 24, no. 2 (May 2016): 343–68.
38 Heller-Roazen, *The Enemy of All*, 11.
39 Walter Rodney, *How Europe Underdeveloped Africa* (Washington, DC: Howard University Press, [1972] 1982).
40 Carl Schmitt, *Political Theology: Four Chapters on the Concept of Sovereignty*, translated by G. Schwab (Chicago: University of Chicago Press, 2005).
41 Achille Mbembe, "Necropolitics," translated by Libby Meintjes, *Public Culture* 15, no. 1 (2003): 27.
42 Schmitt, *Political Theology*, 33–34.
43 Elizabeth Povinelli, *Economies of Abandonment: Social Belonging and Endurance in Late Liberalism* (Durham, NC: Duke University Press, 2011), 3–4.
44 Partha Chatterjee, *The Politics of the Governed: Reflections on Popular Politics in Much of the World* (New York: Columbia University Press, 2004).
45 Peter Drahos and John Braithwaite, *Information Feudalism: Who Owns the Knowledge Economy?* (London: Earthscan, 2002).
46 See, for example, Ramon Lobato and Julian Thomas, *The Informal Media Economy* (Cambridge: Polity, 2015); Alejandro Portes, Manuel Castells, and Lauren A. Benton, eds., *The Informal Economy: Studies in Advanced and Less Developed Countries* (Baltimore: Johns Hopkins University Press, 1989).
47 Shujen Wang, "Harmony or Discord? TRIPS, China, and Overlapping Sovereignties," in *Sarai Reader 2005: Bare Acts* (Delhi: Sarai Media Lab, 2005), 190.

48 Wang, "Harmony or Discord?," 194.
49 Richard Falk, Mark Juergensmeyer, and Vesselin Popovski, eds., *Legality and Legitimacy in Global Affairs* (Oxford: Oxford University Press, 2012), vii.
50 For example, Falk et al., in *Legality and Legitimacy in Global Affairs*, give the example of Kosovo as a humanitarian intervention that was deemed legitimate but was not legally sanctioned (vii).
51 Falk et al., *Legality and Legitimacy in Global Affairs*, 21.
52 Vandana Shiva, *Protect or Plunder: Understanding Intellectual Property Rights* (London: Zed, 2001), 49.
53 Shiva, *Protect or Plunder*, 62.
54 Heller-Roazen, *The Enemy of All*, 61–68. See also Neves and Sarkar, *Asian Video Cultures*, 14.
55 I develop this further in chapter 2, but see especially Partha Chatterjee, "Democracy and Economic Transformation in India," *Economic and Political Weekly*, April 19, 2008, 53–62.
56 Chen Kuan-hsing, *Asia as Method: Toward Deimperialization* (Durham, NC: Duke University Press, 2010). See chapter 5, 211–56.
57 Jürgen Habermas, *The Structural Transformation of the Public Sphere: An Inquiry into a Category of Bourgeois Society* (Cambridge, MA: MIT Press, 1989).
58 Philip C. C. Huang, "Symposium: 'Public Sphere'/'Civil Society' in China?" *Modern China* 19, no. 2 (1993). Other engagements with the public sphere in post-Tiananmen China include Craig Calhoun, *Neither Gods nor Emperors: Students and the Struggle for Democracy in China* (Berkeley: University of California Press, 1997); Stephanie Hemelryk Donald, *Public Secrets, Public Spaces: Cinema and Civility in China* (Lanham, MD: Rowman and Littlefield, 2000).
59 Philip C. C. Huang, "'Public Sphere'/'Civil Society' in China? The Third Realm between State and Society," *Modern China* 19, no. 2 (1993): 216.
60 Nancy Fraser, "Rethinking the Public Sphere: A Contribution to the Critique of Actually Existing Democracy," *Social Text* 25/26 (1990): 56–80.
61 See, for instance, Lauren Berlant, *The Queen of America Goes to Washington City: Essays on Sex and Citizenship* (Durham, NC: Duke University Press, 1997); Warner, *Publics and Counterpublics*.
62 Such invocations of civil society remain common in important recent works. See Guobin Yang, *The Power of the Internet in China* (New York: Columbia University Press, 2009); Robin Visser, *Cities Surround the Countryside: Urban Aesthetics in Postsocialist China* (Durham, NC: Duke University Press, 2010).
63 Nivedita Menon, "Introduction," in Partha Chatterjee, *Empire and Nation: Selected Essays* (New York: Columbia University Press, 2010), 8.
64 Chatterjee, *The Politics of the Governed*.
65 Xi Chen, *Social Protests and Contentious Authoritarianism in China* (Cambridge: Cambridge University Press, 2012), 5.
66 Xi Chen, *Social Protests*, 6.
67 Sundaram, *Pirate Modernity*, 21.

68 Sundaram, *Pirate Modernity*, xiv, 3.
69 Chen Kuan-hsing, *Asia as Method*, 239–40.
70 Chen Kuan-hsing, *Asia as Method*, 212.
71 Partha Chattteree, interviewed by Rudrangshu Mukherjee, *Sephis e-Magazine* 1, no. 1 (2004).
72 As, for example, in Samuel P. Huntington's influential essay "The Clash of Civilizations?" *Foreign Affairs* (summer 1993): 22–49.
73 Lawrence Lessig, *Free Culture: How Big Media Uses Technology and the Law to Lock Down Culture and Control Creativity* (New York: Penguin, 2004), 63.
74 While this may seem like an obvious critique of neoliberalism, the widespread adoption and celebration of the creative industries and what scholars like Koichi Iwabuchi have called "brand nationalism" suggests a different story. Universities, in particular, are among the most eager to support the "creative turn," seeking out ways to instrumentalize, measure, and monetize humanities and social science research.
75 Pang Laikwan, "'China Who Makes and Fakes,'" 119.
76 See, for instance, Chris Berry, *Postsocialist Cinema in Post-Mao China: The Cultural Revolution after the Cultural Revolution* (New York: Routledge, 2004); Dai Jinhua, *Cinema and Desire: Feminist Marxism and Cultural Politics in the Work of Dai Jinhua* (London: Verso, 2002); Arif Dirlik and Zhang Xudong, eds., *Postmodernism and China* (Durham, NC: Duke University Press, 2000); Sheldon Lu, *Chinese Modernity and Global Biopolitics: Studies in Literature and Visual Culture* (Honolulu: University of Hawai'i Press, 2007); Tang Xiaobing, *Chinese Modern: The Heroic and the Quotidian* (Durham, NC: Duke University Press, 2000); Visser, *Cities Surround the Countryside*; Wang Hui, *China's New Order: Society, Politics, and Economy in Transition* (Cambridge, MA: Harvard University Press, 2003).
77 Zhang Xudong, *Postsocialism and Cultural Politics: China in the Last Decade of the Twentieth Century* (Durham, NC: Duke University Press, 2008), 13.
78 Jason McGrath, *Postsocialist Modernity: Chinese Cinema, Literature, and Criticism in the Market Age* (Stanford, CA: Stanford University Press, 2010).
79 Arif Dirlik, "Postsocialism? Reflections on Socialism with Chinese Characteristics," in Arif Dirlik and Maurice Meisner, eds., *Marxism and the Chinese Experience: Issues in Contemporary Chinese Socialism* (Armonk, NY: M. E. Sharpe, 1989), 361–84.
80 Dirlik, "Postsocialism?," 364.
81 See, for example, Carrie Gracie, "China's Xi Jinping Consolidates Power with New Ideology," *BBC News*, October 20, 2017, http://www.bbc.com/news/world-asia-china-41677062.
82 Ralph Litzinger, "Theorizing Postsocialism: Reflections on the Politics of Marginality in Contemporary China," *South Atlantic Quarterly* 101, no. 1 (winter 2002): 36.
83 It recalls, among other examples, the Ten Great Buildings (*shi da jianzhu* 十大建筑) erected by 1959 to commemorate the founding of the PRC ten years prior. Much of the reconstruction was completed in less than one year as part of the Great Leap

Forward's urban initiatives. The project is often invoked as a comparison to understand the speed and scale of demolition and construction in the Olympic era.

84 Michael Curtin, "Media Capital: Toward the Study of Spatial Flows," *International Journal of Cultural Studies* 6, no. 2 (2003): 202–28.

85 In 2009–11, I collaborated with JP Sniadecki on a series of interviews with key voices in the Chinese independent film scene. Interviews recorded include Cui Zi'en, Zhu Rikun, Wang Wo, Xu Tong, Wang Hongwei, among others. Also with JP Sniadecki, I produced the 2014 documentary *The Iron Ministry*. Over the course of three summers, I spent more than 100 hours riding trains across China, and I observed much about contemporary media and migration that informs this research. The film opened at Locarno International Film Festival and has screened at major festivals, museums, and universities around the world: https://www.theironministry.com/.

86 Much of the photographic research was undertaken with the photographer Graham Bury. Over the course of seven months in 2007–8, we walked the streets of Beijing in a neighborhood-by-neighborhood fashion and documented a wide range of street-level media: construction-site billboards, public television sets, advertisements, and large-format displays. Graham passed away during the writing of this book, and the images included in this book are in his memory.

87 Povinelli, *Economies of Abandonment*, x.

Chapter 1: Rendering the City

Epigraphs: Partha Chatterjee interview by Rudrangshu Mukherjee, *Sephis e-Magazine* 1, no. 1 (2004). Denis Wood, *Rethinking the Power of Maps* (New York: Guilford Press, 2010), 1.

1 As David Harvey argues, creative destruction is crucial to the redistribution of capital toward economic elites in the latter part of the twentieth century. While his chief example is the destruction of North Atlantic welfare states, postsocialist creative destruction is also crucial to this larger process and to new forms of common sense. See, for example, "Neoliberalism as Creative Destruction," *Annals of the American Academy of Social Science* 610 (March 2007): 22–44.

2 Ravi Sundaram, *Pirate Modernity: Delhi's Media Urbanism* (New York: Routledge, 2010).

3 There are notable exceptions, including Yomi Braester's *Painting the City Red* (Durham, NC: Duke University Press, 2010). Braester's central innovation, however, is to trace how cinema and theater participated alongside official planning culture—often by promoting ideas of urban change in films or plays before demolition and reconstruction began. As such, his important study gives less attention to how urban planning constitutes its own forms of visual culture beyond its entanglements with cinema and the high arts.

4 I draw on William Mazzarella's distinction between *media* as a material framework that "makes society imaginable and intelligible to itself in the form of external representations," and *mediation* as "processes by which a given social dispensa-

tion produces and reproduces itself in and through a particular set of media." See "Culture, Globalization, Mediation," *Annual Review of Anthropology* 33 (2004): 326.

5 Arjun Appadurai, "The Capacity to Aspire: Culture and the Terms of Recognition," in Vijayendra Rao and Michael Walton, eds., *Culture and Public Action* (Stanford, CA: Stanford University Press), 59–64.

6 Ann Anagnost, *National Past-Times: Narrative, Representation, and Power in Modern China* (Durham, NC: Duke University Press, 1997), 75–98.

7 Collaborative research undertaken with photographer Graham Bury in Beijing in 2007–8.

8 So-called ghost cities are an excessively documented aspect of China's urban growth and speculation. They are a crucial example of the strangeness of peopleless cities built from images that precede social worlds. See, for example, Wade Shepard, "The Future of China's 'Ghost Cities,'" *China Daily* (European edition), June 24, 2016, http://europe.chinadaily.com.cn/epaper/2015-07/03/content_21169332.htm.

9 Joseph Schumpeter, *Capitalism, Socialism, Democracy*, 3rd ed. (New York: Harper and Brothers, 1950), 83.

10 Brian Larkin, "The Politics and Poetics of Infrastructure," *Annual Review of Anthropology* 42 (2013): 327–43. Larkin makes explicit not just the materiality of infrastructure but its aesthetic and poetic qualities, and the related links to the felt experience of modernity: "Many infrastructure projects are copies funded and constructed so that cities or nations can take part in a contemporary modernity by repeating infrastructure projects from elsewhere to participate in a common visual and conceptual paradigm of what it means to be modern" (333).

11 Harvey, "Neoliberalism as Creative Destruction," 23.

12 Lin Chun, *The Transformation of Chinese Socialism* (Durham, NC: Duke University Press, 2006), 2–3.

13 Lin Chun, *The Transformation of Chinese Socialism*, 12.

14 Bishnupriya Ghosh, "The Security Aesthetic in Bollywood's High-Rise Horror," *Representations* 126, no. 1 (spring 2014): 62.

15 Ghosh, "The Security Aesthetic," 62–63.

16 Jacques Derrida, *Spectres of Marx: The State of Debt, the Work of Mourning and the New International* (New York: Routledge, 1994), 63, 201.

17 Ernesto Laclau, "Time Is Out of Joint," *Diacritics* 25, no. 2 (summer 1995): 85–96.

18 Derrida, *Spectres of Marx*, 19–20; See also Laclau, "Time Is Out of Joint," 85–87. Laclau sees "undecidability" as crucial to deconstruction and to the ethical consequences of *Spectres of Marx*. Its role is "to reactivate the moment of decision that underlies any sedimented set of social relations," and thus to enlarge the scope of decision and responsibility (93).

19 Ghosh, "The Security Aesthetic," 60.

20 Ghosh, "The Security Aesthetic," 62. As Ghosh puts it: "Activating a spectrum of perceptions (optical, tactile, kinesthetic, gravitational) . . . at a decided remove from the immediate environs, is particular to twenty-first-century

security technologies." It is this "decided remove" that Ghosh describes as *postphenomenological* in her analysis of high-rise horror films.

21 Robin Visser, "Introduction," in *Cities Surround the Countryside: Urban Aesthetics in Postsocialist China* (Durham, NC: Duke University Press, 2010).

22 Wang Dehua, *Zhongguo chengshi guihua shigang* [An Outline of Chinese Urban Planning] (Nanjing: Dongnan University Press, 2005), 195–216; Zhang Zhen, "Introduction: Bearing Witness: Chinese Urban Cinema in the Era of 'Transformation,'" in Zhang Zhen, ed., *The Urban Generation: Chinese Cinema and Society at the Turn of the Twenty-first Century* (Durham, NC: Duke University Press, 2007), 5.

23 Wu Hung, "Internalizing Changes: Contemporary Chinese Art and Urban Transformation," presentation for the Geske Lectures, Hixson-Lied College of Fine and Performing Arts, Lincoln, Nebraska, February 12, 2009, 7.

24 About weigai, see Daniel Abramson, "The Aesthetics of City-Scale Preservation Policy in Beijing," *Planning Perspectives* 22 (April 2007): 130; Braester, *Painting the City Red*, 110–12. For figures regarding old housing destruction, relocation of residents, new investments in infrastructure, and the like, see Shrawan Kumar Acharya, "Urban Development in Post-Reform China: Insights from Beijing," *Norsk Geografisk Tidsskrift—Norwegian Journal of Geography* 59, no. 3 (2005): 232–33.

25 Abramson, "The Aesthetics of City-Scale Preservation Policy in Beijing," 151.

26 Wu Hung, "Ruins, Fragments, and the Chinese Modern and Postmodern," in *Making History: Wu Hung on Contemporary Art* (Hong Kong: Time Zone 8, 2008), 3–10.

27 Wu Hung, "Ruins, Fragments, and the Chinese Modern and Postmodern," 4.

28 See, for instance, Michael Berry, *A History of Pain: Trauma in Modern Chinese Literature and Film* (New York: Columbia University Press, 2008), 255; also, chapter 6 in Yomi Braester, *Witness against History: Literature, Film, and Public Discourse in Twentieth-Century China* (Stanford, CA: Stanford University Press, 2003).

29 Wu Hung, "Internalizing Changes," 7–8.

30 See Lu Xinyu, *Jilu zhongguo: Dangdai Zhongguo xin jilu yundong* [Documenting China: The New Documentary Movement in China] (Beijing: Sanlian Shudian, 2003), as well as Braester, *Painting the City Red*; Visser, *Cities Surround the Countryside*; Wu Hung, *Remaking Beijing: Tiananmen Square and the Creation of a Political Space* (Chicago: University of Chicago Press, 2005); Zhang Zhen, ed., *The Urban Generation: Chinese Cinema and Society at the Turn of the Twenty-First Century* (Durham, NC: Duke University Press, 2007).

31 Sheldon Lu, "Tear Down the City: Reconstructing Urban Space in Contemporary Chinese Popular Cinema and Avant-Garde Art," in Zhang Zhan, ed., *The Urban Generation: Chinese Cinema and Society at the Turn of the Twenty-First Century* (Durham, NC: Duke University Press, 2007), 138.

32 Lu Xinyu, "Rethinking China's New Documentary Movement: Engagement with the Social," in Chris Berry, Lu Xinyu, and Lisa Rofel, eds., *The New Chinese Documentary Film Movement: For the Public Record* (Hong Kong: Hong Kong University Press, 2011), 16–17.

33 See Chris Berry et al., "Introduction," in *The New Chinese Documentary Film Movement*, 5–6; Braester, *Painting the City Red*, 226–27; Zhang Zhen, "Introduction," in *The Urban Generation*, 19–20.
34 Zhang Zhen, *The Urban Generation*, 3.
35 Braester, *Painting the City Red*, 226.
36 See Wu Hung, *Wu Hung on Contemporary Chinese Artists* (Beijing: Time Zone 8, 2009). Also, Wu Hung, *Transcience: Chinese Experimental Art at the End of the Twentieth Century* (Chicago: David and Alfred Smart Museum of Art, 1999).
37 Wu Hung, *Transcience*, 117.
38 See, for instance, Henry Siling Li, "The Turn to Self: From 'Big Character Posters' to YouTube Videos," *Chinese Journal of Communication* 2, no. 1 (March 2009): 50–60.
39 Wu Hung, *Wu Hung on Contemporary Chinese Artists*, 51–53.
40 Wu Hung, *Wu Hung on Contemporary Chinese Artists*, 48.
41 Dilip Parameshwar Gaonkar, "Toward New Imaginaries: An Introduction," *Public Culture* 14, no. 1 (2002): 4. Additionally, see Cornelius Castoriadis, *The Imaginary Institution of Society*, translated by Kathleen Blamey (Cambridge, MA: MIT Press, 1987); Charles Taylor, *Modern Social Imaginaries* (Durham, NC: Duke University Press, 2004).
42 Gaonkar, "Toward New Imaginaries," 1–9.
43 Wood, *Rethinking the Power of Maps*, 8.
44 Wood, *Rethinking the Power of Maps*, 53.
45 See, for instance, the websites for the Beijing 2008 Olympics, http://en.beijing2008.cn/, and Beijing Commission of Urban Planning, http://www.bjghw.gov.cn/web/static/catalogs/catalog_itl/itl.html, as well as periodicals like *Urban China* (*Chengshi Zhongguo*), http://www.urbanchina.com.cn/.
46 See the Planning and Exhibition Halls website, http://www.bjghzl.com.cn/.
47 Abramson, "The Aesthetics of City-Scale Preservation Policy in Beijing," 144–51.
48 Translation with Weixian Pan. See figure 1.11 for original Chinese text. Photo taken in summer 2011.
49 Anne-Marie Broudehoux, *The Making and Selling of Post-Mao Beijing* (New York: Routledge, 2004). See especially chapters 2 and 3.
50 AbdouMaliq Simone, *For the City Yet to Come: Changing African Life in Four Cities* (Durham, NC: Duke University Press, 2004), 7; my emphasis.
51 Simone, *For the City Yet to Come*, 3.
52 Ariella Azoulay, *The Civil Contract of Photography* (New York: Zone, 2008), 12. I am sensitive to the analogy being drawn here. My suggestion is not that China is colonizing itself—though the massive occupation and concentration camps in Xinjiang requires more analysis in this context—rather, I want to examine the multiscalar forms of imperialism animating radical growth and targeted at the most precarious populations.
53 Azoulay, *The Civil Contract of Photography*, 13–14.
54 Azoulay, *The Civil Contract of Photography*, 14.
55 Azoulay, *The Civil Contract of Photography*, 16–17.

56 Azoulay, *The Civil Contract of Photography*, 17.
57 Azoulay, *The Civil Contract of Photography*, 19.
58 Azoulay, *The Civil Contract of Photography*, 19.
59 Partha Chatterjee, *Lineages of Political Society: Studies in Postcolonial Democracy* (New York: Columbia University Press, 2011).
60 Partha Chatterjee, *The Politics of the Governed: Reflections on Popular Politics in Most of the World* (New York: Columbia University Press, 2004). See especially chapter 3, 53–80.
61 Here I draw on Elizabeth Povinelli's focus on the nature of politics in the context of "dispersed suffering" in *Economies of Abandonment: Social Belonging and Endurance in Late Liberalism* (Durham, NC: Duke University Press, 2011). See "Introduction," especially pages 1–6.
62 Azoulay, *The Civil Contract of Photography*, 17–18.

Chapter 2: Digital Urbanism

Epigraph: Charter 08 was released on December 10, 2008, the anniversary of the Universal Declaration of Human Rights, and signed by three hundred prominent Chinese citizens (and thousands more in subsequent years). It was written in direct homage to Czechoslovakia's Charter 77, serving as a foundational and controversial critique of China's political development in the Olympic era. Several of the signatories were arrested, including Liu Xiaobo. The epigraph continues: "The stultifying results are endemic official corruption, an undermining of the rule of law, weak human rights, decay in public ethics, crony capitalism, growing inequality between the wealthy and the poor, pillage of the natural environment as well as of the human and historical environments, and the exacerbation of a long list of social conflicts, especially, in recent times, a sharpening animosity between officials and ordinary people." See Perry Link's translation, "China's Charter 08," in the *New York Review of Books*, January 15, 2009, https://www.nybooks.com/articles/2009/01/15/chinas-charter-08/.

1 The Chongqing "nail house" was reported in major newspapers in China and throughout the world, even garnering a Wikipedia entry. In April 2007, the *China Daily* recounted the dispute, including its demolition, "'Nail House, in Chongqing Demolished," http://www.chinadaily.com.cn/china/2007-04/03/content_842221.htm.
2 Tania Branigan, "China Embraces Webgame Depicting Family's Fight with Demolition Crew," *The Guardian*, September 16, 2010, http://www.guardian.co.uk/world/2010/sep/16/china-game-family-fight-demolition; you can play the game online at http://www.yx8.cn/11/12697.html.
3 Ravi Sundaram, *Pirate Modernity: Delhi's Media Urbanism* (New York: Routledge, 2010). Digital urbanism is in part a response to the fact that many of the phenomena I engage in my research—billboards, hand-painted signs, low-fi video cultures, sidewalk television, hand-to-hand piracy, and so on—do not figure in imaginations of the digital present. Rather, they tend to be described through

the language of failure and delay, and are marked by a lack of creativity. This is to say that a particular repertoire of artifacts and actions have come to overdetermine the digital. These idealized high-bandwidth networks and high-resolution practices, ensconced in northern metropolitan centers, leave out much of what constitutes technomodernity in China and throughout the world. For more on this discussion, see Joshua Neves and Bhaskar Sarkar, "Introduction," in *Asian Video Cultures: In the Penumbra of the Global* (Durham, NC: Duke University Press, 2017).

4   Sundaram, *Pirate Modernity*, xiv.
5   Chris Berry, "Shanghai Television's Documentary Channel: Chinese Television as Public Space," in Zhu Ying and Chris Berry, eds., *TV China* (Bloomington: Indiana University Press, 2009), 72.
6   Chen Kuan-hsing, *Asia as Method: Toward Deimperialization* (Durham, NC: Duke University Press, 2010), 223.
7   Nancy Fraser, "Rethinking the Public Sphere: A Contribution to the Critique of Actually Existing Democracy," *Social Text* 25/26 (1990): 56–80.
8   Chen Kuan-hsing, *Asia as Method*, 224–30.
9   See Nivedita Menon's "Introduction" to Partha Chatterjee's *Empire and Nation: Selected Essays* (New York: Columbia University Press, 2010), 8. See also Partha Chatterjee, *The Politics of the Governed: Reflections on Popular Politics in Most of the World* (New York: Columbia University Press, 2004).
10 Sundaram, *Pirate Modernity*, 21.
11 Sundaram, *Pirate Modernity*, 22.
12 See, for instance, David Meyer and Sidney Tarrow, eds., *The Social Movement Society: Contentious Politics for a New Century* (Lanham, MD: Rowman and Littlefield, 1998).
13 A recent article in *Jacobin*, for example, charts this tenuous politics of workers' strikes, which are at once illegal and proliferating. See Hao Ren, Zhongjin Li, and Eli Friedman, "The Life and Resistance of a Chinese Worker," *Jacobin*, July 15, 2016, https://www.jacobinmag.com/2016/07/china-strikes-workers-factories-friedman-unions/.
14 Sundaram, *Pirate Modernity*, 23.
15 Sundaram, *Pirate Modernity*, 22–23.
16 I say *increasingly* to reference concrete changes in political reason and expectations, where, for example, market logics consolidate new modes of sociality marked by entrepreneurialism and abandonment, privilege and precarity. But, of course, for many people—even those residing at the heart of the metropole—the promises of democratic modernity were always already false or threatening.
17 Partha Chatterjee, "Democracy and Economic Transformation in India," *Economic and Political Weekly*, April 19, 2008, 57.
18 Chatterjee, "Democracy and Economic Transformation in India," 53. For example, Chatterjee argues that the economic trajectory of Asia "has diverged radically from that of most African countries."

19 Xi Chen, *Social Protest and Contentious Authoritarianism in China* (Cambridge: Cambridge University Press, 2012), 3–26.

20 Xi Chen, *Social Protest and Contentious Authoritarianism*, 27. Similarly, a 2011 article in the *Wall Street Journal* reports that 180,000 such incidents took in place in 2010. See Tom Orlik, "Unrest Grows as Economy Booms," *Wall Street Journal*, September 26, 2011, https://www.wsj.com/articles/SB10001424053111903703604576587070600504108.

21 Hao Ren et al., "The Life and Resistance of a Chinese Worker."

22 Hao Ren et al., "The Life and Resistance of a Chinese Worker," 5.

23 The sociologist Ho-fung Hung makes a similar argument, describing the state's "image as a benevolent Leviathan." He continues: the state "has done these things not because workers have demanded them, but because it cares about 'weak and disadvantaged groups' (as workers are referred to in the official lexicon)." Hung's benevolent Leviathan reiterates the claim that state legitimacy is increasingly tied to a moral and extralegal imperative to ameliorate (some of) the effects of dispossession for precarious people. That this sphere of amelioration or "care" has been largely relocated to informal negotiations and the terrain of political society—and not, that is, the space of proper citizens and the civil contracts promised by idealizations of modernity—marks a considerable conceptual turn. See Ho-fung Hung, "China Fantasies," *Jacobin*, December 10, 2015, https://www.jacobinmag.com/2015/12/china-new-global-order-imperialism-communist-party-globalization. At the same time, this system of paternalistic accommodation also suggests clear limits. The Wukan protests over corruption, land grabs, violent detentions, and deaths, among many other grievances, demonstrate both the process by which the state attempts to absorb unrest and the implicit and explicit forms of repression employed when volatility crosses a certain threshold. See, for example, Lynn Lee, "Wukan: The End of a Democratic Uprising in China," *Al Jazeera*, June 10, 2017, https://www.aljazeera.com/indepth/features/2017/05/wukan-democratic-uprising-china-170531091411268.html.

24 Nikhil Anand, *Hydraulic Citizenship: Water and the Infrastructures of Citizenship in Mumbai* (Durham, NC: Duke University Press, 2017).

25 Nikhil Anand, "Pressure: The PoliTechnics of Water Supply in Mumbai," *Cultural Anthropology* 26, no. 4 (2011): 543.

26 Anand, "Pressure," 545.

27 Examples include Feng Yan's *Bing'ai* (2007), Ou Ning and Cao Fei's *San Yuan Li* (2003), Li Yifan and Yan Yu's *Before the Flood* (2005), Wang Bing's *West of the Tracks* (2003), Zhao Dayong's *Street Life* (2006), Zhao Liang's *Petition* (2006), Shu Haolun's *Nostalgia* (2006), and Cui Zi'en's *We are the . . . of Communism* (2007), among many others.

28 See, for example, Andrew Jacobs, "A Stabbing Rooted in Loss and Despair," *New York Times*, August 10, 2008, https://www.nytimes.com/2008/08/11/sports/olympics/11beijing.html?em=&pagewanted=print; also, Anne-Marie Broudehoux, "Seeds of Dissent: The Politics of Resistance to Beijing's Redevelopment," in Melissa

Butcher and Selvaraj Velayutham, eds., *Dissent and Cultural Resistance in Asian Cities* (New York: Routledge, 2009), 14–32.

29 James Pomfret, "Hopes for Democracy Crushed in the Chinese Rebel Village of Wukan," *Hong Kong Free Press,* July 3, 2016, https://www.hongkongfp.com/2016/07/03/hopes-for-democracy-crushed-in-the-chinese-rebel-village-of-wukan/. Also, Josh Rudolf, "Protesters Condemn Beijing Migrant Crackdown," *China Digital Times,* December 11, 2017, https://chinadigitaltimes.net/2017/12/protesters-condemn-beijing-migrant-crackdown/.

30 AbdouMaliq Simone, *For the City Yet to Come: Changing African Life in Four Cities* (Durham, NC: Duke University Press, 2004), 7.

31 Niu Yuru's reputation was cemented by Hu Jintao in a speech entitled "Renmin xuyao Niu Yuru zheyang de tiexin ren" [Our people need more approachable leaders like Niu Yuru]. Cited in Colin S. C. Hawes, *The Chinese Transformation of Corporate Culture* (New York: Routledge, 2012), 146.

32 See news item July 15, 2008, on the Dazhalan project site: http://www.dazhalan-project.org/news-en/news-en.htm (accessed April 15, 2012). (Note: the Dazhalan project website is no longer operational. Limited documentation of the original website is available through the Wayback Machine, https://web.archive.org/web/20150723051440/http://www.dazhalan-project.org/news-en/news-en.htm.)

33 For further discussion of this and similar forms of "alternative" media, see Chris Berry and Lisa Rofel, "Alternative Archive: China's Independent Documentary Culture," in Chris Berry, Lu Xinyu, and Lisa Rofel, eds., *The New Chinese Documentary Movement: For the Public Record* (Hong Kong: Hong Kong University Press, 2010), 135–54.

34 Began in 2005, the Dazhalan project grew out of the collaborative documentary *Meishi Street*. The project website (www.dazhalan-project.org), which was no longer active in 2017, brought together a wide range of research and dissemination initiatives related to area demolition. Traces of the site can be accessed via the Internet Archive's Wayback Machine. For example, the June 15, 2006, capture can be accessed here: https://web.archive.org/web/20060407080453/http://www.dazhalan-project.org/news-cn/news-cn.htm.

35 I use *dissensus* to mean both widespread dissent—and thus a kind of consensus among those acting from positions beyond rights, norms, and laws—as well as, following Rancière, a fracture or "gap of the sensible itself" that is crucial to political action. As Rancière puts it: "The essence of politics is *dissensus*. Dissensus is not a confrontation between interests or opinions. It is the demonstration (manifestation) of a gap in the sensible itself." Jacques Rancière, *Dissensus: On Politics and Aesthetics* (New York: Continuum, 2010), 38.

36 Yomi Braester, *Painting the City Red: Chinese Cinema and the Urban Contract* (Durham, NC: Duke University Press, 2010), 22.

37 Cited in Thomas Lamarre, "Regional TV: Affective Media Geographies," *Asiascape: Digital Asia* 2 (2015): 94. For the original discussion, see Gilles Deleuze and Félix

Guattari, *Anti-Oedipus: Capitalism and Schizophrenia* (Minneapolis: University of Minnesota Press, 1983), 4.

38 Raymond Williams, *Television: Technology and Cultural Form* (London: Routledge, 2003), 18–19. "It is not only that the supply of broadcasting facilities preceded demand; it is that the means of communication preceded their content."

39 Lamarre, "Regional TV," 94.

40 Rancière, *Dissensus*, 38, 50.

41 Phone interview with a project manager at Beijing Urban Construction Fifth Construction Engineering Co. Ltd., June 24, 2008.

42 Yomi Braester, "Chinese Cinema in the Age of Advertisement: The Filmmaker as Cultural Broker," *China Quarterly* 183 (2005): 562.

43 Melinda Liu, "Restrain the Riffraff: Beijing's Rising-Star Mayor Clamps Down on Public Displays of Excess ahead of the 2008 Olympics," *Newsweek*, October 2, 2007, www.newsweek.com/2007/10/02/restrain-the-riffraff.html.

44 Jason Leow, "Beijing Mystery: What's Happening to the Billboards?" *Wall Street Journal*, June 25, 2007, A-1.

45 RAQs Media Collective, "X Notes on Practice: Stubborn Structures and Insistent Seepage in a Networked World," 2004, https://www.raqsmediacollective.net/images/pdf/e687564d-4109-49f3-a373-fff2119d397f.pdf. Cited in Lawrence Liang, "Porous Legalities and Avenues of Participation," in *Sarai Reader 05: Bare Acts* (Delhi: Sarai Media Lab, 2005), 14.

46 Quoted in Liang, "Porosity and Avenues of Participation," 14–15.

47 See *Beijing 2050* proposal on MAD's official website, accessed December 26, 2018, http://www.i-mad.com/work/beijing-2050/?cid=4.

48 See MAD's website.

49 Xing Danwen, *Urban Fiction*, "Work Statement," accessed December 20, 2012, www.danwen.com/web/works/uf/statement.html.

50 See examples of such construction videos on Cao's YouTube page, http://www.youtube.com/watch?v=jbq_xoQJk-g.

51 Interview with Cao Fei on the PBS series *Art 21*, "Fantasy," season 5 (2009). Watch interview online: https://www.pbs.org/video/art21-fantasy/.

52 Joel Martinsen, "Diary of an Alien in Beijing," *Danwei.org*, January 28, 2011, http://www.danwei.org/art/diary_of_a_grey_in_beijing.php.

53 Martinsen, "Diary of an Alien in Beijing." The blog drew from E2MAN's Weibo account and other Chinese sources. See, for example, "Brother Alien's Microblog Attracts Curious Earthlings," *Changjiang Daily* (via Netease), January 26, 2011, http://news.163.com/11/0126/04/6RA36AIK00014AED.html.

Chapter 3: Bricks and Media

1 Liu Wei, "Movie Magic: Nation's Theater Business Is Booming as More Chinese Take to the Cinemas," *China Daily* (US edition), February 16, 2011, 8.

2 Rey Chow, *Primitive Passions: Visuality, Sexuality, Ethnography, and Contemporary Chinese Cinema* (New York: Columbia University Press, 1995), 8–9.

3   Chow's translation and emphasis.
4   Chow, *Primitive Passions*, 4.
5   Chow, *Primitive Passions*, 8.
6   Spatiality here is not merely a Cartesian grid where things occur and objects take position; rather, it is basic to one's sense of being in the world and cannot be unhinged from history and sociality. This approach draws on David Harvey, *Social Justice and the City* (London: Edward Arnold, 1973); Henri Lefebvre, *The Production of Space*, translated by Donald Nicholson-Smith (Oxford: Blackwell, 1974); Edward Soja, *Thirdspace: Journeys to Los Angeles and Other Real-and-Imagined Places* (Malden, MA: Blackwell, 1996).
7   Chris Berry, Lu Xinyu, and Lisa Rofel, eds., *The New Chinese Documentary Film Movement: For the Public Record* (Hong Kong: Hong Kong University Press, 2010); Sheldon Lu and Mi Jiayan, eds., *Chinese Ecocinema in the Age of Environmental Challenge* (Hong Kong: Hong Kong University Press, 2009); Zhang Zhen, ed., *The Urban Generation: Chinese Cinema and Society at the Turn of the Twenty-First Century* (Durham, NC: Duke University Press, 2007).
8   Such rankings vary quite a bit across various national and international sources, and are clearly oriented toward formal feature film production. For instance, Nigeria's prolific industry is notably missing from this list. The issue is further complicated by the fact that as few as 42 percent of films produced in China reach the big screen—compared to 75 percent in the United States. According to a March 2013 report in the *Wall Street Journal*, one major reason for this discrepancy is the still limited capacity of China's cinemas, which have about one-quarter as many screens as the United States. Additionally, state-sponsored films frequently push both Chinese and international films off the screen. See Lilian Lin, "Why the Majority of Chinese Films Never Make It to Theaters," *Wall Street Journal*, March 22, 2013, accessed November 1, 2013, http://blogs.wsj.com/chinarealtime/2013/03/22/the-many-chinese-films-you-wont-see-in-a-theater/.
9   Lilian Lin, "China Set to Top U.S. in Number of Movie Screens," *Wall Street Journal*, November 14, 2016, https://blogs.wsj.com/chinarealtime/2016/11/14/china-set-to-overtake-u-s-as-worlds-largest-cinema-market/.
10 Patrick Brzeski, "China Box-Office Growth Slowed to 3.7 Percent in 2016, Official Data Shows," *Hollywood Reporter*, January 1, 2017, http://www.hollywoodreporter.com/news/china-box-office-growth-slows-37-percent-2016-official-data-shows-960217; for previous growth, see Clifford Coonan, "China's 2011 Box Office Take Tops $2 Billion," *Variety*, January 10, 2012, http://www.variety.com/article/VR1118048424; *China Film Yearbook* 2011 and 2012.
11 Huang Ying, "Studios Focus on Fundraising," *China Daily*, January 4, 2012, accessed January 15, 2012, http://www.chinadaily.com.cn/bizchina/2012-01/04/content_14375592.htm.
12 Brzeski, "China Box-Office Growth Slowed to 3.7 Percent in 2016."
13 Jack Perkowski, "China's Film Industry," *Forbes*, March 1, 2013, accessed November 1, 2013, http://www.forbes.com/sites/jackperkowski/2013/03/01/chinas

-film-industry/; Lin, "Why the Majority of Chinese Films Never Make It to Theaters."

14 Josh Friedman and Don Lee, "Time Warner Quits China Cinema Deal, Citing Rules," *Los Angeles Times*, November 9, 2006, accessed January 15, 2011, http://articles.latimes.com/2006/nov/09/business/fi-chinafilm9.

15 Kevin Voigt, "China Firm Buys AMC to Form World's Largest Cinema Chain," CNN, May 21, 2012, accessed November 1, 2013, http://www.cnn.com/2012/05/21/business/china-amc-wanda-theater/.

16 Challenges to the quota system through trade negotiations and the WTO seem to have loosened foreign film imports in recent years. In 2011, it is estimated that in addition to the twenty films admitted for profit sharing under the quota, an additional thirty films screened in China's theaters under a flat-fee system. See Coonan, "China's 2011 Box Office Take Tops $2 Billion."

17 See, for example, CCTV News, "Zoujin Beijing laozihao: Daguanlou yingyuan—bainian lai de guangying gushi" [Into the Old Beijing: Daguanlou's One Hundred Years of Light and Shadow]. The segment aired on several CCTV stations including CCTV News (CCTV 13) and CCTV International (CCTV 4), February 15, 2011, accessed December 15, 2011, http://news.cntv.cn/society/20110215/103503.shtml.

18 The Beijing government released a slideshow about the redevelopment of Qianmen ahead of the 2008 Beijing Olympics, accessed July 15, 2008, http://www.ebeijing.gov.cn/feature_2/qianmen/index.html. The page was archived and can be accessed through https://web.archive.org/web/20120313023455/http://www.ebeijing.gov.cn/feature_2/qianmen/index.html.

19 Jing Wang, "Culture as Leisure and Culture as Capital," *positions* 9, no. 1 (2001): 71–72.

20 "Corporate Overview," China Film Group Corporation website, accessed January 5, 2012, http://www.chinafilm.com/gzzy/index_image/20070204/2110.html; Darrell William Davis and Emilie Yueh-yu Yeh, "Re-Nationalizing China's Film Industry: Case Study on the China Film Group and Film Marketization," *Journal of Chinese Cinemas* 2, no. 1 (2008): 42.

21 "Corporate Overview," China Film Group Corporation website.

22 Davis and Yeh, "Re-Nationalizing China's Film Industry," 38.

23 China Film Stellar website, http://www.zyxmmovie.com/other/about.html.

24 Eric Lam, "Imax CEO Sees $1 Billion Box Office in China," *Bloomberg*, September 12, 2013, accessed November 1, 2013, http://www.bloomberg.com/news/2013-09-12/imax-ceo-sees-1-billion-box-office-on-china.html. See also an interview with Richard Gelfond, "Imax Has Target of 450 Screens in China, CEO Says," *Bloomberg TV*, July 15, 2013, http://www.bloomberg.com/video/imax-has-target-of-450-screens-in-china-ceo-says-FIeptHNvQZC5IiLeYc4aTQ.html.

25 Kang Jianmin et al., *The Research Report on Chinese Film Industry 2013* [Zhongguo dianying chanye yanjiu baogao 2013] (Beijing: Zhongguo Dianying Chubanshe, 2013), 126.

26 See Megabox website, http://www.imegabox.com/aboutmega.

27 Achille Mbembe, *On the Postcolony* (Berkeley: University of California Press, 2001), 103.
28 See project overview on Stephen Holl's website, http://www.stevenholl.com/projects/beijing-linked-hybrid.
29 Lin Xiongman, "Wenhuachanye shangye mima: Yingyuan quandy" [The Culture Industries Commercial Secret: The Enclosure of the Cinema], *Jingji ban xiaoshi* (Economics Half-Hour), CCTV 2, September 6, 2010, accessed December 15, 2011, http://jingji.cntv.cn/20100906/104480.shtml; copy of episode also on file with author. For 2012, see Lin, "Why the Majority of Chinese Films Never Make It to Theaters."
30 Chris Berry and Lisa Rofel, "Alternative Archive: China's Independent Documentary Culture," in Berry, Lu Xinyu, and Rofel, eds., *The New Chinese Documentary Film Movement*, 135–37. See also Alternative Archive website, accessed December 15, 2012, http://www.alternativearchive.com/en/main.htm. (Note: The Alternative Archive website is not operational as of 2018, but archived versions of the site can be consulted via the Internet Archive, https://web.archive.org/web/20180822070654/http://alternativearchive.com/en/main.htm).
31 Berry and Rofel, "Alternative Archive"; also, Seio Nakajima, "Film Clubs in Beijing: The Cultural Consumption of Chinese Independent Films," in Paul Pickowicz and Yingjin Zhang, eds., *From Underground to Independent: Alternative Film Culture in Contemporary China* (Lanham, MD: Rowman and Littlefield, 2006).
32 Think Films (Yingxiang Fangying) website, accessed December 15, 2011, http://m-thinking.com/.
33 As with many other informal production and exhibition sites in Beijing, Caochangdi Workstation was closed in 2015 and subsequently moved to a new artist enclave in Changping District, in Beijing's northwest suburbs.
34 See, for instance, recent festival reports, including Lydia Wu, "The Beijing Independent Film Festival Survives," http://dgeneratefilms.com/uncategorized/the-beijing-independent-film-festival-survives#more-10949; Chris Fuchs, "China Censors Indie Cinema," *Taipei Times*, October 30, 2013, http://www.taipeitimes.com/News/feat/archives/2013/10/30/2003575715; David Bandurski, "Authorities Cancel Indie Film Festival," *China Media Project*, April 9, 2013, http://cmp.hku.hk/2013/04/09/32527/; among many others.
35 A similar experience was recounted to me by one of the directors of the Li Xianting Film School. When students arrived in July 2013 to begin courses, the authorities forcibly moved them to a hotel before arranging buses to take the students back to the train station. The organizers quickly responded via text messages and social media, arranging to meet the students elsewhere, and moving the film school outside of Beijing Municipality and into Hebei Province a couple of hours east of Songzhuang.
36 Michelle Kung and Aaron Back, "Chinese Conglomerate Buys AMC Movie Chain in U.S.," *Wall Street Journal*, May 21, 2012, https://www.wsj.com/articles/SB10001424052702303610504577417073912636152.

Chapter 4: Beijing en Abyme

1. Huang Yu and Yu Xu, "Broadcasting and Politics: Chinese Television in the Mao Era, 1958–1976," *Historical Journal of Film, Radio and Television* 17, no. 4 (1997): 567. For an overview of television in China see Hong Junhao, *The Internationalization of Television in China* (Westport, CT: Praeger, 1998), 46–75.
2. Huang Yu, "Peaceful Evolution: The Case of Television Reform in Post-Mao China." *Media, Culture and Society* 16 (1994): 217–41.
3. China Media Monitor, "China Media Facts," accessed November 1, 2009, http://www.cmmintelligence.com/. More recent data suggest a television penetration rate of 94.8 percent in 2015. Data from Statista, "Penetration Rate of Television in China from 2011–2015," https://www.statista.com/statistics/467566/china-tv-penetration-rate/.
4. See, for instance, Ruoyun Bai and Geng Song, eds., *Chinese Television in the Twenty-First Century: Entertaining the Nation* (New York: Routledge, 2014); Zhu Ying and Chris Berry, eds., *TV China* (Bloomington: Indiana University Press, 2009); Zhu Ying, Michael Keane, and Bai Ruoyun, eds., *TV Drama in China* (Hong Kong: Hong Kong University Press, 2008); Michael Curtin, *Playing to the World's Largest Audience: The Globalization of Chinese Film and TV* (Berkeley: University of California Press, 2007).
5. James Lull, *China Turned On: Television, Reform, and Resistance* (New York: Routledge, 1991), 59.
6. Joseph Man Chan and Pang Zhongdan, "Building a Market-Based Party Organ: Television and National Integration in China," in David French and Michael Richards, eds., *Television in Contemporary Asia* (Thousand Oaks, CA: SAGE, 2000), 256.
7. Anna McCarthy, *Ambient Television: Visual Culture and Public Space* (Durham, NC: Duke University Press, 2001), 13.
8. I borrow the idea of the "unhomely" for thinking about the social from Bishnupriya Ghosh's forthcoming work on spectral materialism.
9. Sheldon Lu, *Chinese Modernity and Global Biopolitics: Studies in Literature and Visual Culture* (Honolulu: University of Hawai'i Press, 2007), 205.
10. Ales Erjavec, ed., *Postmodernism and the Postsocialist Condition: Politicized Art under Late Socialism* (Berkeley: University of California Press, 2003), 3.
11. Aihwa Ong, "Introduction: Neoliberalism as Exception, Exception to Neoliberalism," in *Neoliberalism as Exception: Mutations in Citizenship and Sovereignty* (Durham, NC: Duke University Press, 2006), 1–30.
12. Wu Hung, "Television in Contemporary Chinese Art," *October* 125 (2008): 78.
13. Wu Hung, "Television in Contemporary Chinese Art," 67, 72–78.
14. Wu Hung, "Television in Contemporary Chinese Art," 68.
15. Wu Hung, "Television in Contemporary Chinese Art," 69.
16. The title of Dong Xiwen's painting is translated in different ways. For example, the National Museum of China uses *The Founding Ceremony* as the English title,

translated from its Chinese title 开国大典. Here I use Wu Hung's translation in "Television in Contemporary Chinese Art," 69–70.

17 Wu Hung, "Television in Contemporary Chinese Art," 70.
18 Wu Hung, "Television in Contemporary Chinese Art," 70.
19 Huang and Yu, "Broadcasting and Politics," 564–65.
20 Michael Keane, *Created in China: The New Great Leap Forward* (New York: Routledge, 2007), 1–5.
21 This research was undertaken with photographer Graham Bury. More images and project descriptions can be viewed online: www.projectionsproject.com.
22 For more on China's out-of-home TV systems, see Joshua Neves, "The Long Commute: Mobile Television and the Seamless Social," in Bai and Song, *Chinese Television in the Twenty-First Century*, 51–66.
23 Zhang Tongdao, "Chinese Television Audience Research," in Zhu and Berry, *TV China*, 169.
24 McCarthy, *Ambient Television*, 4.
25 Raymond Williams, *Television: Technology and Cultural Form* (New York: Routledge, 2003), 19–25.
26 Shaun Moores, "Television, Geography and Mobile Privatization," *European Journal of Communication* 8, no. 3 (1993): 365–79.
27 Anna McCarthy, *The Citizen Machine: Governing by Television in 1950s America* (New York: New Press, 2010).
28 Beijing All Media and Culture Group website, accessed October 5, 2009, http://www.bamc.com.cn/en/bamc.asp.
29 From a July 19, 2008, phone interview with a BAMC technician. Most information can be corroborated on the English and Chinese versions of the BAMC website, accessed November 5, 2009, http://www.bamc.com.cn/en/mub_9.asp. As of 2018, the City TV website is http://citytv.com.cn/index.aspx.
30 BAMC website, accessed November 5, 2009, http://www.bamc.com.cn/en/mub_13.asp.
31 BAMC website, accessed November 5, 2009, http://www.bamc.com.cn/en/mub_8.asp.
32 Neves, "The Long Commute."
33 André Jansson and Amanda Lagerkvist, "The Future Gaze: City Panoramas as Politico-Emotive Geographies," *Journal of Visual Culture* 8 (2009): 26; emphasis in the original.
34 Nigel Thrift, "Intensities of Feeling: Towards a Spatial Politics of Affect," *Geografiska Annaler* 86B, no. 1 (2004): 75.
35 Cited in Hong Junhao, *The Internationalization of Television in China*, 91.
36 Benedict Anderson, *Imagined Communities: Reflections on the Origin and Spread of Nationalism* (London: Verso, 1983), chapter 3.
37 Anderson, *Imagined Communities*, 25–35; emphasis in the original.
38 Epigraph: Bruce Blanch, "Foxconn Suicides: 'Workers Feel Quite Lonely,'" *BBC News*, May 28, 2010, https://www.bbc.com/news/10182824.

39 Partha Chatterjee, *The Politics of the Governed: Reflections on Popular Politics in Most of the World* (New York: Columbia University Press, 2004), 66.

40 The perils of e-waste labor are well documented in the city of Guiyu. See, for instance, Jim Puckett and Ted Smith, eds., *Exporting Harm: The High-Tech Trashing of Asia* (Seattle: Basel Action Network, 2002), 15–22.

41 Chris Hogg, "Taiwan iPhone-Maker Foxconn Opens Doors after Deaths," BBC News, May 26, 2010, http://www.bbc.co.uk/news/10161633; Tania Branigan, "Latest Foxconn Suicide Raises Concern over Factory Life in China," *The Guardian*, May 17, 2010, http://www.guardian.co.uk/world/2010/may/17/foxconn-suicide-china-factory-life.

42 David Barboza, "Supply Chain for iPhone Highlights Costs in China," *New York Times*, July 5, 2010, http://www.nytimes.com/2010/07/06/technology/06iphone.html.

43 Xinhua News, "Foxconn to Build New Plant with $2b in Chengdu," *China Daily*, October 10, 2010, http://www.chinadaily.com.cn/china/2010-10/22/content_11446060.htm.

44 Jason McGrath, *Postsocialist Modernity: Chinese Cinema, Literature, and Criticism in the Market Age* (Stanford, CA: Stanford University Press, 2008), 188.

45 Bishnupriya Ghosh, "Looking through Coca-Cola: Global Icons and the Popular," *Public Culture* 22, no. 2 (2010): 344.

46 Wang Hui, *China's New Order: Society, Politics, and Economy in Transition* (Cambridge, MA: Harvard University Press, 2003), 43.

47 Arif Dirlik, "Postsocialism? Reflections on 'Socialism with Chinese Characteristics,'" in Arif Dirlik and Maurice Meisner, eds., *Marxism and the Chinese Experience: Issues in Contemporary Chinese Socialism* (Armonk, NY: M. E. Sharpe, 1989), 380.

Chapter 5: Videation

1 Jeffrey Kaye, "In China, Factory Workers Allege Poisoning from iPhone Production," *PBS Newshour*, April 13, 2011, http://www.pbs.org/newshour/bb/world-jan-june11-china_04-13/.

2 Apple Inc., *Apple Supplier Responsibility: 2011 Progress Report*, https://www.apple.com/supplier-responsibility/pdf/Apple_SR_2011_Progress_Report.pdf.

3 Jenny Chan and Pun Ngai, "Suicide as Protest for the New Generation of Chinese Migrant Workers: Foxconn, Global Capital, and the State," *Asia-Pacific Journal: Japan Focus* 8, no. 37 (2010), accessed November 10, 2014, http://japanfocus.org/-Jenny-Chan/3408.

4 Elizabeth Povinelli, *Economies of Abandonment* (Durham, NC: Duke University Press, 2011); Aihwa Ong, *Neoliberalism as Exception: Mutations in Citizenship and Sovereignty* (Durham, NC: Duke University Press, 2006).

5 Pun Ngai, "Chinese Migrant Women Workers in Dormitory Labour System," *Asia Portal*, May 11, 2009, http://www.asiaportal.info/maychinese-migrant-women-workers-a-dormitory-labour-system%AA-pun-ngai/.

6 Cara Wallis, *Technomobility in China: Young Migrant Women and Mobile Phones* (New York: NYU Press, 2015).

7   See, for instance, Leslie T. Chang, *Factory Girls: From Village to City in a Changing China* (New York: Random House, 2008); Peter Hessler, *Country Driving: A Journey through China from Farm to Factory* (New York: HarperCollins, 2010); Pui-Lam Law, ed., *New Connectivities in China: Virtual, Actual and Local Interactions* (London: Springer, 2012); Pun Ngai, *Made in China: Women Factory Workers in a Global Workplace* (Durham, NC: Duke University Press, 2005); Hong Xue, "Local Strategies of Labor Control: A Case Study of Three Electronics Factories in China," *International Labor and Working-Class History* 73 (spring 2008): 85–103; among many others.

8   Guangdong Public TV Channel, "Biling gongchang sushi, Dongguan Wanjiang Zhongxue nvsheng gongyu zao toupai," accessed January 14, 2015, http://v.youku.com/v_show/id_XNTI5NDA2MjUy.html.

9   Lisa Rofel, *Desiring China: Experiments in Neoliberalism, Sexuality, and Public Culture* (Durham, NC: Duke University Press, 2007).

10 Anna Tsing, *Friction: An Ethnography of Global Connection* (Princeton, NJ: Princeton University Press, 2005), 51; my emphasis.

11 Bhaskar Sarkar, "The Melodramas of Globalization," *Cultural Dynamics* 20, no. 1 (2008): 31–51.

12 Jonathan Crary, *24/7: Late Capitalism and Ends of Sleep* (London: Verso, 2013); Tiziana Terranova, "Free Labor: Producing Culture for the Digital Economy," *Social Text 63* 18, no. 2 (2000): 33–34; Yann Moulier Boutang, *Cognitive Capitalism* (Cambridge: Polity, 2011).

13 Donna Haraway, "A Manifesto for Cyborgs: Science, Technology, and Socialist Feminism in the 1980s," *Australian Feminist Studies* 2, no. 4 (1987): 1–42.

14 Michael Hardt, "Affective Labor," *boundary 2* 26, no. 2 (1999): 89–100.

15 Thomas Armstrong, "China's Floating Population," *SCIR*, October 12, 2013, http://scir.org/2013/10/chinas-floating-population/. The article notes that 160 million migrants are without hukou, or household registration, and thus are effectively illegal residents in their own country.

16 Quoted in Neferti X. M. Tadiar, "Life-Times of Disposability within Global Neoliberalism," *Social Text 115* 31, no. 2 (2013): 20; Michel Foucault, *The Birth of Biopolitics: Lectures at the Collège de France, 1978–1979*, translated by Graham Burchell (Basingstoke, UK: Palgrave Macmillan, 2008), 226.

17 Tadiar, "Life-Times of Disposability within Global Neoliberalism," 20–21.

18 Ong, *Neoliberalism as Exception*, 3–4.

19 Maurizio Lazzarato, "Neoliberalism in Action: Inequality, Insecurity and the Reconstitution of the Social," *Theory, Culture, Society* 26, no. 6 (2009): 128.

20 Aihwa Ong, "Boundary Crossings: Neoliberalism as a Mobile Technology," *Transactions of The Institute of British Geographers*, n.s., 32, no. 1 (2007): 3–8.

21 Li Zhang, "Afterword: Postsocialist Assemblages from the Margin," *positions: east asia cultures critique* 20, no. 2 (2012): 660; Aihwa Ong and Li Zhang, "Introduction: Privatizing China; Powers of the Self, Socialism from Afar," in Aihwa Ong and Li Zhang, eds., *Privatizing China: Socialism from Afar* (Ithaca, NY: Cornell University Press, 2008), 1–19.

22 Pun Ngai, "Chinese Migrant Women Workers in Dormitory Labour System."
23 Pun Ngai and Jenny Chan, "The Spatial Politics of Labor in China: Life, Labor, and a New Generation of Migrant Workers, *South Atlantic Quarterly* 112, no. 1 (2013): 181.
24 The German musician and video-essayist Christian von Borries plays on this parallel between corporations and states in his 2014 IPHONECHINA. The video is based on encounters in which von Borries asks people in China: "Imagine Apple is a state. Would you rather live in Apple or live in China?" See, for instance, the 2015 Transmediale Festival program, http://www.transmediale.de/content/iphonechina.
25 Tadiar, "Life-Times of Disposability within Global Neoliberalism," 19.
26 Tadiar, "Life-Times of Disposability within Global Neoliberalism," 21.
27 Tadiar, "Life-Times of Disposability within Global Neoliberalism," 22.
28 Tadiar, "Life-Times of Disposability within Global Neoliberalism," 23.
29 For other essays on the iPhone girl phenomenon, see Helen Grace, "iPhone Girl: Assembly, Assemblages and Affect in the Life of an Image," in Chris Berry, Janet Harbord, and Rachel Moore, eds., *Public Space, Media Space* (London: Palgrave MacMillan, 2013), 135–61; Seth Perlow, "On Production for Digital Culture: iPhone Girl, Electronics Assembly, and the Material Forms of Aspiration," *Convergence* 17 (2011): 245–69.
30 See forum post by markm49uk, "iPhone 3G—Already with Pictures!" August 20, 2008, http://forums.macrumors.com/threads/iphone-3g-already-with-pictures-aka-iphone-girl.547777/.
31 Ma Jun, "Was iPhone Girl a Phony?" *EastSouthWestNorth*, September 4, 2008, http://www.zonaeuropa.com/20080905_1.htm.
32 Ma Jun, "Was iPhone Girl a Phony?"
33 Brian X. Chen, "Factory: 'iPhone Girl' Is for Real, Not Fired," *Wired*, August 27, 2008, https://www.wired.com/2008/08/factory-iphone/.
34 Chang, *Factory Girls*. That this book can be a bestseller is itself indicative of a certain fascination with Chinese productivity.
35 For instance, a 2011 *Wired* story about iPhone labor and suicides asks: "When 17 people take their lives, I ask myself, did I in my desire hurt them? Even just a little?" Joel Johnson, "1 Million Workers. 90 Million iPhones. 17 Suicides. Who's to Blame?" *Wired*, February 28, 2011, accessed April 27, 2012, http://www.wired.com/magazine/2011/02/ff_joelinchina/all/1.
36 Leslie T. Chang, "The Voices of China's Workers," *TEDGlobal*, June 2012, https://www.ted.com/talks/leslie_t_chang_the_voices_of_china_s_workers.
37 Lawrence Liang, "Porous Legalities and Avenues of Participation," in *Sarai Reader 2005: Bare Acts* (Delhi: Sarai Media Lab, 2005), 13.
38 Discourses about the "low-end population" are rampant in China. See, for example, struggles around the recent eviction of migrants in Beijing: Benjamin Haas, "China: 'Ruthless' Campaign to Evict Beijing's Migrant Workers Condemned," *The Guardian*, November 27, 2017, https://www.theguardian.com/world/2017/nov

/27/china-ruthless-campaign-evict-beijings-migrant-workers-condemned. In the global frame, a number of scholars have contributed to this area of research, including Vicki Mayer, *Below the Line: Producers and Production Studies in the New Television Economy* (Durham, NC: Duke University Press, 2011).

39 Jamie Cross, "Technological Intimacy: Re-Engaging with Gender and Technology in the Global Factory," *Ethnography* 12 (2012): 120.

40 See, for instance, Marianne H. Marchand and Anne Sisson Runyan, eds., *Gender and Global Restructuring: Sightings, Sites and Resistances* (London: Routledge, 2000); June Nash and Maria Patricia Fernandez-Kelly, eds., *Women, Men and the International Division of Labour* (New York: SUNY Press, 1983).

41 Cross, "Technological Intimacy," 120–21.

42 Ania Loomba, *Colonialism/Postcolonialism*, 2nd ed. (New York: Routledge, 2005), 222.

43 Cross, "Technological Intimacy," 120–22; Aihwa Ong, *Spirits of Resistance and Capitalist Discipline: Factory Women in Malaysia* (New York: SUNY Press, 1987); Pun Ngai, *Made in China*; Ching Kwan Lee, *Gender and the South China Miracle: Two Worlds of Factory Women* (Berkeley: University of California Press, 1998).

44 Cross, "Technological Intimacy," 121.

45 Aihwa Ong, "Disassembling Gender in the Electronics Age," *Feminist Studies* 13, no. 3 (1987): 621.

46 Cross, "Technological Intimacy," 120.

47 Cross, "Technological Intimacy," 123.

48 Hardt, "Affective Labor," 89.

49 Hardt, "Affective Labor," 89.

50 Hardt, "Affective Labor," 89–93.

51 Maurizio Lazzarato, "From Capital-Labour to Capital-Life," *Ephemera* 4, no. 3 (2004): 187.

52 Related critiques have been lodged from the perspective of gender, among other forms of difference eclipsed by Marxist norms. See, for example, Angela McRobbie, "Reflections on Feminism and Immaterial Labour," *New Formations* 70 (spring 2010): 60–76.

53 Grace, "iPhone Girl," 148.

54 Here I draw on Thomas Lamarre's discussion of how distribution platforms and infrastructures drive "affective media geographies." See Thomas Lamarre, "Regional TV: Affective Media Geographies," *Asiascape: Digital Asia* 2 (2015): 93–126.

55 Michelle Cho suggests that such performativity is key to the specificity of video media in her analysis of K-pop reaction videos. Michelle Cho, "Pop Cosmopolitics and K-Pop Video Cultures," in Joshua Neves and Bhaskar Sarkar, eds., *Asian Video Cultures: In the Penumbra of the Global* (Durham, NC: Duke University Press, 2017), 245–50.

56 Wallis, *Technomobility in China*, 7–8.

57 Wallis, *Technomobility in China*, 6.

58 Ann Anagnost, "The Corporeal Politics of Quality (*Suzhi*)," *Public Culture* 16, no. 2 (2004): 190.

59 Anagnost, "The Corporeal Politics of Quality," 191.
60 I borrow this distinction between "aspiration" and "desire" from Bhaskar Sarkar's forthcoming work on "cosmoplastics."
61 Tadiar, "Life-Times of Disposability within Global Neoliberalism," 20.
62 From the Guggenheim online collection, "Cao Fei, Whose Utopia," http://www.guggenheim.org/new-york/collections/collection-online/artwork/22047.
63 Here I draw on Judith Butler's reworking of Hannah Arendt's "space of appearance." See chapter 2 in Judith Butler, *Notes toward a Performative Theory of Assembly* (Cambridge, MA: Harvard University Press, 2015), 78.
64 Ariella Azoulay, *The Civil Contract of Photography* (New York: Zone, 2008), 19.

Chapter 6: People as Media Infrastructure

1 Brian Larkin, "The Politics and Poetics of Infrastructure," *Annual Review of Anthropology* 42 (2013): 330.
2 Judith Butler, *Notes toward a Performative Theory of Assembly* (Cambridge, MA: Harvard University Press, 2015), 20.
3 Judith Butler, *Frames of War: When Is Life Grievable?* (New York: Verso, 2009), 14. See also Butler, *Notes toward a Performative Theory of Assembly*, 67.
4 AbdouMaliq Simone, "People as Infrastructure: Intersecting Fragments in Johannesburg," *Public Culture* 16, no. 3 (2004): 407.
5 Andrew Mertha, *The Politics of Piracy: Intellectual Property in Contemporary China* (Ithaca, NY: Cornell University Press, 2005), 141–42.
6 Shujen Wang, *Framing Piracy: Globalization and Film Distribution in Greater China* (Lanham, MD: Rowman and Littlefield, 2003), 81.
7 Wang, *Framing Piracy*, 81.
8 Mertha, *The Politics of Piracy*, 142.
9 "Anti-Piracy Fight Posts Remarkable Results," on the Chinese government's official web portal, accessed March 20, 2009, http://english.gov.cn/2006-08/17/content_364351.htm. Similar headlines on the official government site continued in 2018, including "Anti-Pornography and Anti-Piracy Campaign Immensely Successful in First Half of 2018" [2018 *nian shangbannian saohuang dafei gongzuo chengxiao xianzhu*], July 24, 2018, http://www.gov.cn/xinwen/2018-07/24/content_5308906.htm.
10 "Anti-Piracy Campaign on Scenic Spots, Airports in Holiday," accessed March 20, 2009, http://www.china.org.cn/english/travel/182642.htm.
11 This headline was replayed across several sources including *People's Daily*, *China Daily*, and other online news sites. See, for example, "Porn Dealer Given 12-Year Jail Term," *Xinhua*, accessed April 5, 2011, http://www.chinadaily.com.cn/china/2006-11/21/content_739248.htm.
12 Mertha, *The Politics of Piracy*, 144.
13 See, for example, Adrian Johns, *Piracy: The Intellectual Property Wars from Guttenberg to Gates* (Chicago: University of Chicago Press, 2009); Peter Drahos and John Braithwaite, *Information Feudalism: Who Owns the Knowledge Economy?* (London: Earthscan, 2002).

14 Michael Keane, *Created in China: The New Great Leap Forward* (New York: Routledge, 2007).
15 Johns, *Piracy*, 6.
16 See, for instance, Saskia Sassen, *The Global City: New York, London, Tokyo* (Princeton, NJ: Princeton University Press, 2001); Manuel Castells, *The Rise of the Network Society* (London: Wiley-Blackwell, 1996); David Harvey, *The Condition of Postmodernity* (Oxford: Blackwell, 1990); Gina Neff, *Venture Labor: Work and the Burden of Risk in the Innovation Industries* (Cambridge, MA: MIT Press, 2012); Yann Moulier Boutang, *Cognitive Capitalism* (New York: Polity, 2011).
17 Wang, *Framing Piracy*, 74.
18 Gregory F. Treverton, Carl Matthies, Karla J. Cunningham, et al., *Film Piracy, Organized Crime, and Terrorism* (Santa Monica, CA: RAND Corporation, 2009).
19 Nitin Govil, "War in the Age of Pirate Reproduction," in *Sarai Reader 04: Crisis/Media* (Delhi: Sarai Media Lab, 2004), 380, http://archive.sarai.net/files/original/12a426735ae41b79f72edf763898a624.pdf.
20 See chapter 1 in Daniel Heller-Roazen, *The Enemy of All: Piracy and the Law of Nations* (New York: Zone, 2009); also, Deborah Cowen, *The Deadly Life of Logistics* (Minneapolis: University of Minnesota Press, 2014), 136–40.
21 Cowen, *The Deadly Life of Logistics*.
22 Heller-Roazen, *The Enemy of All*, 10–11.
23 Bhaskar Sarkar, "Media Piracy and the Terrorist Boogeyman: Speculative Potentiations," *positions* 24, no. 2 (May 2016): 343–68; Jasbir K. Puar and Amit Rai, "Monster, Terrorist, Fag: The War on Terrorism and the Production of Docile Patriots," *Social Text 72* 20, no. 3 (fall 2002): 117–48.
24 Kavita Philip, "What Is a Technological Author? The Pirate Function and Intellectual Property," *Postcolonial Studies* 8, no. 2 (2005): 199–218.
25 Philip, "What Is a Technological Author?," 211.
26 Quoted in Philip, "What Is a Technological Author?," 212. See also Lawrence Lessig's original text, *Free Culture: How Big Media Uses Technology and the Law to Lock Down Culture and Control Creativity* (New York: Penguin, 2004), 63.
27 Lawrence Liang, "Piracy, Creativity and Infrastructure: Rethinking Access to Culture," *Alternative Law Forum*, July 20, 2009, 11–12, https://papers.ssrn.com/sol3/papers.cfm?abstract_id=1436229.
28 Lawrence Liang, "Porous Legalities and Avenues of Participation," in *Sarai Reader 05: Bare Acts* (Delhi: Sarai Media Lab, 2005), http://archive.sarai.net/files/original/8d57bfa1bcb57c80a7af903363c07282.pdf.
29 Liang, "Porous Legalities and Avenues of Participation," 12.
30 The Leninist principle of democratic centralism is enshrined in Article 3 of the People's Republic of China's constitution (*minzhu jizhong zhi de yuanze*): "The state organs of the People's Republic of China apply the principle of democratic centralism." See the National People's Congress webpage: http://www.npc.gov.cn/npc/xinwen/2018-03/22/content_2052621.htm.
31 Philip, "What Is a Technological Author?," 217.

32 Quoted in Wang, *Framing Piracy*, 75.
33 Shujen Wang, "Harmony or Discord? TRIPS, China, and Overlapping Sovereignties," in *Sarai Reader 05: Bare Acts* (Delhi: Sarai Media Lab, 2005), 191–92, http://archive.sarai.net/files/original/b7138fa2f2bfc4074bf4acce40791f49.pdf.
34 The Blue Goat (*Lan yang*) was a popular if hidden café, bookstore, and DVD store. It changed owners in 2014 and is now only a café.
35 Brian Larkin, *Signal and Noise: Media, Infrastructure, and Urban Culture in Nigeria* (Durham, NC: Duke University Press, 2008).
36 Pang Laikwan, *Cultural Control and Globalization in Asia: Copyright, Piracy and Cinema* (New York: Routledge, 2006), 103.
37 In this period, widespread piracy made video rental redundant before it could take hold. Throughout China, a pirated DVD (about 5–15 RMB per disc in Beijing, depending on the quality) can be purchased for 2 to 5 times less than a movie ticket. Legitimate DVDs cost 1 to 2 times the price of theater going.
38 By the mid-2000s the earlier VCD market was almost entirely replaced by DVDs. DVDs could be commonly purchased in different compression formats, including DVD-5 and DVD-9. The former was cheaper, lower quality, and might include an entire season of a TV show on a single disc, and the latter was higher quality and more costly.
39 See, for instance, Pang, *Cultural Control and Globalization in Asia*, 103.
40 See, for instance, Ryan McMorrow, "For Couriers, China's E-Commerce Boom Can Be a Tough Road," *New York Times*, January 31, 2017, https://www.nytimes.com/2017/01/31/business/china-courier-delivery-labor.html?_r=0; Charles Clover, "China Migration: Delivering the Jack Ma Economy," *Financial Times*, September 16, 2015, https://www.ft.com/content/f014b660-5796-11e59846-de406ccb37f2.
41 Pang, *Cultural Control and Globalization in Asia*, 103.
42 Simone, "People as Infrastructure," 407.
43 Larkin, "The Politics and Poetics of Infrastructure," 336–37.
44 Dru C. Gladney, "Alterity Motives," in Joana Breidenbach and Pal Nyiri, eds., *China Inside Out: Contemporary Chinese Nationalism and Transnationalism* (Budapest: Central European University Press, 2005), 256.
45 Liang, "Piracy, Creativity and Infrastructure."
46 Bhaskar Sarkar, "The Melodramas of Globalization," *Cultural Dynamics* 20 (2008): 31. Sarkar draws on Linda Williams's well-known discussion of "body genres" in "Film Bodies: Gender, Genre, and Excess," *Film Quarterly* 4, no. 4 (1991): 2–13.
47 Sarkar, "The Melodramas of Globalization," 31.
48 Dipesh Chakrabarty, *Provincializing Europe: Postcolonial Thought and Historical Difference* (Princeton, NJ: Princeton University Press, 2000), 47–71.
49 Sarkar, "The Melodramas of Globalization," 32.
50 Sarkar, "The Melodramas of Globalization," 48.
51 Sarkar, "The Melodramas of Globalization."
52 Sarkar, "The Melodramas of Globalization."
53 Williams, "Film Bodies," 9.

54 Ziuaddin Sardar, "The Political Economy of the Fake," in Ackbar Abbas and John Nguyet Erni, eds., *Internationalizing Cultural Studies: An Anthology* (Oxford: Blackwell, 2005), 661.
55 Liang, "Porous Legalities and Avenues of Participation," 6.
56 Homi Bhabha, *The Location of Culture* (New York: Routledge, 1994), 122.
57 Bhabha, *The Location of Culture*.
58 Ackbar Abbas, "Faking Globalization," in Nicholas Mirzoeff, ed., *The Visual Culture Reader*, 3rd ed. (New York: Routledge, 2013), 261. I also take up this argument in the introduction. In a longer passage, Abbas writes: "When something is faked, the global order is not disturbed; in fact, the fake confirms, rather than subverts the global division of labor, made worse now by the fact that developing countries that condemn *themselves* to the (fake) production of First World designs. The fake is not, as it is sometimes represented to be, capable of being politically subversive of the global order."
59 Abbas, "Faking Globalization," 260.
60 Pang Laikwan, *Creativity and Its Discontents: China's Creative Industries and Intellectual Property Rights Offenses* (Durham, NC: Duke University Press, 2012), 188.
61 Pang, *Creativity and Its Discontents*, 192.
62 Quoted in Pang, *Creativity and Its Discontents*, 194.
63 Pang, *Creativity and Its Discontents*, 194.
64 Quoted in Pang, *Creativity and Its Discontents*, 194.
65 Bhabha, *The Location of Culture*, 122.
66 Williams, "Film Bodies."
67 Bhabha, *The Location of Culture*, 126.
68 Bhabha, *The Location of Culture*, 129.
69 Bhabha, *The Location of Culture*, 131.
70 Simone, "People as Infrastructure," 407.
71 Larkin, "The Politics and Poetics of Infrastructures," 329.
72 Butler, *Notes toward a Performative Theory of Assembly*, 78.
73 See especially the "Introduction" of Joshua Neves and Bhaskar Sarkar, eds., *Asian Video Cultures: In the Penumbra of the Global* (Durham, NC: Duke University Press, 2017).
74 Quoted in Butler, *Notes toward a Performative Theory of Assembly*, 73.
75 Butler, *Notes toward a Performative Theory of Assembly*, 88. Also, while beyond the scope of this discussion, it should be noted that this point—acting together under conditions of equality—contributes to the definition of "political society" in a way that refuses its anti-egalitarian potentials.
76 Butler, *Notes toward a Performative Theory of Assembly*, 83, 89.
77 Abbas, "Faking Globalization," 286–87.
78 Michel Foucault, *Society Must Be Defended: Lectures at the Collège de France, 1975–1976*, translated by David Macey (New York: Picador, 2003), 247.

BIBLIOGRAPHY

Abbas, Ackbar. "Faking Globalization." In *The Visual Culture Reader*, 3rd ed., edited by Nicholas Mirzoeff, 282–95. New York: Routledge, 2013.

Abbas, Ackbar. *Hong Kong: Culture and the Politics of Disappearance*. Minneapolis: University of Minnesota Press, 1997.

Abramson, Daniel Benjamin. "The Aesthetics of City-Scale Preservation Policy in Beijing." *Planning Perspectives* 22 (April 2007): 129–66.

Abramson, Daniel Benjamin. "Beijing's Preservation Policy and the Fate of the Siheyuan." *Traditional Dwellings and Settlements Review* 13, no. 1 (fall 2001): 7–22.

Abramson, Daniel Benjamin. "Mega Projects as Urbanism." *Building Research and Information* 37, no. 3 (2009): 335–39.

Abramson, Daniel Benjamin. "Urban Planning in China: Continuity and Change." *Journal of the American Planning Association* 71, no. 1 (spring 2006): 197–215.

Acharya, Shrawan Kumar. "Urban Development in Post-Reform China: Insights from Beijing." *Norsk Geografisk Tidsskrift—Norwegian Journal of Geography* 59, no. 3 (2005): 228–36.

Alampay, Erwin, ed. *Living the Information Society in Asia*. Singapore: Institute of Southeast Asian Studies, 2009.

Altman, Rick. "Dickens, Griffith, and Film Theory Today." *South Atlantic Quarterly* 88 (1989): 321–59.

An Hongkun. "Xin Beijing, xin Aoyun, xin shimin" [New Beijing, New Olympics, New Citizens]. In *Renwen Aoyun*, edited by Peng Yongjie, Zhang Zhiwei, and Han Donghui, 495–98. Beijing: Dongfang Chubanshe, 2003.

Anagnost, Ann. "The Corporeal Politics of Quality (*Suzhi*)." *Public Culture* 16, no. 2 (2004): 189–208.

Anagnost, Ann. *National Past-Times: Narrative, Representation, and Power in Modern China*. Durham, NC: Duke University Press, 1997.

Anand, Nikhil. *Hydraulic Citizenship: Water and the Infrastructures of Citizenship in Mumbai*. Durham, NC: Duke University Press, 2017.

Anand, Nikhil, "Pressure: The PoliTechnics of Water Supply in Mumbai." *Cultural Anthropology* 26, no. 4 (2011): 542–64.

Anderson, Benedict. *Imagined Communities: Reflections on the Origin and Spread of Nationalism*. London: Verso, 1983.

Aoki, Keith. "Considering Multiple and Overlapping Sovereignties: Liberalism, Libertarianism, National Sovereignty, 'Global' Intellectual Property, and the Internet." *Indiana Journal of Global Legal Studies* 5 (1998): 443–73.

Appadurai, Arjun. "The Capacity to Aspire: Culture and the Terms of Recognition." In *Culture and Public Action*, edited by Vijayendra Rao and Michael Walton. Stanford, CA: Stanford University Press, 2004.

Appadurai, Arjun. "Mediants, Materiality, Normativity." *Public Culture* 27, no. 2 (2015): 221–37.

Appadurai, Arjun. *Modernity at Large: Cultural Dimensions of Globalization*. Minneapolis: University of Minnesota Press, 1996.

Apple Inc. *Apple Supplier Responsibility: 2011 Progress Report*. 2011. https://www.apple.com/supplier-responsibility/pdf/Apple_SR_2011_Progress_Report.pdf.

Azoulay, Ariella. *The Civil Contract of Photography*. New York: Zone, 2008.

Bai, Ruoyun, and Geng Song, eds. *Chinese Television in the Twenty-First Century: Entertaining the Nation*. New York: Routledge, 2014.

Barmé, Geremie. *In the Red: On Contemporary Chinese Culture*. New York: Columbia University Press, 1999.

Barry, Andrew. *Political Machines: Governing a Technological Society*. London: Continuum, 2001.

Baudrillard, Jean. *Simulacra and Simulation*, translated by Sheila Faria Glaser. Ann Arbor: University of Michigan Press, 1994.

Beijing chengshi zongti guiha (1991 nian zhi 2010 nian) [Master Plan for Beijing City 1991–2010]. Beijing Municipal Government, www.zhengwu.beijing.gov.cn.

Beijing chengshi zongti guiha (2004 nian zhi 2020 nian) [Master Plan for Beijing City 2002–2020]. Beijing Commission of Urban Planning, www.bjghw.gov.cn/web/static/catalogs/catalog_233/233.html.

Beniger, James. *The Control Revolution: Technological and Economic Origins of the Information Society*. Cambridge, MA: Harvard University Press, 1986.

Berlant, Lauren. "The Theory of Infantile Citizenship." In *The Queen of America Goes to Washington City: Essays on Sex and Citizenship*. Durham, NC: Duke University Press, 1997.

Berry, Chris. *Postsocialist Cinema in Post-Mao China: The Cultural Revolution after the Cultural Revolution*. New York: Routledge, 2004.

Berry, Chris. "Shanghai Television's Documentary Channel: Chinese Television as Public Space." In *TV China*, edited by Chris Berry and Ying Zhu, 71–89. Bloomington: Indiana University Press, 2009.

Berry, Chris, and Mary Farquhar. *China on Screen: Cinema and Nation*. New York: Columbia University Press, 2006.

Berry, Chris, Nicola Liscutin, and Jonathan D. Mackintosh, eds. *Cultural Studies and Cultural Industries in Northeast Asia: What a Difference a Region Makes*. Hong Kong: Hong Kong University Press, 2009.

Berry, Chris, Lu Xinyu, and Lisa Rofel, eds. *The New Chinese Documentary Film Movement: For the Public Record*. Hong Kong: Hong Kong University Press, 2011.

Berry, Chris, Souyoung Kim, and Lynn Spigel, eds. *Electronic Elsewheres: Media, Technology, and the Experience of Social Space*. Minneapolis: University of Minnesota Press, 2010.

Berry, Michael. *A History of Pain: Trauma in Modern Chinese Literature and Film*. New York: Columbia University Press, 2008.
Berry, Michael. *Speaking in Images: Interview with Contemporary Chinese Filmmakers*. New York: Columbia University Press, 2005.
Berry, Michael. *Xiao Wu, Platform, Unknown Pleasures: Jia Zhangke's "Hometown Trilogy."* London: BFI, 2009.
Bhabha, Homi. *The Location of Culture*. New York: Routledge, 1994.
Bordwell, David, Janet Staiger, and Kristin Thompson, *Classical Hollywood Cinema: Film Style and Mode of Production to 1960*. New York: Columbia University Press, 1985.
Boutang, Yann Moulier. *Cognitive Capitalism*. Cambridge: Polity, 2011.
Braester, Yomi. "Chinese Cinema in the Age of Advertisement: The Filmmaker as Cultural Broker. *China Quarterly* 183 (2005): 549–64.
Braester, Yomi. *Painting the City Red: Chinese Cinema and the Urban Contract*. Durham, NC: Duke University Press, 2010.
Braester, Yomi. *Witness against History: Literature, Film, and Public Discourse in Twentieth-Century China*. Stanford, CA: Stanford University Press, 2003.
Bray, David. *Social Space and Governance in Urban China: The Danwei System from Origins to Reform*. Stanford, CA: Stanford University Press, 2005.
Broudehoux, Anne-Marie. *The Making and Selling of Post-Mao Beijing*. New York: Routledge, 2004.
Broudehoux, Anne-Marie. "Seeds of Dissent: The Politics of Resistance to Beijing's Redevelopment." In *Dissent and Cultural Resistance in Asian Cities*, edited by Melissa Butcher and Selvaraj Velayutham, 14–32. New York: Routledge, 2009.
Bruno, Giuliana. *Atlas of Emotion: Journeys in Art, Architecture, and Film*. London: Verso, 2002.
Bruno, Giuliana. *Streetwalking on a Ruined Map: Cultural Theory and the City Films of Elvira Notari*. Princeton, NJ: Princeton University Press, 1993.
Butler, Judith. *Frames of War: When Is Life Grievable?* New York: Verso, 2009.
Butler, Judith. "Imitation and Gender Insubordination." In *Inside/Out: Lesbian Theories, Gay Theories*, edited by Diana Fuss, 13–31. New York: Routledge, 1991.
Butler, Judith. *Notes toward a Performative Theory of Assembly*. Cambridge, MA: Harvard University Press, 2015.
Calhoun, Craig. *Neither Gods nor Emperors: Students and the Struggle for Democracy in China*. Berkeley: University of California Press, 1997.
Campanella, Thomas J. *The Concrete Dragon: China's Urban Revolution and What It Means for the World*. New York: Princeton Architectural Press, 2008.
Canclini, Néstor García. *Consumers and Citizens: Globalization and Multicultural Conflicts*. Minneapolis: University of Minnesota Press, 2001.
Cao Hongtao and Zhu Chuanheng, eds. *Dangdai Zhongguo de chengshi jianshe* [Urban Construction in Contemporary China]. Beijing: Zhongguo Shehui Kexue Chubanshe, 1990.
Castells, Manuel. *Networks of Outrage and Hope: Social Movements in the Internet Age*. Malden, MA: Polity, 2012.

Castells, Manuel. *The Rise of the Network Society*. London: Wiley-Blackwell, 1996.

Castells, Manuel, and Jordi Borja. *Local and Global: The Culture of Cities in the Information Age*. London: Earthscan, 1997.

Castoriadis, Cornelius. *The Imaginary Institution of Society*, translated by Kathleen Blamey. Cambridge, MA: MIT Press, 1987.

Chakrabarty, Dipesh. *Provincializing Europe: Postcolonial Thought and Historical Difference*. Princeton, NJ: Princeton University Press, 2000.

Chan, Jenny, and Pun Ngai. "Suicide as Protest for the New Generation of Chinese Migrant Workers: Foxconn, Global Capital, and the State," *Asia-Pacific Journal: Japan Focus* 8, no. 37 (2010). https://apjjf.org/-Jenny-Chan/3408/article.html.

Chan, Joseph Man, and Pang Zhongdang. "Building a Market-Based Party Organ: Television and National Integration in China." In *Television in Contemporary Asia*, edited by David French and Michael Richards, 233–66. Thousand Oaks, CA: SAGE, 2000.

Chang, Leslie T. *Factory Girls: From Village to City in a Changing China*. New York: Spiegel and Grau, 2008.

Chang Runjie. "Kan Aoyun, you Beijing" [Watching the Olympics, Touring Beijing]. In *Renwen Aoyun*, edited by Peng Yongjie, Zhang Zhiwei and Han Donghui, 426–30. Beijing: Dongfang Chubanshe, 2003.

Chatterjee, Partha. "Democracy and Economic Transformation in India." *Economic and Political Weekly*, April 19, 2008, 53–62.

Chatterjee, Partha. *Empire and Nation: Selected Essays*. New York: Columbia University Press, 2010.

Chatterjee, Partha. *Lineages of Political Society: Studies in Postcolonial Democracy*. New York: Columbia University Press, 2011.

Chatterjee, Partha. *The Politics of the Governed: Reflections on Popular Politics in Most of the World*. New York: Columbia University Press, 2004.

Chattopadhyay, Swati. "The Art of Auto-Mobility: Vehicular Art and the Space of Resistance in Calcutta." *Journal of Material Culture* 14, no. 1 (2009): 107–39.

Chattopadhyay, Swati. *Representing Calcutta: Modernity, Nationalism, and the Colonial Uncanny*. New York: Routledge, 2005.

Chattopadhyay, Swati. *Unlearning the City: Infrastructure in a New Optical Field*. Minneapolis: University of Minnesota Press, 2012.

Chattopadhyay, Swati, and Bhaskar Sarkar. "Introduction: The Subaltern and the Popular." *Postcolonial Studies* 8, no. 4 (2005): 357–63.

Chen Kuan-hsing, *Asia as Method: Toward Deimperialization*. Durham, NC: Duke University Press, 2010.

Chen Kuan-hsing, ed., *Trajectories: Inter-Asia Cultural Studies*. New York: Routledge, 1998.

Chen Kuan-Hsing, and Chua Beng-Huat, eds. *The Inter-Asia Cultural Studies Reader*. New York: Routledge, 2007.

Chen Lüsheng. *Xin Zhongguo meishu tushi, 1949–1966* [An Illustrated History of Art in the New China, 1949–1966]. Beijing: Zhongguo Qingnian Chubanshe, 2000.

Chen, Mel. *Animacies: Biopolitics, Racial Mattering, and Queer Affect*. Durham, NC: Duke University Press, 2012.

Cheng Jihua, ed. *Zhongguo diarying fazhan shi* [History of the Development of Chinese Cinema]. 2 vols. Beijing: Zhongguo Dianying Chubanshe, 1998.

Cho, Michelle. "Pop Cosmopolitics and K-Pop Video Cultures." In *Asian Video Cultures: In the Penumbra of the Global*, edited by Joshua Neves and Bhaskar Sarkar, 240–65. Durham, NC: Duke University Press, 2017.

Choi, Jung Bong. "Of the East Asian Cultural Sphere: Theorizing Cultural Regionalization." *China Review* 10, no. 2 (2010): 109–36.

Chow, Rey. *The Age of the World Target: Self-Referentiality in War, Theory, and Comparative Work*. Durham, NC: Duke University Press, 2006.

Chow, Rey. *Entanglements, or Transmedial Thinking about Capture*. Durham, NC: Duke University Press, 2012.

Chow, Rey. *Primitive Passions: Visuality, Sexuality, Ethnography, and Contemporary Chinese Cinema*. New York: Columbia University Press, 1995.

Chu Weihua. *Zhongguo dushi pingmin dianying* [The Cinema of Chinese Urban Citizens]. Beijing: Zhoungguo Dianying Chubanshe, 2008.

Chua Beng-Huat, ed. *Consumption in Asia: Lifestyles and Identities*. New York: Routledge, 2000.

Chua Beng-Huat and Koichi Iwabuchi, eds. *East Asian Pop Culture: Analyzing the Korean Wave*. Hong Kong: Hong Kong University Press, 2008.

Chun, Wendy Hui Kyong. *Control and Freedom: Power and Paranoia in the Age of Fiber Optics*. Cambridge, MA: MIT Press, 2006.

Clark, Paul. *Chinese Cinema: Culture and Politics Since 1949*. Cambridge: Cambridge University Press, 1987.

Clarke, David B., ed. "Introduction: Previewing the Cinematic City." In *The Cinematic City*, 1–18. London: Routledge, 1997.

Conquergood, Dwight. "Rethinking Ethnography: Towards a Critical Cultural Politics." *Communication Monographs* 58 (1991): 179–94.

Cooper, Melinda. *Life as Surplus: Biotechnology and Capitalism in the Neoliberal Era*. Seattle: University of Washington Press, 2008.

Cowen, Deborah. *The Deadly Life of Logistics*. Minneapolis: University of Minnesota Press, 2014.

Crary, Jonathan. *24/7: Late Capitalism and the Ends of Sleep*. London: Verso, 2013.

Cross, Jamie. "Technological Intimacy: Re-Engaging with Gender and Technology in the Global Factory." *Ethnography* 12 (2012): 119–43.

Curtin, Michael. "Media Capital: Towards the Study of Spatial Flows." *International Journal of Cultural Studies* 6, no. 2 (2003): 202–28.

Curtin, Michael. *Playing to the World's Largest Audience: The Globalization of Chinese Film and TV*. Berkeley: University of California Press, 2007.

Dai Jinhua. *Cinema and Desire. Feminist Marxism and Cultural Politics in the Work of Dai Jinhua*, edited by Jing Wang and Tani E. Barlow. London: Verso, 2002.

Davis, Darrell William, and Emilie Yueh-yu Yeh. "Re-Nationalizing China's Film Industry: Case Study on the China Film Group and Film Marketization." *Journal of Chinese Cinemas* 2, no. 1 (2008): 37–51.

Dayan, Daniel, and Elihu Katz. *Media Events: The Live Broadcasting of History*. Cambridge, MA: Harvard University Press, 1992.

de Certeau, Michel. *The Practice of Everyday Life*. Berkeley: University of California Press, 2002.

Deleuze, Gilles. *Negotiations: 1972–1990*, translated by Martin Joughlin. New York: Columbia University Press, 1995.

Deleuze, Gilles, and Félix Guattari, *Anti-Oedipus: Capitalism and Schizophrenia*. Minneapolis: University of Minnesota Press, 1983.

Derrida, Jacques. *Spectres of Marx: The State of Debt, the Work of Mourning and the New International*. New York: Routledge, 1994.

Di Fang. "Outdoor Ads Banned in Beijing's Special Areas." *China Daily*, September 13, 2004. www.chinadaily.com.cn/english.

Dirlik, Arif, and Maurice Meisner, eds. *Marxism and the Chinese Experience: Issues in Contemporary Chinese Socialism*. London: M. E. Sharpe, 1989.

Dirlik, Arif, and Zhang Xudong, eds. *Postmodernism and China*. Durham, NC: Duke University Press, 2000.

Donald, Stephanie Hemelryk. *Public Secrets, Public Spaces: Cinema and Civility in China*. Lanham, MD: Rowman and Littlefield, 2000.

Dong Guanqi, ed. *Gudu Beijing: Wushi nian yanbian lu* [The Old Capital of Beijing: A Record of Fifty Years of Evolution]. Nanjing: Dongnan Daxue Chubanshe, 2006.

Dong, Madeleine Yue. *Republican Beijing: The City and Its Histories*. Berkeley: University of California Press, 2003.

Drahos, Peter, and John Braithwaite. *Information Feudalism: Who Owns the Knowledge Economy?* London: Earthscan, 2002.

Dutton, Michael. *Beijing Time*. Cambridge, MA: Harvard University Press, 2008.

Dutton, Michael. *Streetlife China*. Cambridge: Cambridge University Press, 1998.

Erjavec, Ales, ed. *Postmodernism and the Postsocialist Condition: Politicized Art under Late Socialism*. Berkeley: University of California Press, 2003.

Falk, Richard, Mark Juergensmeyer, and Vesselin Popovski, eds. *Legality and Legitimacy in Global Affairs*. Oxford: Oxford University Press, 2012.

Fang Ke. *Dangdai Beijing jiucheng genxin: Diaocha, yanjiu, tansuo* [Contemporary Redevelopment in Beijing's Inner City: Survey, Analysis, Investigation]. Beijing: Zhongguo Jianzhu Gongye Chubanshe, 2000.

Farquhar, Judith. *Appetites: Food and Sex in Post-Socialist China*. Durham, NC: Duke University Press, 2002.

Foucault, Michel. *The Birth of Biopolitics: Lectures at the Collège de France, 1978–1979*, translated by Graham Burchell. Basingstoke, UK: Palgrave Macmillan, 2008.

Foucault, Michel. *The History of Sexuality*. Vol. 1: *An Introduction*, translated by Robert Hurley. New York: Pantheon, 1978.

Foucault, Michel. *Society Must Be Defended: Lectures at the Collège de France, 1975–1976*, translated by David Macey. New York: Picador, 2003.

Foucault, Michel. "The Subject and Power." *Critical Inquiry* 8, no. 4 (1982): 777–95.

Fraser, Nancy. "Rethinking the Public Sphere: A Contribution to the Critique of Actually Existing Democracy." *Social Text* 25/26 (1990): 56–80.

French, David, and Michael Richards, eds. *Television in Contemporary Asia*. Thousand Oaks, CA: SAGE Publications, 2000.

Friedberg, Anne. *The Virtual Window: From Alberti to Microsoft*. Cambridge, MA: MIT Press, 2006.

Friedberg, Anne. *Window Shopping: Cinema and the Postmodern*. Berkeley: University of California Press, 1993.

Friedman, John. *China's Urban Transition*. Minneapolis: University of Minnesota Press, 2005.

Gao Minglu, ed. *Inside/Out: New Chinese Art*. Berkeley: University of California Press, 1998.

Gaonkar, Dilip Parameshwar. "Toward New Imaginaries: An Introduction." *Public Culture* 14, no. 1 (2002): 1–19.

Gaonkar, Dilip Parameshwar, and Elizabeth Povinelli. "Technologies of Public Forms: Circulation, Transfiguration, Recognition." *Public Culture* 15, no. 3 (2003): 385–97.

Ghosh, Bishnupriya. *Global Icons: Apertures to the Popular*. Durham, NC: Duke University Press, 2011.

Ghosh, Bishnupriya. "Looking through Coca-Cola: Global Icons and the Popular." *Public Culture* 22, no. 2 (2010): 332–68.

Ghosh, Bishnupriya. "The Security Aesthetic in Bollywood's High-Rise Horror." *Representations* 126, no. 1 (spring 2014): 58–84.

Ginsburg, Faye D., Lila Abu-Lughod, and Brian Larkin, eds. *Media Worlds: Anthropology on New Terrain*. Berkeley: University of California Press, 2002.

Gladney, Dru C. "Alterity Motives." In *China Inside Out: Contemporary Chinese Nationalism and Transnationalism*, edited by Joana Breidenbach and Pal Nyiri, 237–92. Budapest: Central European University Press, 2005.

Govil, Nitin. "War in the Age of Pirate Reproduction." In *Sarai Reader 04: Crisis/Media*, 378–83. Delhi: Sarai Media Lab, 2004. http://archive.sarai.net/files/original/12a426735ae41b79f72edf763898a624.pdf.

Grace, Helen. "iPhone Girl: Assembly, Assemblages and Affect in the Life of an Image." In *Public Space, Media Space*, edited by Chris Berry, Janet Harbord, and Rachel Moore, 135–61. London: Palgrave MacMillan, 2013.

Greenhalgh, Susan, and Edwin A. Winckler. *Governing China's Population: From Leninist to Neoliberal Biopolitics*. Stanford, CA: Stanford University Press, 2005.

Habermas, Jürgen. *The Structural Transformation of the Public Sphere: An Inquiry into a Category of Bourgeois Society*, translated by Thomas Burger. Cambridge, MA: MIT Press, 1989.

Halbwachs, Maurice. *On Collective Memory*, translated by Lewis A. Coser. Chicago: University of Chicago Press, 1992.

Han Xiaohui, ed. *Chengshi piping: Beijing juan* [Urban Criticism: Beijing]. Beijing: Wenhua Yishu Chubanshe, 2002.

Hansen, Miriam Bratu. "America, Paris, the Alps: Kracauer (and Benjamin) on Cinema and Modernity." In *Cinema and the Invention of Modern Life*, edited by Leo Charney and Vanessa Schwartz. Berkeley: University of California Press, 1995.

Hansen, Miriam Bratu. *Babel and Babylon: Spectatorship in American Silent Film*. Cambridge, MA: Harvard University Press, 1994.

Haraway, Donna. "A Manifesto for Cyborgs: Science, Technology, and Socialist Feminism in the 1980s." *Australian Feminist Studies* 2, no. 4 (1987): 1–42.

Hardt, Michael. "Affective Labor." *boundary 2* 26, no. 2 (1999): 89–100.

Harootunian, Harry. *History's Disquiet: Modernity, Cultural Practice, and the Question of Everyday Life*. New York: Columbia University Press, 2000.

Harvey, David. *The Condition of Postmodernity: An Enquiry into the Origins of Cultural Change*. Cambridge: Blackwell, 1990.

Harvey, David. "Neoliberalism as Creative Destruction." *Annals of the American Academy of Social Science* 610 (March 2007): 22–44.

Harvey, David. *Social Justice and the City*. London: Edward Arnold, 1973.

Harvey, David. *The Urban Experience*. Baltimore: Johns Hopkins University Press, 1989.

Hawes, Colin S. C. *The Chinese Transformation of Corporate Culture*. New York: Routledge, 2012.

He Guangsen, ed. *Olympic Architecture: Beijing 2008*, translated by He Guangsen et al. Beijing: China Architecture and Building Press, 2008.

He Shenjing and Fulong Wu. "Property-Led Redevelopment in Post-Reform China: A Case Study of Xintiandi Redevelopment Project in Shanghai." *Journal of Urban Affairs* 27, no. 1 (February 2005): 1–23.

Heller-Roazen, Daniel. *The Enemy of All: Piracy and the Law of Nations*. New York: Zone, 2009.

Hjorth, Larissa, Jean Burgess, and Ingrid Richardson. *Studying Mobile Media: Cultural Technologies, Mobile Communication and the iPhone*. London: Routledge, 2012.

Ho, Josephine. "Shan-Zhai: Economic/Cultural Production through the Cracks of Globalization." Plenary speech, Crossroads: 2010 Cultural Studies Conference, Hong Kong. http://cultstud.org/xr2010/crossroad/pdf/Josephine%20Ho.pdf.

Hobsbawm, Eric. *Primitive Rebels: Studies in Archaic Forms of Social Movement in the Nineteenth and Twentieth Centuries*. London: Norton, 1965.

Hong Junhao. *The Internationalization of Television in China*. Westport, CT: Praeger, 1998.

Hong Xue. "Local Strategies of Labor Control: A Case Study of Three Electronics Factories in China." *International Labor and Working-Class History* 73 (spring 2008): 85–103.

Hou Jianmei. "Meili Beijing, you wo yige: Renwen Aoyun yu zhiyuanzhe" [Beautiful Beijing, Count Me In: Humanistic Olympics and the Volunteers]. In *Renwen Aoyun*, edited by Peng Yongjie, Zhang Zhiwei, and Han Donghui, 525–28. Beijing: Dongfang Chubanshe, 2003.

Hou Renzhi. "Beijing jiucheng pingmian sheji de gaizao" [Reconstructing the Surface Design of Beijing's Old City]. In *Lishi dilixue de lilun yu shixian* [Theory and Practice of Historical Geography], edited by Hou Renzhi, 202–26. Shanghai: Shanghai Renmin Chubanshe, 1979.

Hou Renzhi. "The Transformation of the Old City of Beijing, China." In *World Patterns of Modern Urban Change*, edited by Michael P. Conzen, 217–39. Chicago: University of Chicago, Department of Geography, 1986.

Hu Huilin. *The Development of Cultural Industries and National Cultural Security* [Wenhua chanye fazhan yu guojia wenhua anquan]. Guangdong: Guangzhou Renmin Chubanshe, 2005.

Huang Du. *Hou Wuzhi* [Post-Material: Interpretations of Everyday Life by Contemporary Chinese Artists]. Beijing, Shijie Huaren Yishu, 2000.

Huang, Philip C. C. "'Public Sphere'/'Civil Society in China? The Third Realm Between State and Society." *Modern China* 19, no. 2: 216–40.

Huang, Philip C. C., ed. "Symposium: 'Public Sphere'/'Civil Society,' in China?" *Modern China* 19, no. 2 (1993).

Huang Yu. "Peaceful Evolution: The Case of Television Reform in Post-Mao China." *Media, Culture and Society* 16 (1994): 217–41.

Huang Yu and Yu Xu. "Broadcasting and Politics: Chinese Television in the Mao Era, 1958–1976." *Historical Journal of Film, Radio and Television* 17, no. 4 (1997): 563–74.

Hung, Ho-fung. "China Fantasies." *Jacobin*, December 10, 2015. https://www.jacobinmag.com/2015/12/china-new-global-order-imperialism-communist-party-globalization.

Huntington, Samuel P. "The Clash of Civilizations?" *Foreign Affairs* (summer 1993), 22–49.

Iwabuchi, Koichi, ed. *Feeling Asian Modernities: Transnational Consumption of Japanese TV Dramas*. Hong Kong: Hong Kong University Press, 2004.

Jameson, Fredric. "Cognitive Mapping." In *Marxism and the Interpretation of Culture*, edited by Cary Nelson and Lawrence Grossberg. Chicago: University of Illinois Press, 1990.

Jameson, Fredric. *The Geopolitical Aesthetic: Cinema and Space in the World System*. Bloomington: Indiana University Press, 1992.

Jameson, Fredric. "Notes on Globalization as a Philosophical Issue." In *The Cultures of Globalization*, edited by Fredric Jameson and Masao Miyoshi, 54–77. Durham, NC: Duke University Press, 1998.

Jansson, André, and Amanda Lagerkvist. "The Future Gaze: City Panoramas as Politico-Emotive Geographies." *Journal of Visual Culture* 8, no. 1 (2009): 25–53.

Jiang Jun. "Why MAD Is Mad." In *Mad Dinner*, edited by Brendan McGetrick and Chen Shuyu, 350–57. Barcelona: Actar, 2007.

Jianshebu Zhengce Yanjiu Zhongxin [Policy Research Center of the Construction Bureau], ed. *Zuixin chengshi fangwu chaiqian zhinan* [The New Guide to Demolition and Relocation of Urban Housing]. Beijing: Zhongguo Jianzhu Gongye Chubanshe, 2004.

Johns, Adrian. *Piracy: The Intellectual Property Wars from Guttenberg to Gates.* Chicago: University of Chicago Press, 2009.

Johns, Adrian. "Pop Music Pirate Hunters." *Dædalus* 131, no. 2 (2002): 67–77.

Johnson, Ian. *Wild Grass: Three Stories of Change in Modern China.* New York: Pantheon, 2004.

Karaganis, Joe, ed. *Media Piracy in Emerging Economies.* New York: Social Science Research Council, 2011.

Keane, Michael. "Broadcasting Policy, Creative Compliance and the Myth of Civil Society in China." *Media, Culture and Society* 23 (2001): 783–98.

Keane, Michael. *Created in China: The New Great Leap Forward.* New York: Routledge, 2007.

Kim, Youna, ed. *Media Consumption and Everyday Life in Asia.* New York: Routledge, 2008.

Koichi Iwabuchi, ed. *Feeling Asian Modernities: Transnational Consumption of Japanese TV Dramas.* Hong Kong: Hong Kong University Press, 2004.

Koichi Iwabuchi. *Recentering Globalization: Popular Culture and Japanese Transnationalism.* Durham, NC: Duke University Press, 2002.

Koichi Iwabuchi. "Reconsidering East Asian Connectivity and the Usefulness of Media and Cultural Studies." In *Cultural Studies and Cultural Industries in Northeast Asia: What a Difference a Region Makes,* edited by Chris Berry, Nicola Liscutin, and Jonathan D. Mackintosh, 25–36. Hong Kong: Hong Kong University Press, 2010.

Kostof, Spiro. "His Majesty the Pick: The Aesthetics of Demolition." In *Streets: Critical Perspectives on Public Space,* edited by Zeynep Celik, Diane Favro, and Richard Ingersoll, 9–22. Berkeley: University of California Press, 1994.

Kraus, Richard Curt. *The Party and the Arty in China: The New Politics of Culture.* Lanham, MD: Rowman and Littlefield, 2004.

Laclau, Ernesto. "Time Is Out of Joint." *Diacritics* 25, no. 2 (summer 1995): 85–96.

Ladd, Brian. *The Ghosts of Berlin: Confronting German History in the Urban Landscape.* Chicago: University of Chicago Press, 1997.

Lamarre, Thomas. "Regional TV: Affective Media Geographies." *Asiascape: Digital Asia* 2 (2015): 93–126.

Larkin, Brian. "The Politics and Poetics of Infrastructure." *Annual Review of Anthropology* 42 (2013): 327–43.

Larkin, Brian. *Signal and Noise: Media, Infrastructure, and Urban Culture in Nigeria.* Durham, NC: Duke University Press, 2008.

Law, Pui-Lam, ed. *New Connectivities in China: Virtual, Actual and Local Interactions.* London: Springer, 2012.

Lazzarato, Maurizio. "From Capital-Labour to Capital-Life." *Ephemera* 4, no. 3 (2004): 187–208.

Lazzarato, Maurizio. "Neoliberalism in Action: Inequality, Insecurity and the Reconstitution of the Social." *Theory, Culture, Society* 26, no. 6 (2009).

Leaf, Michael, and Li Hou. "The 'Third Spring' of Urban Planning in China: The Resurrection of Professional Planning in the Post-Mao Era." *China Information* 20, no. 3 (November 2006): 553–85.

Lee, Ching Kwan. *Gender and the South China Miracle: Two Worlds of Factory Women*. Berkeley: University of California Press, 1998.

Lefebvre, Henri. *The Production of Space*, translated by Donald Nicholson-Smith. Oxford: Blackwell, 1974.

Lessig, Lawrence. *Free Culture: How Big Media Uses Technology and the Law to Lock Down Culture and Control Creativity*. New York: Penguin, 2004.

Li Xiaoping. "The Chinese Television System and the Television News." *China Quarterly* 126 (1991): 340–55.

Li Zhang. "Afterword: Flexible Postsocialist Assemblages from the Margin." *positions: east asia cultures critique* 20, no. 2 (2012).

Li Zhongjin, Eli Friedman, and Hao Ren, eds. *China on Strike: Narratives of Workers' Resistance*. Chicago: Haymarket, 2016.

Liang, Lawrence. "Piracy, Creativity and Infrastructure: Rethinking Access to Culture." *Alternative Law Forum*, July 20, 2009. https://papers.ssrn.com/sol3/papers.cfm?abstract_id=1436229.

Liang, Lawrence. "Porous Legalities and Avenues of Participation." In *Sarai Reader 05: Bare Acts*. Delhi: Sarai Media Lab, 2005. http://archive.sarai.net/files/original/8357bfa1bcb57c80a7af903363c07282.pdf.

Lin Chun. *The Transformation of Chinese Socialism*. Durham, NC: Duke University Press, 2006.

Link, Perry, trans. "China's Charter 08." *New York Review of Books*, January 15, 2009. https://www.nybooks.com/articles/2009/01/15/chinas-charter-08/.

Litzinger, Ralph. "Theorizing Postsocialism: Reflections on the Politics of Marginality in Contemporary China." *South Atlantic Quarterly* 101, no. 1 (winter 2002): 33–55.

Liu, Melinda. "Restrain the Riffraff: Beijing's Rising-Star Mayor Clamps Down on Public Displays of Excess Ahead of the 2008 Olympics." *Newsweek*, October 2, 2007. www.newsweek.com/2007/10/02/restrain-the-riffraff.html.

Lobato, Ramon. *Shadow Economies of Cinema: Mapping Informal Film Distribution*. London: Palgrave, 2012.

Lobato, Ramon, and Julian Thomas, *The Informal Media Economy*. Cambridge: Polity, 2015.

Loomba, Ania. *Colonialism/Postcolonialism*, 2nd ed. New York: Routledge, 2005.

Lu, Sheldon Hsiao Peng. *Chinese Modernity and Global Biopolitics: Studies in Literature and Visual Culture*. Honolulu: University of Hawai'i Press, 2007.

Lu, Sheldon Hsiao Peng. "Tear Down the City: Reconstructing Urban Space in Contemporary Chinese Popular Cinema and Avant-Garde Art." In *The Urban Generation*, edited by Zhang Zhen, 136–60. Durham, NC: Duke University Press, 2007.

Lu, Sheldon H., and Jiayan Mi, eds. *Chinese Ecocinema: In the Age of Environmental Challenge*. Hong Kong: Hong Kong University Press, 2009.

Lu Xinyu. *Jilu zhongguo: Dangdai Zhongguo xin jilu yundong* [Documenting China: The New Documentary Movement in China]. Beijing: Sanlian Shudian, 2003.

Lu Xinyu. "Rethinking China's New Documentary Movement: Engagement with the Social." In *The New Chinese Documentary Film Movement: For the Public Record*, edited by Lu Xinyu, Chris Berry, and Lisa Rofel. Hong Kong: Hong Kong University Press, 2011.

Lull, James. *China Turned On: Television, Reform, and Resistance.* New York: Routledge, 1991.

Marchand, Marianne H., and Anne Sisson Runyan, eds. *Gender and Global Restructuring: Sightings, Sites and Resistances.* London: Routledge, 2000.

Mattelart, Armand. *Mapping World Communication: War, Progress, Culture.* Minneapolis: University of Minnesota Press, 1994.

Mayer, Vicki. *Below the Line: Producers and Production Studies in the New Television Economy.* Durham, NC: Duke University Press, 2011.

Mazzarella, William. "Culture, Globalization, Mediation." *Annual Review of Anthropology* 33 (2004): 345–67.

Mbembe, Achille. "Necropolitics," translated by Libby Meintjes. *Public Culture* 15, no. 1 (2003): 11–40.

Mbembe, Achille. *On the Postcolony.* Berkeley: University of California Press, 2001.

McCarthy, Anna. *Ambient Television: Visual Culture and Public Space.* Durham, NC: Duke University Press, 2001.

McCarthy, Anna. *The Citizen Machine: Governing by Television in 1950s America.* New York: New Press, 2010.

McGrath, Jason. *Postsocialist Modernity: Chinese Cinema, Literature, and Criticism in the Market Age.* Stanford, CA: Stanford University Press, 2010.

McHale, Brian. "Cognition *En Abyme*: Models, Manuals, Maps." *Partial Answers* 4, no. 2 (2006): 175–89.

McRobbie, Angela. "Reflections on Feminism and Immaterial Labour." *New Formations* 70 (spring 2010): 60–76.

Menon, Nivedita. "Introduction." In *Empire and Nation: Selected Essays,* by Partha Chattejee. New York: Columbia University Press, 2010.

Mertha, Andrew. *The Politics of Piracy: Intellectual Property in Contemporary China.* Ithaca, NY: Cornell University Press, 2005.

Meyer, David, and Sidney Tarrow, eds. *The Social Movement Society: Contentious Politics for a New Century.* Lanham, MD: Rowman and Littlefield, 1998.

Moores, Shaun. "Television, Geography and Mobile Privatization." *European Journal of Communication* 8, no. 3 (1993): 365–79.

Nash, June, and Maria Patricia Fernandez-Kelly, eds. *Women, Men, and the International Division of Labor.* New York: SUNY Press, 1983.

Neff, Gina. *Venture Labor: Work and the Burden of Risk in the Innovation Industries.* Cambridge, MA: MIT Press, 2012.

Neves, Joshua. "Beijing en Abyme: Outside Television in the Olympic Era," *Social Text* 107 29, no. 2 (summer 2011): 21–46.

Neves, Joshua. "The Long Commute: Mobile Television and the Seamless Social." In *Rethinking Chinese Television*, edited by Ruoyun Bai and Geng Song. New York: Routledge, 2014.

Neves, Joshua. "Media Archipelagos: Inter-Asian Film Festivals." *Discourse* 34, nos. 2–3 (2012): 230–39.

Neves, Joshua. "New Specificities." *Cinema Journal* 52, no. 4 (2013): 147–54.

Neves, Joshua, and Bhaskar Sarkar, eds. *Asian Video Cultures: In the Penumbra of the Global*. Durham, NC: Duke University Press, 2017.

Ong, Aihwa. "Boundary Crossings: Neoliberalism as a Mobile Technology." *Transactions of the Institute of British Geographers*, n.s., 32, no. 1 (January 2007): 3–8.

Ong, Aihwa. "Disassembling Gender in the Electronics Age." *Feminist Studies* 13, no. 3 (1987): 609–26.

Ong, Aihwa. *Flexible Citizenship: The Cultural Logics of Transnationality*. Durham, NC: Duke University Press, 1999.

Ong, Aihwa. *Neoliberalism as Exception: Mutations in Citizenship and Sovereignty*. Durham, NC: Duke University Press, 2006.

Ong, Aihwa. *Spirits of Resistance and Capitalist Discipline: Factory Women in Malaysia*. New York: SUNY Press, 1987.

Ong, Aihwa, and Li Zhang, eds. *Privatizing China: Socialism from Afar*. Ithaca, NY: Cornell University Press, 2008.

Pang Laikwan. *Creativity and Its Discontents: China's Creative Industries and Intellectual Property Rights Offenses*. Durham, NC: Duke University Press, 2012.

Pang Laikwan. *Cultural Control and Globalization in Asia: Copyright, Piracy and Cinema*. New York: Routledge, 2006.

Pang Laikwan. "Piracy/Privacy: The Despair of Cinema and Collectivity in China." *boundary 2* 31, no. 3 (2004): 101–21.

Parks, Lisa. *Cultures in Orbit: Satellite and the Televisual*. Durham, NC: Duke University Press, 2005.

Peng Hongwei. *+0086: Beijing Cool: From the Pages of China's Coolest Magazine*. Hong Kong: Time Zone 8, 2009.

Perlow, Seth. "On Production for Digital Culture: iPhone Girl, Electronics Assembly, and the Material Forms of Aspiration," *Convergence* 17 (2011): 245–69.

Philip, Kavita. "What Is a Technological Author? The Pirate Function and Intellectual Property." *Postcolonial Studies* 8, no. 2 (2005): 199–218.

Pickowicz, Paul, and Yingjin Zhang, eds. *From Underground to Independent: Alternative Film Culture in Contemporary China*. Lanham, MD: Rowman and Littlefield, 2006.

Portes, Alejandro, Manuel Castells, and Lauren A. Benton, eds. *The Informal Economy: Studies in Advanced and Less Developed Countries*. Baltimore: Johns Hopkins University Press, 1989.

Povinelli, Elizabeth. *Economies of Abandonment: Social Belonging and Endurance in Late Liberalism*. Durham, NC: Duke University Press, 2011.

Price, Monroe E., and Daniel Dayan. *Owning the Olympics: Narratives of the New China*. Ann Arbor: University of Michigan Press, 2008.

Puar, Jasbir K., and Amit Rai, "Monster, Terrorist, Fag: The War on Terrorism and the Production of Docile Patriots." *Social Text* 72 20, no. 3 (fall 2002): 117–48.

Puckett, Jim, and Ted Smith, eds. *Exporting Harm: The High-Tech Trashing of Asia*. Seattle: Basel Action Network, 2002.

Pun Ngai. "Chinese Migrant Women Workers in Dormitory Labour System." *Asia Portal*, May 11, 2009. http://www.asiaportal.info/maychinese-migrant-women-workers-a-dormitory-labour-system% EF% 80% AA-pun-ngai/.

Pun Ngai. *Made in China: Women Factory Workers in a Global Workplace*. Durham, NC: Duke University Press, 2005.

Pun Ngai and Jenny Chan. "The Spatial Politics of Labor in China: Life, Labor, and a New Generation of Migrant Workers." *South Atlantic Quarterly* 112, no. 1 (2013): 179-90.

Rajadhyaksha, Ashish. *The Last Cultural Mile: An Inquiry into Technology and Governance in India*. Bangalore: Centre for Internet and Society, 2011.

Rancière, Jacques. *Dissensus: On Politics and Aesthetics*. New York: Continuum, 2010.

Rodney, Walter. *How Europe Underdeveloped Africa*. Washington, D.C.: Howard University Press, 1982.

Rofel, Lisa. *Desiring China: Experiments in Neoliberalism, Sexuality, Public Culture*. Durham, NC: Duke University Press, 2007.

Rofel, Lisa. *Other Modernities: Gendered Yearning in China after Socialism*. Berkeley: University of California Press, 1999.

Rose, Steve, Terry Hill, Andrew Chan, et al. *Solutions for a Modern City: ARUP in Beijing*. London: Black Dog, 2008.

Sardar, Ziauddin. *The Consumption of Kuala Lumpur*. London: Reaktion, 2000.

Sardar, Ziauddin. "The Political Economy of the Fake." In *Internationalizing Cultural Studies: An Anthology*, edited by Ackbar Abbas and John Nguyet Erni, 658-62. Oxford: Blackwell Publishing, 2005.

Sarkar, Bhaskar. "Media Piracy and the Terrorist Boogeyman: Speculative Potentiations." *positions* 24, no. 2 (May 2016): 343-68.

Sarkar, Bhaskar. "The Melodramas of Globalization." *Cultural Dynamics* 20 (2008): 31-51.

Sarkar, Bhaskar. *Mourning the Nation: Indian Cinema in the Wake of Partition*. Durham, NC: Duke University Press, 2009.

Sarkar, Bhaskar. "Postcolonial and Transnational Perspectives." In *The SAGE Handbook of Film Studies*, edited by James Donald and Michael Renov. London: SAGE, 2008.

Sassen, Saskia. *The Global City: New York, London, Tokyo*. Princeton, NJ: Princeton University Press, 2001.

Sassen, Saskia. "Place and Production in the Global Economy." In *The Globalization and Development Reader: Perspectives on Development and Social Change*, edited by J. Timmons Roberts and Amy Bellone Hite, 195-215. London: Blackwell, 2007.

Schmitt, Carl. *Political Theology. Four Chapters on the Concept of Sovereignty*, translated by G. Schwab. Chicago: University of Chicago Press, 2005. (Originally published 1922.)

Schumpeter, Joseph. *Capitalism, Socialism, Democracy*, 3rd ed. New York: Harper and Brothers, 1950.

Shi Mingzheng. *Zouxiang jindaihua de Beijingcheng: Chengshi jianshe yu shehui biange* [Modernizing Beijing: Urban Development and Social Change]. Beijing: Beijing Daxue Chubanshe, 1995.

Shiel, Mark, and Tony Fitzmaurice, eds. *Cinema and the City: Film and Urban Societies in a Global Context*. Oxford: Blackwell, 2001.

Shiva, Vandana. *Protect or Plunder: Understanding Intellectual Property Rights*. London: Zed, 2001.

Siegel, Greg. "Double Vision: Large-Screen Video Display and Live Sports Spectacle." *Television and New Media* 3, no. 1 (February 2002): 49–73.

Simone, AbdouMaliq. *For the City Yet to Come: Changing African Life in Four Cities*. Durham, NC: Duke University Press, 2004.

Simone, AbdouMaliq. "People as Infrastructure: Intersecting Fragments in Johannesburg." *Public Culture* 16, no. 3 (2004): 407–29.

Sit, Victor F. S. [Xue Fenxuan]. *Beijing: The Nature and Planning of a Chinese Capital*. Chichester, UK: Wiley, 1995.

Soja, Edward. *Thirdspace: Journeys to Los Angeles and Other Real-and-Imagined Places*. Malden, MA: Blackwell, 1996.

Sorensen, André. *The Making of Urban Japan: Cities and Planning from Edo to the Twenty-First Century*. New York: Routledge, 2002.

Steinfeld, Edward S. *Playing Our Game: Why China's Rise Doesn't Threaten the West*. Oxford: Oxford University Press, 2010.

Sun Wanning. *Leaving China: Media, Migration, and Transnational Imagination*. Lanham, MD: Rowman and Littlefield, 2002.

Sundaram, Ravi. *Pirate Modernity: Delhi's Media Urbanism*. New York: Routledge, 2010.

Tadiar, Neferti X. M. "Life-Times of Disposability within Neoliberalism." *Social Text* 115 31, no. 2 (summer 2013): 19–48.

Tang Xiaobing. *Chinese Modern: The Heroic and the Quotidian*. Durham, NC: Duke University Press, 2000.

Taylor, Charles. *Modern Social Imaginaries*. Durham, NC: Duke University Press, 2004.

Terranova, Tiziana. *Network Culture: Politics for the Information Age*. London: Pluto, 2004.

Thrift, Nigel. "Intensities of Feeling: Towards a Spatial Politics of Affect." *Geografiska Annalar* 86B, no. 1 (2004): 57–78.

Thrift, Nigel. *Knowing Capitalism*. London: SAGE, 2005.

Thrift, Nigel. *Non-Representational Theory: Space, Politics, Affect*. New York: Routledge, 2008.

Treverton, Gregory F., Carl Matthies, Karla J. Cunningham, et al. *Film Piracy, Organized Crime, and Terrorism*. Santa Monica, CA: RAND Corporation, 2009.

Tsing, Anna. *Friction: An Ethnography of Global Connection*. Princeton, NJ: Princeton University Press, 2005.

Tung, Anthony M. *Preserving the World's Great Cities: The Destruction and Renewal of the Historic Metropolis*. New York: Clarkson Potter, 2001.

Tweedie, James, and Yomi Braester. *Cinema at the City's Edge: Film and Urban Space in East Asia*. Hong Kong: Hong Kong University Press, 2010.

Vidler, Anthony. *The Architectural Uncanny: Essays in the Modern Unhomely.* Cambridge, MA: MIT Press, 1992.

Vidler, Anthony. *Warped Space: Art, Architecture, and Anxiety in Modern Culture.* Cambridge, MA: MIT Press, 2003.

Visser, Robin. *Cities Surround the Countryside: Urban Aesthetics in Postsocialist China.* Durham, NC: Duke University Press, 2010.

Voci, Paola. *China on Video: Smaller-Screen Realities.* New York: Routledge, 2010.

Wallis, Cara. *Technomobility in China: Young Migrant Women and Mobile Phones.* New York: NYU Press, 2015.

Wang Dehua. *Zhongguo chengshi guihua shigang* [An Outline of Chinese Urban Planning]. Nanjing: Dongnan University Press, 2005.

Wang Guangtao. *Beijing lishi wenhua mingcheng de baohu yu fazhan* [Preservation and Development of Beijing as a Historical City]. Beijing: Xinhua Chubanshe, 1999.

Wang Guohua. *Beijing chengqiang cunfei ji: Yige lao difangzhi gongzuozhe de zilia jicun* [Records of Beijing's City Wall and Its Disappearance: A Compilation of Materials by an Old Gazeteer Worker]. Beijing: Beijing Chubanshe, 2007.

Wang Hui. *China's New Order: Society, Politics, and Economy in Transition.* Cambridge, MA: Harvard University Press, 2003.

Wang, Jing. *Brand New China: Advertising, Media, and Commercial Culture.* Cambridge, MA: Harvard University Press, 2008.

Wang, Jing. "Culture as Leisure and Culture as Capital." *positions* 9, no. 1 (2001).

Wang, Jing. *High Culture Fever: Politics, Aesthetics, and Ideology in Deng's China.* Berkeley: University of California Press, 1996.

Wang Jun. *Caifang shang de chengshi* [Interviews with a City]. Beijing: Sanlian, 2008.

Wang Jun. *Cheng ji* [City Record]. Beijing: Sanlian Shudian, 2003.

Wang, Shujen. "Big Shot's Funeral: China, Sony, and the WTO." *Asian Cinemas* 14, no. 2 (2003): 145–54.

Wang, Shujen. *Framing Piracy: Globalization and Film Distribution in Greater China.* Lanham, MD: Rowman and Littlefield, 2003.

Wang, Shujen. "Harmony or Discord? TRIPS, China, and Overlapping Sovereignties." In *Sarai Reader 05: Bare Acts*, 189–201. Delhi: Sarai Media Lab, 2005. http://archive.sarai.net/files/original/b7138fa2f2bfc4074bf4acce40791f49.pdf.

Warner, Michael. *Publics and Counterpublics.* New York: Zone, 2002.

Wasserstrom, Jeffrey N. *China's Brave New World—And Other Tales for Global Times.* Bloomington: Indiana University Press, 2007.

Wei Chenglin, ed. *Beijing zhongzhouxian chengshi sheji* [Urban Design of Beijing's Central Axis]. Beijing: Jijie Gongye Chubanshe, 2005.

Williams, Linda. "Film Bodies: Gender, Genre, and Excess." *Film Quarterly* 4, no. 4 (1991): 2–13.

Williams, Raymond. *Television: Technology and Cultural Form.* New York: Routledge, 2003.

Winichakul, Thongchai. *Siam Mapped: A History of the Geo-Body of a Nation.* Honolulu: University of Hawai'i Press, 1994.

Wong, Winnie, *Van Gogh on Demand: China and the Readymade*. Chicago: University of Chicago Press, 2013.

Wood, Denis. *Rethinking the Power of Maps*. New York: Guilford, 2010.

Wu, Fulong. "China's Changing Urban Governance in the Transition Towards a More Market-Oriented Economy." *Urban Studies* 39, no. 7 (2002): 1071–93.

Wu, Fulong, ed. *Globalization and the Chinese City*. New York: Routledge, 2006.

Wu Hung. "Internalizing Changes: Contemporary Chinese Art and Urban Transformation." Presentation for the Geske Lectures, Hixson-Lied College of Fine and Performing Arts, Lincoln, NE, February 12, 2009.

Wu Hung. *Making History: Wu Hung on Contemporary Art*. Hong Kong: Time Zone 8, 2008.

Wu Hung. *Remaking Beijing: Tiananmen Square and the Creation of a Political Space*. Chicago: University of Chicago Press, 2005.

Wu Hung. "Ruins, Fragmentation, and the Chinese Modern/Postmodern." In *Inside/Out: New Chinese Art*, edited by Gao Minglu, 59–66. Berkeley: University of California Press, 1998.

Wu Hung. "Television in Contemporary Chinese Art." *October* 125 (2008): 65–90.

Wu Hung. *Transience: Chinese Experimental Art at the End of the Twentieth Century*. Chicago: Chicago University Press, 1999.

Wu Hung. *Wu Hung on Contemporary Chinese Artists*. Chicago: David and Alfred Smart Museum of Art, 1999.

Wu Liangyong. *Rehabilitating the Old City of Beijing: A Project in the Ju'er Hutong Neighborhood*. Vancouver: University of British Columbia Press, 1999.

Wu Wenguang. "*Xianchang*: He jilu fangshi yuguan de shu" [*Xianchang*: A Book Concerning Documentary Methods]. In *Xianchang*, edited by Wu Wenguang, 274–75. Tianjin: Shehui Kexueyuan Chubanshe, 2000.

Xi Chen. *Social Protest and Contentious Authoritarianism in China*. Cambridge: Cambridge University Press, 2012.

Xin Xu. "Modernizing China in the Olympic Spotlight: China's National Identity and the 2008 Beijing Olympiad." *Sociological Review* 54, no. 2 (2006): 90–107.

Yang, Guobin. *The Power of the Internet in China*. New York: Columbia University Press, 2009.

Yoshimoto, Mitsuhiro. "The Difficulty of Being Radical: The Discipline of Film Studies and the Postcolonial World Order." *boundary 2* 18, no. 3 (1991): 242–57.

Yusuf, Shahid, and Tony Saich. *China Urbanizes: Consequences, Strategies, and Policies*. Washington, DC: World Bank, 2008.

Zha Jianying. *China Pop: How Soap Operas, Tabloids, and Bestsellers Are Transforming a Culture*. New York: New Press, 1995.

Zhang Hongxing and Lauren Parker, eds. *China Design Now*. London: Victoria and Albert Museum, 2010.

Zhang Jinggan. *Beijing guihua jianshe wushi nian* [Fifty Years of Planning and Construction in Beijing]. Beijing: Zhongguo Shudian, 2001.

Zhang Tongdao, "Chinese Television Audience Research." In *TV China*, edited by Chris Berry and Ying Zhu, 168–80. Bloomington: Indiana University Press, 2009.

Zhang Xudong. *Postsocialism and Cultural Politics: China in the Last Decade of the Twentieth Century*. Durham, NC: Duke University Press, 2008.

Zhang Yingjin. "Bearing Witness: Chinese Urban Cinema in the Era of 'Transformation' (*Zhuanxing*)." In *The Urban Generation: Chinese Cinema and Society at the Turn of the Twenty-First Century*, edited by Zhang Zhen, 1–45. Durham, NC: Duke University Press, 2007.

Zhang Yingjin. *Cinema, Space, and Polylocality in a Globalizing China*. Honolulu: University of Hawai'i Press, 2010.

Zhang Yingjin. *The City in Modern Chinese Literature and Film: Configurations of Space, Time, and Gender*. Stanford, CA: Stanford University Press, 1996.

Zhang Zhen. *An Amorous History of the Silver Screen*. Chicago: University of Chicago Press, 2005.

Zhang Zhen, ed. *The Urban Generation: Chinese Cinema and Society at the Turn of the Twenty-First Century*. Durham, NC: Duke University Press, 2007.

Zhang Zhenqian and Yang Yuanying, eds. *WTO yu Zhongguo dianying* [The WTO and Chinese Cinema]. Beijing: Zhongguo Dianying Chubanshe, 2002.

Zhu, Jieming. *The Transition of China's Urban Development: From Plan-Controlled Economy to Market-Led*. Westport, CT: Praeger, 1999.

Zhu Ying. *Chinese Cinema during the Era of Reform: The Ingenuity of the System*. Westport, CT: Praeger, 2003.

Zhu Ying. *Television in Post-Reform China: Serial Dramas, Confucian Leadership and the Global Television Market*. New York: Routledge, 2008.

Zhu Ying and Chris Berry, eds. *TV China*. Bloomington: Indiana University Press, 2009.

Zhu Ying, Michael Keane, and Bai Ruoyun, eds. *TV Drama in China*. Hong Kong: Hong Kong University Press, 2008.

Zhu Ying and Stanley Rosen, eds. *Art, Politics, and Commerce in Chinese Cinema*. Hong Kong: Hong Kong University Press, 2010.

INDEX

Page numbers followed by *f* refer to illustrations.

Abbas, Akbar, 3, 19, 190–91, 221n58; on China's design ambitions, 6; on the "x-colonial," 4, 5, 196
Abramson, Daniel, 50, 51
accumulation, dispossession and, 37
advertising, 130, 138
aesthesis (ambient and affective experience), 184, 194
aesthetics, 52, 77, 80, 194; of development, 68; digital, 53, 55; documentary, 42; geopolitical, 96; of ruins, 41, 42; spatial aesthetics of cinemas, 95; state, 139; urban, 40; of vulgarity, 109
Aftershock (Feng, 2010), 101
Ah Gan, 124
Ai Weiwei, 2, 87
Alibaba, 183
Alternative Archive project, 112
AMC Entertainment, 100, 118
Anagnost, Ann, 165
Anand, Nikhil, 67
Anderson, Benedict, 140–41
Andreu, Paul, 55
animation, 130
anthropology, 27, 193
Appadurai, Arjun, 35, 36
Apple corporation, 107, 163; copycats of Apple brand products, 10; fake stores, 2; immaterial labor and, 162; "iPhone girl" meme (2008) and, 158; Wintek scandal and, 150
architecture, 4, 41, 52–53, 80, 85, 109
Arendt, Hannah, 168, 195
art, digital, 63, 93

ASEAN countries, 20
Asia as Method (Chen), 18
Asian studies, 27
aspiration–desire distinction, 165–66, 222n60
Assembly (Feng, 2007), 101
Australia, 115
authenticity, 5, 8, 29, 192
authoritarianism, 66–67
avant-garde, 6, 22
Avengers: Age of Ultron (Whedon, 2015), 101*f*
Azoulay, Ariella, 57–60, 168

Beijing, city of, 30, 76, 172; Apple stores in, 163; billboard excesses as contentious issue in, 82, 82*f*; bookstores/cafés, 179–80, 181*f*, 224n34; Chaoyang District, 139*f*, 180; cine clubs, 76, 113, 114; demolition and relocation projects in, 40; Dongcheng District, 34*f*, 36, 52*f*, 180; Haidian District, 27, 179, 180; *hutong* housing, 40, 43, 52; masterplans, 48*f*, 49, 50, 51*f*, 52; media urbanism of, 33; National Centre for the Performing Arts (the Egg) 70, 92*f*, 117; National Stadium (the Bird's Nest), 35*f*, 55, 70, 71, 137*f*; "New Beijing" (*xin Beijing*), 36; North–South dichotomy within China and, 159–60; Olympic urbanization in, 27; proliferation of screens and images in, 30–31; Qianmen neighborhood, 101, 103, 214n18; 798 Art Zone, 27, 84, 113, 130; Songzhuag Arts Village, 84;

Beijing (*continued*)
  transformation into a global capital, 103; Urban Planning Exhibition Hall, 49, 50f; Xicheng District, 180; Zhongguancun high-tech zone, 130. *See also* cinemas, Beijing theatrical
Beijing All Media and Culture Group (BAMC), 135–36
Beijing Bastards (Zhang, 1993), 42
Beijing Besieged by Waste (Wang Jiuliang, 2011), 43
Beijing Bicycle (Wang Xiaoshuai, 2001), 42
Beijing: Candidate City (Olympic short film), 56
Beijing Film Academy, 113
Beijing Film Panorama, 117
Beijing Independent Film Festival (BJIFF), 115, 116f, 117
Beijing Indie Film Workshop, 113
Beijing Normal University, film screenings at, 113
Beijing Olympic Summer Games (2008), 2, 3, 26, 75, 174; *Fuwa* (Olympic mascot), 56, 136; Municipal Commission of Urban Planning and, 68; opening and closing ceremonies, 56; promotional films leading up to, 143–44; satellite broadcasts of, 148; screen atop Worker's Stadium, 111f; tourism and, 54f
Beijing Olympic Winter Games (2022), 3, 25f, 26
Beijing Queer Film Festival, 115
Beijing Storm Company, 114
Beijing Taxi (Wang Miao, 2010), 43
Beijing Television, 120, 130
Beijing 2050 (MAD architectural proposal), 85–87, 86f
Beijing Welcomes You (Lu, 2000), 87
belonging, 46, 93, 122f; citizenship and, 67, 141; everyday forms of, 60; illicit and illegitimate forms of, 140, 188; urban belonging, 9, 22, 67, 84, 170, 185, 193

Benjamin, Walter, 199n14
Berlant, Lauren, 17
Berry, Chris, 63, 112, 113
Berry, Michael, 41
Bertolucci, Bernardo, 144
Beshty, Walead, 113
Bhabha, Homi, 190, 192, 199n8
Bhatt, Vikram, 38
Bhoot (Varma, 2003), 38
Bicycle Thief, The (De Sica, 1948), 186
bie guan ("side building") project, 112, 117
Big Battle, The: Nail House vs. Demolition Team [*Dingzihu dazhan chaiqiandui*] (online video game), 61–62, 62f, 75
Big Movie [*Da Dianying*] (Ah, 2006), 124, 125f
Big Shot's Funeral [*Da wan'r*] (Feng, 2001), 42, 144
billboards, 30, 49, 55; construction-site, 27, 38f, 63, 81f, 84f; opposition to proliferation of advertisements on, 81–82; orchestrated address from, 81; Qianmen beautification project and, 83f
biopiracy, 14
biopolitics, 11, 65, 155, 162, 165
biopower, 59, 162
Bird's Nest: Herzog & de Meuron in China (film), 56
Birth of Biopolitics, The (Foucault), 154
blockbuster films, 55, 109, 110, 144, 177, 183; geopolitical distribution and, 118–19; Hollywood and Bollywood, 180; state-led projects, 30, 95, 106
Blue Goat [*Lan yang*] bookstore/café (Haidian District), 113, 181f, 224n34
blueprints, 33, 34, 41, 47–48, 57; civil contract of photography and, 60; deconstruction of, 42; experimental investigation of, 87; present deferred into the future by, 46; rendering contrasted with, 53; social imaginaries and, 48; visual culture of, 35
Bluetooth connectivities, 138, 163
Bollywood, 38, 180, 189

Borries, Christian von, 220n24
Bo Xilai, 2
Boys from Fengkuei, The (Hou, 1983), 186
Boys over Flowers (TV program), 77
Braester, Yomi, 41, 43, 204n3
Brand New China (Wang, 2008), 21
brand performance, 192
Broadway Cinemas (Hong Kong franchise), 100
Broadway Cinematheque (Film Culture Center), 109f, 110
Brown, Wendy, 155
Bumming in Beijing: The Last Dreamers (Wu, 1990), 42
Bury, Graham, 204n86, 217n21
Butler, Judith, 169, 170, 194, 195

Cala, My Dog! (Lu Xuechang, 2002), 42
camouflage, 192, 193
Canclini, Néstor, 19
Caochangdi Workstation, 114f, 114-15
Cao Fei, 72, 87, 90
capitalism, 123, 149, 188; "cognitive capitalism," 153, 174; modernization and, 189; postindustrial, 156; postsocialism and, 23-24; "print capitalism," 140; state capitalism, 64, 86
cardboard baozi tale (2007), 1, 2, 4, 199n2
Castoriadis, Cornelius, 48
CCTV (China Central Television), 1, 26, 57, 70, 214n18; history of, 120; newscast of party congress, 127, 128f; relocation to center of Beijing, 130
CDs, pirated, 180
Cell Phone (Feng, 2003), 42
censorship, 65, 113, 188, 194
CGI (computer-generated imagery), 49
CGV Cinema (South Korean chain), 100, 107
Chakrabarty, Dipesh, 188-89, 193
Chan, Jackie, 117
Chan, Jenny, 155

Chang, Leslie, 158-59, 164
Chaoyang District LED Sky Screen, 139f
Charming Beijing (Olympic short film), 56
Charter 08, 61, 208
Chatterjee, Partha, 33, 57, 65, 66; on divergent economic trajectories of Asia and Africa, 209n18; "political society" idea, 15-16, 17, 18, 59-60, 64, 141; on state legitimacy and precarity, 66
Chattopadhyay, Swati, 19
Cheah, Pheng, 17
Chen Guangcheng, 2
Chen Kaige, 42
Chen Kuan-hsing, 18, 63
Cherry Lane cine club, 113
China, People's Republic of (PRC), 2, 12; anxieties over "rise" of, 165; "contentious authoritarianism" in, 17-18; design and innovation ambitions of, 6, 21; globalization and, 189; "Going Out Policy," 21; "low-end population" of, 159, 220n38; migratory population, 153; National Anti-Pornography and Anti-Piracy Office, 9, 31, 171, 172f, 173, 196; reform and opening (*gaige kaifang*), 23, 25, 120; satellites and space program of, 147-48; South China Sea excursions, 13; State Food and Drug Administration, 1; as world historical agent, 98; WTO joined by, 171, 174
China critique, 37
China Documentary Film Festival (Zhongguo jilupian jiaoliu zhou), 28, 115, 117
China Film Archive Cinema, 104f
China Film Group Corporation (CFGC), 100, 105-6, 118
China Film South, 106f
China Film Stellar, 100, 105, 106, 106f
China Independent Film Festival, 115
Chinese Seal (Olympic short film), 56
Cho, Michelle, 221n55

INDEX **247**

Chow, Rey, 95–96
chronotopes, 43
Cicero, Marcus Tullius, 10, 175
cinema, 49, 120, 123, 164; art films, 101, 110, 186, 187; Chinese independent cinema, 183; Olympic shorts, 56. *See also* blockbuster films; documentary
Cinema Paradiso (Tornatore, 1988), 118
cinemas, Beijing theatrical, 93, 94–95; alternative cinematic space, 112–17, 116*f*; art house cinemas, 95; box office explosion in China, 98–101, 99*f*, 213n8; cineplexes, 95, 107*f*, 107–8, 110; Daguanlou [Grand Shadowplay Theater] (China's oldest theater), 101–3, 102*f*; domestic theater chain performance, 106*f*; formal exhibition sites, 105–12, 107*f*, 108*f*, 109*f*; informal screens, 95; outdoor theaters, 95; quotas for foreign releases, 100, 214n16; technologized spatiality and, 95–98, 97*f*; theater chains, 100
cinema studies, 27
cities, global, 90, 174, 178
citizenship, 8, 31, 194; becoming-illegal forms of, 67; citizen-alien, 91–93; fake, 155; fractured, 64, 168; hydraulic, 67; shifting conditions of, 151. *See also* piratical citizenship
city panoramas, 140
civilization campaigns, 47
civil society, 8, 16, 17, 196; cultural forms and, 197; as normative analytical category, 63; political society distinguished from, 59; shift to global political society, 26; violent modernization of, 18; West-East binary and, 64
class divisions, 63
Clifford, James, 28
cognitive mapping, 48, 92
colonialism, 4, 5, 11, 191, 196
Communist Party, Chinese, 3, 24, 130, 140; democratic centralism of, 176, 223n30; Eleventh Party Congress (1978), 40
community, 28, 76, 148, 161; imagined, 141; loss of, 41, 72; workers' dormitories as "gated communities," 155
computers, 80, 142, 176
Confucius Institutes, 21
Conquering Ding Jun Mountain (Ren, 1905), 100
consumption, 6, 12; of fakes, 5; mass consumer society, 123; middle-class, 165; modeling of consumer lifestyles, 36, 191
contact zones, 14, 56, 150, 165
Cool Japan, 118
Cooper, Melinda, 155
copyright, 13, 171, 172–73, 174, 185, 190
corruption, 2, 41, 72, 190; in developing world, 66; protests against, 71
counterfeit goods, 3, 177
counterpublics, 8, 17
courtyard (*siheyuan*) housing, 19, 53, 68, 71, 80. *See also hutong*
Created in China (Keane, 2007), 21
Creative Industries in China (Keane, 2013), 21
Creativity and Its Discontents (Pang, 2012), 7, 21, 191
creativity/creative industries, 8, 21, 22, 158; "brand nationalism" and, 203n74; capitalist, 191; creative destruction, 33, 37, 204n1; local communities and, 188; political economic logic of, 196; producer-consumers and, 176
Cross, Jamie, 161, 167
Cui Zi'en, 204n85
cultural production, 12, 31, 42, 91; blueprints and, 47; commodity chain and, 152; demolition and reconstruction in, 41; images of ruins in, 40; marketized, 23, 123; media urbanism and, 34; politics of transitional spaces and, 92; underdevelopment and, 11
Cultural Revolution, 41, 97, 118, 120, 121, 126

cultural studies, 8, 23, 29, 56, 156, 194, 200n26
Culture Salon cine club, 113
cyanotype images, 33, 34f, 36, 38f

Dadi Century Films, 100
Daguanlou [Grand Shadowplay Theater] (China's oldest theater), 103, 109
Dancing Beijing (Olympic short film), 56
daoban (pirated), 3
Davis, Darrell William, 106
Days, The [*Dongchun de rizi*] (Wang, 1993), 182f
Dazhalan Project, 75–76, 211n34
dazibao ("big character posters"), 44
Degrees of Transparency [*Toumingdu*] (TV program), 1
Deleuze, Gilles, 4, 77
Delhi, city of, 65
democracy, 8, 12, 58; debates on cultures of, 23; exported modernity and, 15; informal, 64; as institution of politics, 61; modernity and, 63; noncitizens and, 90; piratical citizenship and, 62; political society beyond, 66; post-democracy, 177; rule of law and, 93; standards of political theory and, 17; suspended in state of exception, 11; village democracy in China, 115
Democracy Wall, 44
demolition, 40, 41, 42, 46; built environment shifted into the past by, 45; *chai* ("demolish") character, 41, 122f; of Daguanlou movie theater, 103; Olympic preparations and, 68, 72; of Qianmen neighborhood, 78, 79f, 80; velocity of, 43
Deng Xiaoping, 25, 120, 173
Derrida, Jacques, 39
De Sica, Vittorio, 186
design, 45, 190; computer-aided, 55; design culture, 3, 6; digital, 93; as multimodal social capacity, 92; urban, 110

desire, 152, 153, 163, 191; "desiring China," 152; of factory workers, 159, 161; for the fake, 193; role in construction of new humans in China, 165
developing nations, 5, 20, 66, 225n58; architecture of globalization and, 4; IP laws of, 178; mimicry and, 22, 188
development, 3, 50, 55; aesthetics of, 68–72; audiovisuality of, 51; colonialism and, 11; constant critiques of China's development, 20; culture in tension with, 30, 35; fakes as symptom of, 3, 8; future associated with, 35; modernization and, 25; noncitizens and, 72; technological, 26; underdevelopment, 11; Western-oriented discourse of, 57
Development of Cultural Industries and National Cultural Security, The (Hu, 2005), 21
dGenerate films, 76, 117
difference, 9, 35; "almost . . . but not quite," 190, 199n8; citizen-alien as form of iconic difference, 91; historical, 148; mimicry and, 192; persistence of, 189; racial/economic/sexual, 17
digital culture, 4, 27, 62, 163, 196
digital design, 47, 52, 93
digital projection, 111
digitization, 5
Dirlik, Arif, 23–24, 148
disappearance, logic of, 41, 60
Disappearance Foretold, A (Meys and Zhang, 2008), 78, 78f, 79f, 80, 103
disorientation, 4
displacement, 19, 39, 58, 59, 77
dispossession, urban, 37, 40, 66; memes about, 75; ruins and, 41
dissensus, 30, 63, 76, 93, 211n35
distribution, 63, 76, 84; distribution impulse, 77; global film distribution, 118; of infrastructure, 93; production of, 77; restructuring of film distribution system, 111; of the social, 13

INDEX 249

documentary, 42, 60, 117; documentary impulse, 43, 47, 76; video, 63, 93. See also *Pirated Copy [Manyan]*
documentation, 76, 77, 80
Document on Hygiene No. 3 (Zhang, 1991), 126, 126f
Dong Xiwen, 127, 216n16
"dormitory labor regimes," 151, 155
Dream Weavers: Beijing 2008 [Zhu Meng, 2008] (Gun, 2008), 42, 56, 68, 69f, 70–72, 143–44
Du Haibin, 147
DVDs, 163, 165, 168, 170, 173, 180; authentic and pirated DVDs sold in Beijing shops, 179–80, 181f; destruction of confiscated DVDs, 172f; DVD region coding, 7f; hand-to-hand exchange of, 170, 183, 185–87, 194; in *Pirated Copy*, 185–86, 187f; pornography alongside global art cinema, 185f; prices of pirated DVDs, 224n37; "secret" DVD shops, 183; VCD market replaced by, 224n38

East Palace, West Palace (Zhang Yuan, 1996), 42
Eating the City (Song, 2006), 87
Economies of Abandonment (Povinelli), 11
Edko Films, 110
Egg and Stone (Huang Ji, 2012), 115
Electric Shadows (Xiao, 2004), 42, 97f, 118
Eleventh Chinese Radio and Television Conference (1983), 140
elite-subaltern relations, 165
eminent domain, 22
enclosure movement, new cinemas and, 110, 112
environment, degradation of the, 65, 142
equality, 20, 37, 174, 194; acting together under conditions of, 195, 225n75; inequality in existing democracies, 63; "transition" and inequality, 148
ethnicity, critical studies of, 24

ethnocentrism, 17
E2MAN, 91–92, 92f
Eurocentrism, 15
Europe, Eastern, 176
European Union, 115
everyday life, 4, 49, 141, 148; alien's view of, 91; archiving of the everyday, 47; becoming-illegal forms of, 6, 29; digital imaginaries in, 61; embodied experience and, 184; of factory migrants, 151, 155; networks and experiences in *Pirated Copy*, 186–88; technology in, 63; television and, 121, 130–31, 141, 145; widespread illegality of, 176, 184
e-waste, 123, 142
exception, state of, 11–12

Factory Girls (Chang), 158, 164, 220n34
Faked in China (Fan, 2015), 21
fakes/faking, 2–3, 29, 64, 177; Chinese terms for, 3; condition of globalization and, 5–6; of DVDs, 165; fake news, 2, 3; global division of labor and, 225n58; new modes of replication and, 4–5; political economy of the fake in Malaysia, 189–90; "prepolitical" concerns about, 7–8; pricing of fakes, 191; time and, 189
"Faking Globalization" (Abbas), 4, 190
Falk, Richard, 13
Falling from the Sky [Tianjiang] (Zhang, 2009), 147f, 147–48
Falun Gong, 145–46
Family Stuff (Huang and Ma, 2007–8), 121–22, 122f
Fan Bingbing, 117
Fanhall Films, 115, 179
Fan Yang, 21
Farewell My Concubine (Chen, 1995), 42
fascism, resurgence of, 2
Fast & Furious (Wan, 2015), 101f
feminist scholars, 160
Feng Mengo, 87

Feng Xiaogang, 42, 117, 144
Fifth Generation filmmakers, 43
film festivals, 30, 96, 114, 168; Beijing Independent Film Festival (BJIFF), 115, 116f, 117; Beijing Queer Film Festival, 115; China Documentary Film Festival (Zhongguo jilupian jiaoliu zhou), 28, 115, 117; International Film Festival Rotterdam, 179
Film Movement Society, 113
Film Piracy, Organized Crime, and Terrorism (RAND Corporation report), 5
financialization, 153
F Is for Fake (Welles, 1973), 5
Fish and Elephant (Li Yu, 2001), 43
floating media, 162–65
"floating" populations (*liudong renkou*), 72, 83, 154, 155
Flowers of War (Zhang, 2011), 101
food safety, 1, 2, 66
Fordist production, 160
For Fun (Ning, 1992), 42
Formula 3 cine club, 113
Forrest Gump (Zemeckis, 1994), 124
For the City Yet to Come (Simone), 57
Foucault, Michel, 154, 155
Founding of a Party, The (Han and Huang, 2011), 26
Founding of a Republic, The (Han and Huang, 2009), 26, 42, 101, 127
Founding of the Nation, The (Dong, 1952), 127, 216n16
Foxconn corporation, 155, 156; suicides of workers, 142, 150; workers as public TV viewers, 141
fractal replication, 4
Free Culture (Lessig, 2004), 176
free culture movements, 175, 176
"free world," 20
Future Beijing [*Weilai Beijing*] (short film), 49
futurity, 3, 8, 35, 48
Fuwa (Olympic mascot) cartoons, 56

gambiara (local make-do practice), 7
Gandelsonas, Mario, 4, 196
Gao, Grandma, 69f, 70–71, 92
Gaonkar, Dilip, 48
Gelfond, Richard, 107
gender, 63, 160, 184
geopolitics, 20, 21, 153
Ge You, 144
Ghosh, Bishnupriya, 38–39, 40, 56, 144, 205n20
ghost cities, 37, 205n8
Gladney, Dru C., 184
globalization, 5, 12, 26, 121, 148, 179; architecture of, 4; China's marketized transformation and, 23; Chinese model of development and, 37; developing nations goaded and belittled, 22; dualities and, 178; faking of, 3, 153, 196; fiction of law and, 13; financial, 39; hegemonic claims of, 8, 66, 177; legality/legitimacy and, 7; pornographies of, 31, 188–93; socialist residues and, 123; violent social effects of, 150
Go Lala Go! (Xu, 2010), 42
Goodbye, Mr. Loser (Peng and Yan, 2015), 105f
Good Morning, Beijing (Pan, 2003), 42
Govil, Nitin, 175
Grace, Helen, 162
graffiti, 44, 84, 84f
Gramsci, Antonio, 59
Grandmaster, The (Wong, 2013), 101
Great Leap Forward, 203n83
Green Tea (Zhang Yuan, 2003), 42
Guangdong Dadi, 100, 106f
Guattari, Félix, 77
Gu Kailai, 2
Gun Jun, 42
Gutiérrez Alea, Tomás, 11

Habermas, Jürgen, 16
hands, social network of, 9, 170, 188, 193–97

INDEX 251

Han Sanping, 26, 100
Haraway, Donna, 153
Hardt, Michael, 161–62
Hart Salon cine club, 113
Harvey, David, 37, 204n1
He Jianjun, 147, 197
Heller-Roazen, Daniel, 10, 15, 175
heritage zones, 80
Herzog, Werner, 110
heterotopias, 10
Heywood, Neil, 2
historicism, 188
History 1–History 2 distinction, 188–89, 192, 193, 197
Ho, Josephine, 10
Holl, Steven, 56, 110
Hollywood, 144, 189
homelessness, 41
Hong Kong, 76, 180
Hon Hai Precision Industrial Company, 156
horror genre, 192
Hou Hsiao-Hsien, 186
House of Flying Daggers, The (Zhang, 2004), 124
housing, 12, 19, 59, 65, 196, 197; demolition of, 22, 46f; *hukou* system and, 155; illegal, 177, 185; new, 70; prefabricated, 83; relocation, 75; skyrocketing prices of, 91; squatters and, 14; subsidized, 154; unaffordable, 72; worker, 84f. *See also* courtyard (*siheyuan*) housing; *hutong*
How Europe Underdeveloped Africa (Rodney), 11
Huang, Philip C. C., 16
Huang Bo, 124
Huang Jianxing, 26, 42
Huang Qingjun, 121
Huang Yu, 130
Huat, Chua Beng, 19
Huayi Brothers, 100
Hu Huilin, 21

hukou (urban registration) system, 84, 155, 177, 219n15
hutong (narrow streets and alleyways), 40, 43, 52, 68, 84; demolished, 46f; "illegal destruction" in, 78. *See also* courtyard (*siheyuan*) housing

Iberia Center for Contemporary Art, 113
If You Are the One (Feng, 2008), 101
illegality, 3, 8, 28, 119, 177; "bad" illegalities, 197; clashes over, 95; of everyday life, 176; partial sovereignty and, 178; proliferation of, 92, 178, 194, 195; shifting conditions of, 151
illegitimacy, 3, 8, 119, 194; clashes over, 95; shifting conditions of, 151
I Love Beijing (Ning, 2000), 42, 47f
I Love You (Zhang Yuan, 2001), 42
imaginaries, social, 48, 119, 153
imagined community, 140
IMAX cinemas, 100, 107, 109
imitation, 5, 22, 28, 190; contradictory role of, 29; enforced, 6, 197; as global phenomenon, 20; Northern creativity and Southern imitation, 159
imperialism, 160, 207n52
Implemental Photography (Wang and Liu, 2007), 126–27, 128f
in-betweenness, 18, 52, 178
India, 64, 98, 144; Bangalore as technology center, 176; globalization and, 189; special economic zones in, 161
Indie Film Workshop, 113
industrialization, 166
Informal Media Economy, The (Lobato and Thomas), 7
information and communication technologies for development (ICT4D), 188
"information feudalism," 12
infrastructures, 19, 55, 141, 169, 178; beyond content, 152; cinema-going and, 95; of dissensus, 77; distribution, 93; felt experience of modernity

and, 205n10; human, 188; infrastructure studies, 193; pirate, 183–84, 194; sensational, 118–19; technological, 197; transportation, 53. *See also* media infrastructures
innovation, 6, 21; brand innovation, 191; knowledge-innovation economy, 174; national security and, 200n27; in TV and urban space, 130
intellectual property (IP), 13, 29, 31, 169, 197; counterfeit, 11; IPR regulations, 188; laws of developed and developing countries, 178; Liang's critique of, 8, 9; piracy and, 175; violations of, 1
interactivity, 168, 170, 183
interlacing, of audiovisual modes, 138–39
international law, 196
internet, 55, 75, 138, 153, 176
In the Mood for Love (Wong, 2000), 124
In the Realm of the Senses (Oshima, 1976), 186
intimacy, technological, 18, 25, 160–62, 167
Into the City (Feng, 2004), 87
IPHONECHINA (Borries, 2014), 220n24
"iPhone girl" meme (2008), 156, 157f, 158–59, 164
Iraq, US invasion of, 13
Iron Ministry, The (Sniadecki, 2014), 28, 204n85
Iwabuchi, Koichi, 203n74

Jack Ma economy, 183
Jameson, Fredric, 48–49
Jansson, André, 140
Japan, 20
Jian Bing Man (Wu, 2015), 101f
jianghu ("rivers and lakes") culture, 9
Jiang Zemin, 2, 127
Jia Zhangke, 42, 144–45
Jinyi International Cinema, 104f
Johns, Adrian, 174

jugaad (local make-do practice), 7
Jurassic World (Trevorrow, 2015), 101f

Karaganis, Joe, 7
Keane, Michael, 21, 130
Kieslowski, Krzysztof, 186
knowledge economy, 22, 86
Korea, South, 20, 21, 107
Korean Wave, 118
kuaidi (express delivery), 170

labor: affective labor, 161–62; gender and, 160; global division of, 5, 37, 191, 225n58; guilt narrative about Asian factory labor, 159, 220n35; immaterial, 162
Lacan, Jacques, 192
Laclau, Ernesto, 205n18
Lagerkvist, Amanda, 140
Lamarre, Thomas, 77, 163
Larkin, Brian, 19, 169, 184, 193
Last Emperor, The (Bertolucci, 1987), 144
law, 9, 13, 62, 64, 75, 178, 197; copyright, 188; international law, 10, 11, 13, 175, 196; as political infrastructure, 15; Roman law, 10, 175; rule of law, 8, 15, 61, 93, 208; sovereign as inside and outside of, 14
Lazzarato, Maurizio, 154, 155
Lee, Ching Kwan, 160
legitimacy, 13, 175, 192; "after legitimacy," 29; becoming legitimate, 197; contested, 14, 194; creation of, 9; legality-legitimacy intersection, 29, 31; legality trumped by, 13; at odds with legality, 29; overlapping forms of, 14, 179, 196; performance of, 191; politics of, 195; television as apparatus of, 127, 132
legitimation, 14
leitmotif (*zhuxuanli*) films, 42, 94–95
Lessig, Lawrence, 21, 175–77, 190
Let the Bullets Fly (Jiang, 2010), 101
Liang, Lawrence, 8, 9, 159, 175, 176–77

INDEX 253

"Life-Times of Disposability within Global Neoliberalism" (Tadiar), 155
Lin Chun, 37
Linked Hybrid MOMA project (Holl), 56, 109f, 110
Little Dieter Needs to Fly (Herzog, 1998), 110
littorum, 15
Litzinger, Ralph, 24
Liu Debin, 111
Liu Wei, 126
Liu Xiang, 68
Liu Xiaobo, 2, 208
Liu Xinhua, 126
Living Dance Studio, 114
Li Xianting Film Fund, 28, 113, 115, 215n35
Li Yu, 43
Li Zhang, 154–55
Lobato, Ramon, 7
Loomba, Ania, 160
Lost in Beijing (Li Yu, 2007), 43
Lost in Hong Kong (Xu, 2015), 101
Lou Ye, 43, 182
Lu, Sheldon, 41
Lu Hao, 87
Lull, James, 121, 142
Lumière brothers, 109
Lury, Celia, 191
Lu Xinyu, 41, 63
Lu Xuechang, 42
Lu Xun, 95–96, 98, 118

Made in China (Pun Ngai, 2005), 161
make-do practices, 7, 8, 117, 176, 177, 197
Malaysia, 6, 160, 189
Man from Macau II, The (Wong and Chang, 2015), 101f
Maoism, 23
Mao Zedong: copycat statues of, 177; death of, 120; portraits of, 41, 85
Marx, Karl, 188
Marxism, 160

Matrix, The (Wachowski brothers, 1999), 124
Mazzarella, William, 204n4
Mbembe, Achille, 11, 109
McCarthy, Anna, 122
McGrath, Jason, 23, 41, 144
media, 35, 204n4; affective media geographies, 77, 163, 221n54; informal media networks, 180; "mainstream" media studies, 164; media event, 144; media logic, 62; "politics before media," 65; spectralizing effect of, 39
media assemblage, 162, 163, 168
media culture, 114, 120, 163
media infrastructures, 62, 63, 67, 197; distribution and, 77; embodied nature of, 187; people as, 18, 31, 170, 193, 196, 197
Media Piracy in Emerging Economies (Karaganis), 7
mediation, 35, 152, 204n4
media urbanism, 11, 18, 34, 93; audiovisuality of development and, 51; creative industries and, 21; distribution of images and, 77; material and imaginary practices in, 30; Olympic era linked to, 1; Olympics and, 26; technological social projects and, 28
medium specificity, 122, 123, 164, 221n55
Megabox theater chain, 100, 107f, 107–8
Meishi Street (Ou and Cao, 2006), 72, 73–74f, 75–78, 80, 90, 103, 211n34
melodrama, 188, 192
memes, 156, 157f, 158–60
Memories of Underdevelopment [*Memorias del Subdesarrollo*] (Gutiérrez Alea, 1968), 11
memory, 94, 95, 193; of demolished places, 46; destruction of urban memory, 41; TV viewing and collective memory, 126
Memory Project, 115
Menon, Nivedita, 17

Mermaid, The (Chow, 2016), 100, 101
Mertha, Andrew, 171, 173
Meys, Olivier, 78
migrant workers, 52, 72, 111f, 152; dormitory housing for, 151, 155; media in everyday lives of, 151; mobile telephony and, 164; outside of *hukou* system, 219n15
migration, 59, 70, 148, 154, 155, 204n85
mimesis, 191
mimicry, 188–93
minjian shehui ("folk" society), 18
minorities, 66, 175
mise en abyme, 122, 123, 124, 144; closed structure of social body, 142; as governmental technology, 127
MK Pictures, 107
mobile phones, 120, 121, 163, 164, 170
model/media city, 62, 70
Modern China (journal), 16
modernity, 16, 19, 118, 176; contradictory elements of, 25; digital, 152; Euro-American, 64; exported, 15; infrastructure and, 205n10; postsocialist, 23; technomodernity, 63, 209n3; Western-dominated ideal of, 19–20
modernization, 22, 71, 72, 86, 140
Mojin: The Lost Legend (2015), 101f
Mongolian Ping Pong [Lü caodi] (Ning, 2006), 144
Monkey King: Hero Is Back (Tian, 2015), 101f
Monster Hunt (Hui, 2015), 101
Moores, Shaun, 135
Motion Picture Association of America (MPAA), 175
"Movie Magic" (*China Daily*, 2011), 94
Mumbai (India), city of, 38
My Future Is Not a Dream (factory band), 166
"My Future Is Not a Dream" (song), 150

nail houses (*dingzihu*), 2, 61, 208n1
Nakajima, Seio, 113

National Film Museum, 108–9
nationalism, 123
National Stadium, The (Olympic short film), 56
necropolitics, 11
neoliberalism, 2, 14, 123, 190, 196, 205n74; developing nations and, 22; exception and, 154–55; individualism and, 195; innovation industries, 200n19; postsocialism and, 163, 165, 166, 195; social (il)legitimacy fostered by, 14
neorealism, 186
New Beijing CBD (Shi, 2007), 87
New Chinese Documentary Film Movement, The (Berry, Lu, and Rofel, 2011), 112
New Documentary Movement, 35, 42, 83, 96, 114, 147
Ngai, Pun, 155, 160, 161
Ng See-Yuan, 106
1920 (Bhatt, 2008), 38
Ning Hao, 144
Ning Ying, 42
No Regret about Youth (Zhou, 1992), 42
North, Global, 63, 153; creativity associated with, 159; North–South relations, 191; "third world figure" and benevolence of, 159–60
Not One Less [Yi ge bu neng shao] (Zhang, 1999), 144

"Old and Dilapidated (or Hazardous) Housing Renewal" (*Wei jiu fang gaizao*), 40
Olympic era, of China, 1, 3, 18, 23–26, 131; blueprints and, 48; Olympic slogans, 53; street piracy in, 183; television and, 145; transformation of China (*zhuanxing*), 33; visual culture of, 49; "Water Cube" (*shuilifang*), 54f, 55, 57. *See also* Beijing Olympic Summer Games (2008)
100 Flowers Hidden Deep (Chen, 2001), 46f
One Man Olympics, The (film), 56
Ong, Aihwa, 13, 154–55, 160, 161

On the Beat (Ning, 1995), 42
"on the scene" (*xianchang*) videomaking, 42
"on-the-spot realism" (*jishi zhuyi*), 42
ontology, 39
optical disc cultures, 170
organized crime, 175
orientalism, 1, 19
"original-fake," 5
Oshima, Nagisa, 186
Osram China Lighting factory (Guangdong), 166
Ou Ning, 72, 112, 113
Outlaws of the Marsh [Shuihuzhuan] (Shi Nai'an), 9
Outside (Wang Wo, 2007), 43
"outsourcing," 153

Painted Skin 2 (Wu, 2012), 101
Pang Laikwan, 7, 21, 180, 191
Pan Jianlin, 42
past and future vectors, 30, 33, 37; disappearance of the present and, 26, 35; tradition versus future, 35
patriarchy, 160
Pear (Zhang Ciyu, 2010), 113
Pearl River Delta, 40, 172
Peking University, film screenings at, 113
people as media infrastructure, 18, 31
performance art, 91
performativities, 3, 98; of brand image, 191; citizenship and, 67; underperformativity, 13; video medium specificity and, 164, 221n55
Perpetual Motion (Ning, 2005), 42
Petition [Shangfeng] (Zhao Liang, 2008), 43, 147
Philip, Kavita, 175, 176, 178
Phoenix TV, 130
photography: amateur, 77; civil contract of, 57, 60, 168; *Family Stuff* exhibition, 121–22, 122f; *Implemental Photography* (Wang and Liu, 2007), 126–27, 128f

piracy, 3, 6, 13, 26, 59, 179; accessibility and, 188; antipiracy campaigns and discourse, 7, 28, 36, 171, 173, 177, 184; biopiracy, 14; crisis resolution and anxieties about, 66; cultural commons and, 175–76; cultural objects and practices remade by, 183; of DVDs, 110; film distribution and, 28; as "global pricing problem," 8; good and bad, 176, 177; hand-to-hand circulation and sociality of, 18, 22, 33, 170, 183, 185, 186, 208n3; as illegal but socially legitimate, 9, 201n31; international law and, 10, 11; Liang's critiques of piracy discourse, 159; new economic zones opened by, 12–13; pirate culture, 4; pirates as "enemy of all," 10, 11, 175, 196; pirate TV, 139–40, 145; political/technological/economic changes and, 173–74; pricing of fakes, 191; street piracy, 6, 18, 22; terrorism associated with, 5; as theft, 174–75; too-early temporality of, 190
Pirated Copy [Manyan] (He, 2004), 147, 169–70, 172, 175, 187f, 192, 194; cult status of, 179; DVD title screen, 179f; everyday networks depicted in, 186–88; opening scene, 185–86; police interrogation scene, 186
Pirate Modernity: Delhi's Media Urbanism (Sundaram), 7, 18, 65
piratical citizenship, 9, 22, 30, 149, 185; distribution and, 72, 75–78; emergence of, 123; as form of political subjectivity, 62; global proliferation of, 66; media urbanism and, 93; political society and, 141; seepage and, 85
political society, 15–16, 18, 19, 60, 149, 177; civil society distinguished from, 59; equality and, 225n75; everyday life and, 194; global, 64; global proliferation of, 66; illicit life and, 185; informal media networks and, 183; media

urbanism and, 93; pirate sociality and, 197; as politics of legitimacy, 195; shift from civil society to, 26; technocultural networks in, 65, 163
Politics of the Governed, The (Chatterjee), 16
Poly Theaters, 111
pornification (*seqinghua*), 184–85
pornography, 2, 9, 26, 179, 183, 186; antipornography campaigns, 28, 170–73, 172f; discursive performativity of, 184; linked with copyright violations, 173; mimicry and, 193; pornographies of globalization, 31, 170, 188–93; punishment of pornographers in China, 196; temporality of, 189, 192
Portable Cities series (Yin, 2002–3), 87
postcolonial societies, 25, 63, 119, 177
postcolonial studies, 29, 57, 194
postcommunism, 24–25
postdemocracy, 177
postmodernity, 23
postphenomenological gaze, 40, 205n20
postsocialism, 23–24, 40, 63, 119; command logic of management, 152; defined, 148; as dubious historical marker, 25; neoliberalism and, 163, 165, 166, 195; normalization of, 177; single-party governance and, 64, 65; symbolism of, 87; television and, 140–41
Povinelli, Elizabeth, 11, 28, 150, 208n61
precarity, 6, 66, 153, 193, 194, 209n16
presence, partial, 192
preservation, 40, 42, 49, 50–51, 52; Beijing master plan (2020) projections for, 48f; "city-scale preservation," 50; debates over politics of, 41; ecological, 20; tourism and, 55; Urban Generation filmmakers and, 43
Primitive Passions (Chow), 95
print shops, 80
private spheres, 141
privatization, 52, 71, 106, 112, 120, 135
propaganda art, 127

protests/strikes, illegal, 65, 67, 71, 209n13, 210n20
Public Culture (journal), 17, 48f
public-private distinction, 43, 65, 123, 133, 141, 195
publics, formal and informal, 133, 143, 147
public service announcements, 49, 138
public space, 39, 63, 148, 187; breakdown between private and public space, 43; television and, 121, 131, 135, 141
public sphere, 16, 63, 141; as overdetermined concept, 17; publics outside of liberal public sphere, 177; West–East binary and, 64
"'Public Sphere'/'Civil Society,' in China?" symposium (1993), 16
Pulp Fiction (Tarantino, 1994), 170, 186, 188

Qianmen Demolition and Reconstruction Project, 78, 80
Qing Dynasty, 52
Qiu Zhijie, 126

race: critical studies of, 24; divisions based on, 63
racism, 20
radio, 140
Rancière, Jacques, 61, 77–78, 211n35
RAQS Media Collective, 30, 85
reconstruction, 40, 41, 46; blueprints and, 47; of Daguanlou movie theater, 103; Olympic preparations and, 68; projections of the future city and, 51; of Qianmen neighborhood, 78, 79f, 80; velocity of, 43
Red Cliff (Woo, 2008), 101
regionalization, 121
rendering, 33–34, 53, 55
Ren Qingtai (aka Ren Jingfeng), 102
repetition, 4, 26, 149, 193; in factory work, 150; at heart of underglobalization, 48; mise en abyme and, 122; modernization and, 124

representation, 9, 12, 60, 65, 184, 193
resistance, 8, 24, 194, 200n26; to *chaiqian*, 76; local, 178; romanticized view of, 23, 58; subaltern, 98; technology and state intervention, 161; of women factory workers, 160
reverse engineering, 190
Ricci, Antonio, 186
RMB *City: A Second Life City Planning* (Cao, 2008), 87, 90, 90f
roads, widening of, 51
Road to the Green Olympics, The (film), 56
Robbins, Bruce, 17
Rodney, Walter, 11
Rofel, Lisa, 112, 113, 152, 165
Rong Rong, 43
Rosecrance, Richard, 5–6
ruins, 33, 34, 39, 40–47, 57; aesthetics of, 41, 42; civil contract of photography and, 60; evacuation of the present by, 43–44; preserved, 41; Rong Rong's images of, 43, 44f; space and time of, 46; taboo in pre-modern China on portrayal of, 40–41; Zhang Dali's ruins graffiti and sculptures, 44f, 44–45
rural-urban disparities, 123

Said, Edward, 1
saohuang dafei [antipornography and antipiracy] campaigns (1989–present), 170–73, 171f, 172f, 197
Sardar, Ziauddin, 6, 19, 188–89, 190
Sarkar, Bhaskar, 4, 165, 188, 189, 195, 201n31
Sassen, Saskia, 13, 178
satellite cities, 50, 51f
Schmitt, Carl, 11, 12, 14
screen intimacy, 152
"seamless social," 138
Second Life, 87, 90
security, 8, 39–40; innovation linked to national security, 200n27; technologies of, 38

"seepage," 30, 85
semiotics, 23, 194
sensorium, 29, 36, 93; counter-planning discourses and, 87; the spectral and, 39; of the technologized city, 30, 34
Sex, Lies and Videotape (Soderbergh, 1989), 187
sex industry, 164
sexuality, divisions based on, 63
Shadow Magic (Hu, 2000), 98
Shanghai, city of, 120, 172
Shanghai United Cinema, 100, 106, 106f
shanzhai ("mountain fortress") culture, 3, 7, 9, 10, 196
Shenzhen, city of, 76
Shi Guorui, 87
Shiva, Vandana, 14
Short Film about Killing, A (Kieslowski, 1988), 186
Shower (Zhang Yang, 1999), 42
Silicon Valley, 176
Silver Medalist (Ning, 2009), 101
Simone, AbdouMaliq, 17, 19, 57, 170, 193
simultaneity, 140
Sino-African Summit (2006), 81
site specificity, 42
Sniadecki, J. P., 28, 204n85
socialism: advances of socialist era, 37; market socialism, 56, 95, 112; nostalgia for, 123; sonic and visual culture of, 130
socialist realism, 42
social media, 153, 170, 184, 215n35
social movement society, 65
Soderbergh, Steven, 187
soft power, cultural, 98, 118
Song Dong, 43, 87
Sorry Baby (Feng, 1999), 42
South, Global, 12, 29, 37, 153; imitation associated with, 159; North–South relations, 191
sovereignties, 13, 15, 196; law in relation to, 14; overlapping, 14, 178; territorial, 175

Soviet Union (USSR), 16, 148
space of appearance, 168, 195
spatiality, technologized, 95–98, 110, 213n6
Special Economic Zones (SEZ), 40, 65, 123, 151, 154
special topics programs (*zhuantipian*), 42
spectatorship, 59, 95, 96, 135, 192; alternative history of TV spectatorship, 126; cinematic, 22; social space of, 106; state-designed collective spectatorship, 132, 133
spectral, the, 37–38, 56; labor and laborers, 31, 149; of political society, 60
Spectres of Marx (Derrida), 205n18
speculation, real-estate, 38, 71
Spring Subway (Zhang Yibai, 2002), 42
Square, The (Zhang Yuan, 1994), 42
squatter communities, 141–42
state, the, 3, 15, 22, 29, 34; cinema theaters and, 109; citizenship and, 57, 58, 59, 72; civil society and, 63, 64, 65; development and, 19; digital urbanism and, 85; economy partially owned by, 123; experience and imaginaries coded by, 119; image as benevolent Leviathan, 210n23; importance of culture for, 36; informal practices incorporated by, 8; legitimacy of, 66, 67; modernity and, 19; modernizing of, 18; party state, 65, 66; piracy and, 10; piratical citizenship and, 62; political society and, 14, 60; protections afforded by, 37; sovereignty and, 13; spatial practices of, 103; stability and, 25; state capitalism, 64; state-corporate capital, 59, 163; state-led cultural projects, 27, 30; state-market, 30, 33, 40, 47, 112; state-society relations, 17, 30, 146; technology and state intervention, 117; television and, 31, 127, 128f, 139, 142, 144; violence of, 16

State Administration of Radio, Film, and Television (SARFT), 105, 117
Steal This Film (2006), 8
stealth marketing, 91
Steinfeld, Edward S., 4
street realism, 44
Studio Z cine club, 113
subjectivity, 18, 66, 152, 155; human disposability and, 156; investor model of, 14; political, 14, 17, 62, 66, 98, 168, 193; precarious, 168; transformative subject, 163
suburbs, 4, 108
subway liines, 30, 36, 70, 80
Summer Palace (Lou, 2006), 43
Sundaram, Ravi, 7, 18, 19; media urbanism concept, 30, 34, 62; public culture in crisis and, 66; on technology in everyday life, 63
supply chain, East-West, 163
surveillance, 8, 38, 65
survivalism, 7, 23
sustainability, 55
Sutherland, Donald, 144
suzhi (quality) idea, 165

Tadiar, Neferti X. M., 9, 14, 19, 155, 156
Taiwan, 18, 20, 108, 180
Taussig, Michael, 191
Taylor, Charles, 48
technocultures, 191
technologies, 130, 194; networked, 120; production and consumption of, 152; screen technologies, 27, 136, 142, 158, 163; security, 38; social projects and, 28; technologized spatiality, 95–98; technomobility, 151; technomodernity, 153; television as political technology, 148. *See also* intimacy, technological
technologized city, 3, 22, 39, 86, 90, 93; migrant factory workers in, 152; ruins and blueprints as sensorium of, 30, 34
technology transfer, 6

Technomobility in China: Young Migrant Women and Mobile Phones (Wallis, 2013), 164
television, 27, 28, 49, 164; ambient, 22, 26, 30, 93; as "citizen machine," 136; City TV (*chengshi dianshi*), 135–36, 137f, 138–40; closed-circuit, 131f, 132, 133; in contemporary cinema, 142–48, 143f, 145f, 146f, 147f; history of Chinese TV, 120; LED Sky Screen (Chaoyang District, Beijing), 139f; Metro TV (*ditie dianshi*), 136, 138f; Mobile TV (*yidong dianshi*), 136, 137f; outside the home, 123, 130, 141; pirate TV, 139–40, 145; as public culture, 130–35, 131f, 134f, 135f; regional TV in East Asia, 77; role in contemporary art, 124; screen postsocialism, 140–41; sidewalk TV in "old" Beijing, 129f, 131; the state and, 31; technological change and, 120–21; "Water Cube" design and, 55. *See also* CCTV
Ten Great Buildings (*shi da jianzhu*), 85, 203n83
territoriality, 13
terrorism, 5, 8–9, 175
Think Films (Yingxiang Fangying), 113, 114
third world, 66
"third world figure," 159
Thomas, Julian, 7
Three Shadows Photography Art Center, 113
Thrift, Nigel, 140
Tiananmen Square massacre (1989), 16, 25, 148, 172
torrent sites, distribution through, 76
Touch of Sin, A (Jia, 2014), 151f
tourism, 52, 53, 54f, 55
transition, concept of, 148
TRIPS (Trade-Related Aspects of Intellectual Property Rights), 12, 178
Tsang, Eric, 124

Tsing, Anna, 152, 156
22filmcafé cine club, 113
"Two Histories of Capital, The" (Chakrabarty), 188

Ullens, Baron Guy, 113
Ullens, Myriam, 113
Ullens Center for Contemporary Art (UCCA), 113
Ultimate Movie Experience (UME), 100, 105f, 106, 107
underglobalization, 2, 11, 19–23, 28, 119, 194; democratic potentialities and, 64; logic of repetition and, 48; political subjectivity in era of, 62; proliferation of illegality and, 178; risk and abandonment in processes of, 142; seepage and, 85; television and, 123
Under the Skyscrapers (Du, 2002), 147
unhomely social, 123, 141–42, 148–49, 152, 216n8
United States, 13, 115, 174, 175, 213n8
Unknown Pleasures [*Ren Xiao Yao*] (Jia, 2002), 145f, 145–47, 146f
urban fabric, 55
Urban Fiction [*Dushi yanyi*] project (Xing, 2004–present), 87, 88f, 89f
Urban Generation, The (Zhang Zhen, 2007), 43
Urban Generation filmmakers, 43, 96
urbanism, digital, 57, 60, 62–63, 87, 93, 208n3; cinema-going and, 98; seepage and, 85
urbanization, 37–38, 72, 123
Urban Landscape—New Beijing (Zhan, 2003–7), 87
urban planning, 18, 50; lifeless visual culture of, 87; as mode of visual culture, 51; visual culture of, 204n3

Van Gogh on Demand (Wong, 2014), 21
Varma, Ram Gopal, 38
videation, 152, 163, 168

video: digital video, 30, 80; documentary, 93; first domestic video exhibition in China, 126; tube video, 147; video culture, 31, 152, 162; viral videos, 168
Villager Documentary Project, 114
violence, 10, 14; intellectual property and, 8; state violence in China, 16; structural, 20
Visser, Robin, 40, 41
visual culture, of urban planning, 5, 26, 30, 47, 51; cinema-going and, 95; cognitive maps of disappearing places, 92; as media and mediation, 35; Olympic-era, 49; politics of, 18; street life and, 52
visuality, 4, 58, 83, 98; micro/local communications and, 164; modernity and, 118; technologized, 95
visual studies, 27

Waiting Alone (Wu Shixian, 2005), 42
Wallis, Cara, 164
Wanda Cinemas, 100, 106, 106f, 118
Wang, Shujen, 13, 171, 178
Wang Hongwei, 204n85
Wang Hui, 148
Wang Jin, 126
Wang Jing, 21, 103
Wang Jinsong, 43
Wang Jiuliang, 43
Wang Jun, 41
Wang Lang, 126
Wang Miao, 43
Wang Qishan, 82
Wang Wo, 43, 143, 204n85
Wang Xiaoshuai, 42, 182
Wang Zhan, 43
Warlords, The (Chan, 2007), 101
Warner, Michael, 17
Warner Brothers, 100
"Water Cube" [*shuilifang*] (Beijing), 54f, 55, 56

web 2.0, 147, 168
Weekend Lovers [*Zhoumo qingren*] (Lou, 1993), 182f
Weerasethakul, Apichatpong, 113
We Got It (Olympic short film), 56
Weibo, 91, 164
Welles, Orson, 5
West, the, 20
West-East binary, 20, 64, 154
"What Is a Technological Author?" (Philip), 175
Whose Utopia (Cao, 2006), 166f, 166–68, 167f
Williams, Raymond, 135
Wired magazine, 158, 220n35
women: resistance of female factory workers, 160–61; as "third world" subjects, 160
Wong, Winnie, 21
Woo, John, 117
Wood, Dennis, 33, 49
worker suicides, 31
Workstation, 113
work units, 120, 131, 138
World, The (Jia, 2004), 42–43, 147
World Bank, 20
World Trade Organization (WTO), 3, 12, 20, 171, 172, 174, 178, 214n16
Wu, Lydia, 117
Wu Hung, 40, 43, 124, 127
Wu Qiong, 145
Wu Shixian, 42
Wu Wenguang, 42, 113, 114
Wu Xia (Chan, 2011), 102f
wuxia (martial arts) literature and cinema, 9

x-colonialism, 4, 5, 196
Xianxiang Theater (Songzhuang), 116f
Xiao Jiang, 42, 118
Xiao Wu (Jia, 1997), 145
Xia Yu, 118
Xi Chen, 17–18, 63, 66–67

INDEX 261

Xi Jinping, 24
Xing Danwen, photographs of, 87, 88f, 89f
Xinjiang, 207n52
Xu Bing, 43
Xu Jinglei, 42
X-urbanism, 4–5, 196
Xu Tong, 204n85

Yao Chen, 124
Yeh, Emilie Yueh-yu, 106
Ying Da, 144
Yin Xiuzhen, 43, 44, 87
Yuanchuang Art Center, 115
Yu Bo, 186
Yung Ho Chang, 113
Yunnan Multicultural Visual Festival (Yunfest), 115
Yu Xu, 130

Zhang Ciyu, 113
Zhang Dali, 43, 44–45
Zhang Jinli, 72, 73f, 75–77, 83, 85
Zhang Peili, 126
Zhang Tongdao, 132, 133
Zhang Xianming, 113
Zhang Xudong, 23
Zhang Yang, 42
Zhang Yaxuan, 78
Zhang Yibai, 42
Zhang Yimou, 144
Zhang Yingjin, 41
Zhang Yuan, 42
Zhang Zanbo, 147, 148
Zhang Zhen, 41, 43
Zhang Ziyi, 117
Zhan Wang, 44, 87, 113
Zhao Liang, 43, 147
Zhao Weiwei, 145
Zheng Xiaoyu, 1
Zheteng (Wang, 2010), 143, 143f
Zhou Xiaowen, 42
Zhu Rikun, 204n85
Zi Beijia, 1

www.ingramcontent.com/pod-product-compliance
Lightning Source LLC
Chambersburg PA
CBHW070757230426
43665CB00017B/2397